Shanghaied in San Francisco

Bill Pickelhaupt

Judith Robinson, Editor

Flyblister Press
San Francisco, California
1996

Flyblister Press acknowledges the following for granting permission to reprint items as indicated:
Pearl D. Coffman: *American in the Rough,* by William M. Coffman, © 1955 by Simon-Schuster. Copyright reverted to Mr. Coffman in 1960.
San Francisco Maritime Museum N.H.P.: For use of oral histories gathered by Jack McNairn in 1959 and 1960 and later transcribed. These transcribed accounts form the basis for first-hand stories of shanghaiing.
Sea Breezes magazine: "Liverpool to Melbourne and 'Frisco About the Year 1875," by Sackville Smyth, July 1937 issue.
University of California at Berkeley Oral History Office: *Recollections of the San Francisco Waterfront*, by Thomas Crowley, Sr. Interviewed by Willa Klug Baum and Karl Kortum, University of California Press, 1967.

A good faith effort has been made to acquire permission for use of quotations of material by John H. (Jack) Shickell and drawings by Gordon Grant.

Original source of front cover art work unknown. The line-drawing appeared in a March 1962 article of *Westways* magazine by Richard H. Dillon.
Back cover art is from the shipping articles for the ship *Kate Hooper*, which departed San Francisco November 14, 1856. The drawing was an advertisement for Goin & Ellis, shipping masters.

Library of Congress Catalog Card Number: 96-96781
First printed December 1996
10 9 8 7 6 5 4 3 2 1

Printed in the United States of America

Flyblister Press draws its name from an old four-person rowboat, made of paper, owned by a San Francisco rowing club in the 1880s. A wag, seeing the peeled paint of the craft, dubbed her the *Flyblister*. The boat was very fast due to its light weight, and carried her crews to numerous victories.

Flyblister Press
1706 Irving Street, San Francisco, Ca. 94122

Acknowledgments

Writing a book about an illegal activity which ended over eighty years ago is a difficult proposition at best. Fortunately a wealth of assistance became available as the project unfolded.

The greatest help was afforded by David Hull and his staff at the San Francisco Maritime Museum Library. David made the wonderful collection of the library available to me and spent many hours discussing problems with the project. The mere existence of that library was of the utmost importance when the San Francisco Public Library's Main Branch was closed while the bulk of my research was under way.

Nancy Olmsted's encouragement and insight into San Francisco's waterfront history were invaluable tools. Her knowledge of and collection of photographs were equally invaluable to me.

Stan Carroll of the San Francisco History Room at the city's Main branch made a very valuable suggestion when I searched for a topic—the Barbary Coast. While my research followed the path of shanghaiing, his idea helped tremendously. Thanks in large measure go to Stan's brilliant staff for their enthusiastic support, especially Pat Akre's assistance with photographs.

Steve Canright of the National Maritime Museum is owed a huge debt of gratitude for pointing out the transcripts of Jack McNairn's oral histories.

Robert MacKimmie helped with initial design and located key photographs from the collection of the California Historical

Society, while keeping up his own hectic schedule. Thank you, Robert.

Judith Robinson played a very big role in making sense of the data I gathered. Her organizational efforts helped pull it all together.

The Bancroft Library assisted with photographs and Mechanics' Library staff was very patient with my continued requests to look at their collection of San Francisco City Directories. Amy Holloway at the African-American Museum of San Francisco provided information on John T. Callender.

Thanks to Archie Green for pointing out the art work which graces the front cover.

Malcolm E. Barker contributed significantly to design of this book. Bill Secrest, John Boessenacker, Kevin Mullen, Walt Schneebeli, Mike Griffith of the United States District Court, Charles Fracchia, Dr. Albert Shumate and Dan Bacon all made important contributions. Special thanks to Kevin Starr.

Diane Laflin made a significant contribution when she showed me the Laflin Record. The Laflin Record confers the stamp of reality and truth to the entire work.

Last but by no means least, Courtney S. Clarkson deserves special recognition for encouraging me to pursue historical research, particularly for an earlier work. Thank you, Courtney. I am indebted to you.

Table of Contents

Illustrations

Foreword

Today, after long struggle, the question of civil rights is by and large in the consciousness of most Americans. Hence the city described by Bill Pickelhaupt in this vivid, well-researched narrative seems, in one sense, light years away. The fact that free men of America or other nationalities could be enticed, drugged, then shanghaied into what amounted to penal servitude before the mast for indefinite periods of time seems, like slavery itself, to belong to another and very remote era. And yet, even as this book appears, cases regarding the enforced servitude of Asian immigrants in Southern California sweatshops are pending before the courts. The question of enforced servitude, even slavery itself, remains a pressing issue in many parts of the world. In various forms, the practice of shanghaiing has not become a thing of the past.

For all its sordid illegality, the culture and practice of shanghaiing—the boardinghouses, the saloons, the dance halls and bordellos, the crimps themselves, the swiftly sailing Whitehalls which serviced the ships—was an established part of the culture of old San Francisco. Indeed, as Pickelhaupt demonstrates, the official establishment of the city and its political bosses had a tendency to look the other way when it came to what was in effect the kidnapping and enslavement of working men. The culture of shanghaiing, moreover, was but one part of the harsh exploitation of maritime labor on the Pacific Coast which continued into the twentieth century.

Organized in March 1885 in San Francisco, the Coast Seamen's Union fought the exploitation of maritime labor as best it could. In July 1891 the Coast Seamen's Union joined the Steamship Sailors Union to form the Sailors Union of the Pacific, which elected former sailor Andrew Furuseth to its presidency. For the next quarter of a century ensued the struggle to correct such abuses as the beating of sailors, the frequent defrauding of sailors wages and shanghaiing itself. Not until Senator Robert La Follette of Wisconsin introduced the Seamen's Act into Congress, which was signed into law by Woodrow Wilson on Mach 4, 1915, were the last vestiges of enforced servitude outlawed on American ships.

Meanwhile, there flourished in San Francisco, the rough, rowdy, frequently violent and sometimes colorful world described by Bill Pickelhaupt in this engaging book. Writers such as Frank Norris and Jack London found in the shanghaiing culture of the port of San Francisco a world of elemental brutality—yet vivid drama. Today, San Francisco prides itself on its identity as a world-renowned center for the arts, dining, retail and other amenities. It is important to remember, however, that this city of refinement came into being and passed its middle years as a bareknuckled Pacific port. Assembling the historical materials of this era and fashioning them into narrative, Bill Pickelhaupt helps us understand San Francisco in a new light.

Kevin Starr
author of the *Americans and the California Dream* series

Preface

Shanghaiing. The word carries a power which frightens and fascinates. It attracts and repulses us. But how much do we know about this practice which supposedly thrived on San Francisco's waterfront in the 19th century?

I came across the subject of shanghaiing in 1994 while writing a small book about the old rowing clubs of San Francisco. There seemed to be murky connections with shanghaiing and the Whitehall boatmen who were early members of some of these clubs. How widespread was the practice of shanghaiing? Could shanghaiing exist without the assistance of San Francisco's politicians? I decided to investigate further.

Using Richard H. Dillon's *Shanghaiing Days* as a guide, names of sailors' boardinghouse keepers were identified. Retail clothiers along the waterfront were also involved in providing men as sailors, willingly or otherwise. Then a photograph of a man who was a bare-knuckle boxer and boardinghouse keeper fleshed out the picture. The man, Thomas Chandler, not only shanghaied sailors and fought bare-knuckle bouts, he served on the San Francisco Democratic County Committee for over thirty years. Then shanghaiers who had terms in the California State Assembly and Senate revealed themselves. They spent more terms in the state legislature than in San Quentin. I was on to something.

The incentive to shanghai men was the advance money paid by shipowners through their agents and captains to men and women who supplied sailors to man a ship. No questions were asked—present a body and the first two months of that man's wages were yours. Sometimes the body did not have to be warm. Corpses were sometimes shanghaied.

Not just white males provided crews for ships in a questionable way. Although white males, almost all of them immigrants from outside the United States, formed the bulk of the community, white and Hispanic men and women joined in an early economic form of equality. Blacks shanghaied "coloreds," Hispanics shanghaied Hispanics, Chinese shanghaied Japanese and whites shanghaied everyone, regardless of color. Dorothy Paupitz, age seventy-eight, still sent young men to an uncertain fate, even after going through four husbands herself. (She did not shanghai her husbands—two died and two went insane).

Thomas Crowley, Sr., founder of Crowley Maritime, got his start as a Whitehall boatman on San Francisco Bay. He knew all the crimps on the waterfront. Old Man Crowley admitted he was one himself during his beginning. When he took a victim to his new home, "If they gave me any trouble, I hit 'em with the boat's footstretchers. That would quiet 'em down."

While I was cataloguing oral histories at the San Francisco Maritime Museum Library what inspired me originally was reading first-hand accounts of men who drank drugged liquor and woke up one hundred miles outside the Golden Gate. Culled in 1959 and '60 by Jack McNairn, these stories have never been published before. They make-up a compelling part of our maritime heritage—but a part some people would rather forget.

Another clue, and a huge incentive to pursue shanghaiing as a research topic, was discovery of listings in San Francisco City Directories of something called the Seamen's Boarding House Masters' Association. When Tommy Chandler, a man I knew was a crimp, turned up as president of this association, I knew I was on to something fascinating. I found a photograph of him and two other crimps and the course was clear--the story of San Francisco's shanghaiing past had to be told even if the tale had to be pieced together. New research in the pages of the *Daily Alta*, from 1867-1890 yielded missing pieces with which a narrative could be stiched.

The payment book of a crimp also was uncovered. James Laflin arrived in San Francisco in 1849 on the Gold Rush ship *Arkansas*. Laflin served as cabin boy on the passage around Cape Horn from New York. When the *Arkansas* became the Old Ship Saloon, Laflin worked there as bartender. He shanghaied men for over fifty years in San Francisco. A four hundred forty page record book was discovered which documents payments made by Laflin for shipowners' agents to the various shanghaiers who brought in men to form the whaling crews Laflin specialized in. The period included is December 1886-December 1890. Over six thousand officers and men shipped through James Laflin's shipping office in that four-year period—and when a crimp brought a man in he signed for the money received. "Shanghai" Brown, "Shanghai" Nelson and dozens of other unsavory characters left a sample of their penmanship for history to view.

The voyage of discovery into San Francisco's seedy past has yielded results beyond my wildest imagination. The fabric of shanghaiing spread to the highest levels of state government, and influenced national legislation and international affairs. Yet shanghaiing did not die until the crimps had drained as much money from it as they could. When sailing ships had pretty much passed from the scene in 1915, shanghaiing died.

Bill Pickelhaupt
August 1996
San Francisco

Introduction

San Francisco has always had an aura of mystery unlike any city in the world, fueled by the possibility of living with freedoms little dreamed of elsewhere, of enjoying pleasures in a semi-lawless environment. Those illusions continue to be part of the city's attraction.

Part of the enduring mystery stems from stories that quickly spread about the city as it grew on the edge of the North American continent beginning with the Gold Rush in 1848-9. A manifestation of this lawlessness was the common practice of stealing men away to sea. They seemingly disappeared from the face of the earth for long periods of time, sometimes never to be seen again. The practice gave a new word to the English language—shanghaiing—replacing the older term of crimping. A cast of characters ranging from unscrupulous crimps and lowly runners to skilled boatmen, respected sea captains and ship owners were its principals. Politicians, capitalist businessmen and the police were needed to allow shanghaiing to florish—for, though evil as the practice seems to us today, law-abiding citizens turned a blind eye.

Shanghaiing flourished in San Francisco between 1850 and 1910. It lent a real danger to the mystique—and the misery—of the boom town. The practice prompted enactment of laws at the state and national levels to put an end to shanghaiing, but fortunes could be made selling sailors, so these laws were weakly enforced. The political power and influence of the crimps who made their living shanghaiing prevented effective enforcement of such laws.

Crimps included men with names such as "One-Eyed" Curtin, "Horseshoe" Brown, "Shanghai" Kelly, John "Shanghai Chicken" Devine; women like Dorothy Paupitz and Anna Gomes, and many more. Sailors' boardinghouses, where the tired, lonely seamen thought they would find clean beds and fresh food were, in fact, traps for the unaware. The saloons and brightly lit gambling and dancing halls where sailors went for entertainment on the waterfront and the nearby Barbary Coast were traps where the hapless victims were transported by Whitehall boats to ships about to weigh anchor. These excellent harbor craft were developed in New York City around the War of 1812, and frequently taken twenty-five miles or more outside the Golden Gate. When the senseless sailors awoke from a drugged state as a result of knockout potions slipped into drinks, they found themselves in the focsles of sailing ships bound for Shanghai, Liverpool and ports east.

This book follows the path of the crimps and politicians during their reign in San Francisco from 1850 until 1910. The first three chapters introduce many of the personalities involved in shanghaiing, from men as notorious as James "Shanghai" Kelly, folk-villain John "Shanghai Chicken" Devine and more respectable shanghaiers like bare-knuckle boxer Thomas Chandler and James Laflin, the smartest crimp of them all. The century-old mystery of the fate of "Shanghai" Kelly will also be revealed. The fourth chapter brings the other side of the shanghaiing equation—first-hand accounts of men who were shanghaied. Most of these accounts are published for the first time, and may be found in the San Francisco Maritime Museum Library.

Whitehall boatmen, the subject of chapter five, formed the crucial connection between sailors' boardinghouses on shore—the supply side of the shanghaiing formula—and ships that needed sailors. In addition to the activities of transporting shanghaied sailors and smuggling liquor and opium, Whitehall boatmen ferried passengers and cargo between ship and shore. They sometimes went more than twenty-five miles outside the Golden Gate in search of business. That business may have been to persuade a British captain to buy supplies from a particular meat market or ship chandlery, or the more serious activity of enticing inbound sailors to desert their ships after plying the men with bad whiskey and filling their heads with stories of high wages, a good drunk or wild women, if they only followed their new found friend.

Chapters six and seven document the crimps who were also politicians, and their powerful friends like Chris "Blind Boss" Buckley, the Democratic Party boss of San Francisco in the 1880s, or William T. Higgins, Republican Party boss in the 1870s and '80s. In the face of legislation at the state level in California and at the federal level, San Francisco's shanghaiing community managed not only to survive but thrive for over forty years after the first federal legislation, the Shipping Commissioner's Act of 1872, attempted to put a stop to shanghaiing.

Tables in the Appendix give an understanding of the demographics of the shanghaiing trade. Over seventy photographs and line-drawings, many not seen for over one-hundred years, help bring the days of *Shanghaied In San Francisco* to life.

Chaos on the Waterfront

Sailors are treated as, and are, chattels.
Daily Alta California, 1867

Instead of being an intelligent freeman, the sailor is a slave, not only to his purposely excited passions but to a race of beings known as landlords, or boardinghouse keepers.
Daily Alta California, 1868

The practice of shanghaiing men as sailors was a phenomenon of the American period in San Francisco's history. After the Americans' takeover of the town in 1846, desertion by sailors from visiting whaling ships or other vessels became more and more common. The Gold Rush of 1848-9 aggravated the problem tremendously.

The business of shanghaiing was carried on by the lowly and not so lowly. Many partners in the activity during its heyday were prominent businessmen and women, and those fueled by political ambition, in San Francisco. There was money to be made in the market for human bodies and understandings were reached—and bribes were given to keep the pipeline flowing. But it was primarily public indifference to the sailor's plight that allowed greater exploitation by crimp and captain, threatening sailors' civil rights.

The first person to set up shop in the sailor's port of call, the village of Yerba Buena, was an Englishman, William A. Richardson, who in 1822 had left a British ship that sailed through the narrow opening that would come to be known as the Golden Gate, into the harbor at Yerba Buena Cove. After the American takeover in 1846, a captain who lost crew in the sparsely inhabited port found it very difficult to find replacements.

The Gold Rush of 1848-9 in San Francisco coincided with an important shipping innovation—the glory days of clipper ships. Clippers demanded more and more crewmen to handle their greater complement of sail. Yet, with the Gold Rush fewer willing men were available to man the ships. Not only clipper ships had problems finding crewmen—all ships were short-handed. One need only look into Yerba Buena Cove, choked with hundreds of ships in the early 1850s, to realize the severe shortage of sailors that existed. Into the void stepped shanghaiers, men who supplied sailors for a price.

By late 1853, the term "shanghaeing" was being used in print to describe the practice of robbing and kidnapping seamen. In November of that year, the *Daily Alta* recounted the story of a sailor, Fred Campbell, induced to ship; after he received his advance money, his liquor was drugged by men bent on shanghaiing him. Campbell's money and clothes were removed and he was presented to three Whitehall boatmen, to be transported to the waiting ship *Bonita*. One of the boatmen slipped off and notified police who arrested the three shanghaiers. Campbell's sea chest had also been rifled and filled with stones. [1]

Another early tale is that of "an excitement" on Front Street. A boardinghouse keeper attempted to "shanghae" a drunken sailor. The sailor was freed and the boardinghouse keeper "flogged." [2]

By 1855, Reverend William Taylor used the phrase shanghaiing to denounce the practice at an open-air sermon in Portsmouth

Harbor Police Set Off After a Whitehall Boat, circa 1890s . . .
The Harbor Police, at both the North Station on Davis Street and the
South Station on Steuart Street, had the duty of watching shipping, in
addition to their street patrols. Here, guided by moonlight, two officers
push off from a wharf to intercept a Whitehall boat approaching a ship.
The fact that the sails are already furled suggests the ship has been in
the harbor for at least a short time. Although boatmen were known to
be involved in smuggling, the extra man in the Whitehall indicates
someone is about to be shanghaied.

Square. The origin of the term shanghaiing is that a voyage to Shanghai, China, was not a direct one: if a sailor was sent to Shanghai, he would have to go all the way around the world to return to San Francisco. Service on at least two or three ships was necessary and would take nearly two years. A shanghai voyage was feared as a long journey with no assurance of returning alive. Sailors had to be forced or tricked into a trip to Shanghai—they were shanghaied.

The practice of kidnapping men to serve in the army, navy or merchant marine had been around for centuries by the time the Americans took over the affairs of Yerba Buena from the Mexicans. The term crimping had been used as early as 1638 for the use of force or trickery to get men to serve in the army, navy or merchant marine. [3]

The Americans took over the town council of the village from the Mexican authorities in 1846 as part of the spoils of the Mexican War. Following the advice of the merchant community, the first law passed by the council made it a criminal offense for a sailor to jump ship or for the residents of Yerba Buena to harbor a runaway sailor. The fine for enticing a sailor from his ship ranged between $20-$500 or a jail sentence of no more than 30 days. The fine and jail term for harboring a runaway sailor were the same. Sailors who deserted were arrested: in March 1850, four sailors were brought to the court of Judge Almond for deserting from the ship *Mount Vernon*, just in from Boston. "They were all held to answer." [4]

In 1848, the town merchants' association took matters into their own hands in an effort to maintain crews for the merchant ships on which the fledgling port's commercial interests depended. It contracted with a group of young men to return runaway sailors at $25 a head. But with the onset of the Gold Rush, that task became impossible. Sailors could barely wait to leave their ships to flee to the gold fields and try their luck with a pick and shovel. The young sailor-catchers, however, formed the nucleus of the Hounds, a group of young toughs who briefly terrorized San Francisco. And a precedent was established in San Francisco—for payment on the head of sailors to serve aboard ships. [5]

With the Gold Rush, San Francisco was an instant city. A severe shortage of housing existed for years. Into the housing void stepped men who built or operated boardinghouses. These boardinghouses served men newly arrived from all over the world on their way to the diggings. As miners drifted back to the city during the off-season, when winter rains and snow prevented mining, many of them stayed in boardinghouses. Some of these boardinghouses would turn a miner into a sailor when the resident's bill for lodging and food grew too high. If the demand for sailors was brisk, a resident would not be around long. Beatings were a common method of persuasion: if the new sailor resisted, the burly boardinghouse runner convinced the reluctant man it was in his best interest to cooperate.

Boatmen played an essential role in the commerce of the new city. In the late 1840s and early 1850s, the shallow waters of Yerba Buena Cove made it essential that a way be found to move people and goods between the ships anchored in deeper waters and the shore. Boatmen filled that need. For decades, only ships tied at a wharf could do without the services of a boatman. The boatman was an indispensable part of San Francisco's mercantile community.

Taking sailors' boardinghouse runners and sailors removed from an inbound ship or new sailors, shanghaied or otherwise, to an outbound ship was a job Whitehall boatmen were well suited for. They could carry five or more men in their boats and the boats handled rough water well. Whitehall boats could be sailed or rowed.

San Francisco's early political leaders, many of whom were merchants like entrepreneur Samuel Brannan and William T.

Coleman, vigilante leader in 1851, 1856 and 1877 and a shipowner, recognized the necessity of having available crew for the vessels that fed the city's commerce. Ship captains shared the same interests. It was a ship captain, Ned Wakeman, who placed the noose around the neck of the first victim of the Committee of Vigilance of 1851. Another infamous captain, Robert "Bully" Waterman, had cruelly maltreated the crew of the clipper ship *Challenge* on a passage from New York. He was greeted by an angry mob of 200 when the ship arrived in San Francisco, October 29, 1851, calling for the captain's hanging. Crewmen who had jumped ship while it was still in the stream waiting to anchor tipped off San Franciscans to Waterman's misdeeds. But Vigilantes, summoned by their notorious bell, saved "Bully's" skin—not, as some accounts related, because they wanted justice, but to save one of their own, a man guilty of atrocities upon the men of his ship. [6]

A common interest held the sailors' boardinghouse masters, their runners, the boatmen and the merchant/political men of San Francisco together. Men were needed as crewmen so the commerce of the burgeoning city could grow. The town merchants had notions that San Francisco would outstrip New York, Paris and London in world commerce. That could not happen if crews could not be found for ships. If the merchants' shanghaiing friends broke the rules, it was all right, as long as the port functioned and goods moved. The sea was the only viable route for travel to the new port which was isolated from the rest of the nation by miles of inhospitable land which would not be traversed by railroads until completion of the transcontinental railroad in 1869.

Shanghaiing and the sailors' boardinghouse system were a chaotic affair the first several years of San Francisco's existence. Henry Smith, one of San Francisco's first two constables after the American takeover, ran a sailors' boardinghouse. According to William Martin Camp, in his book *San Francisco: Port of*

Courtesy San Francisco Maritime N.H.P.

Vallejo, Broadway, and Pacific Wharves in 1863 . . . When Dave Crowley Sr. started his Whitehall boat trade in 1873, San Francisco's north waterfront looked very much like this. In the foreground, just beyond Daniel Gibbs' Warehouse, Front Street stood on wooden pilings, creating a protection for small boats, such as the Whitehall boat seen catching the wind to head out.

Two deepwater vessels have cockbilled their lower yards to move cargo down into drays on the 800-foot Vallejo Street Wharf.

In 1872-3, J.S. Dolliver's shipping offices occupied the building at the southwest corner of Vallejo and Davis streets. Next door, at the time of this photo in 1863, the firm of Scott and Babcock also shanghaied sailors, using the more polite term of shipping offices. Abel F. Scott attempted to bribe the jury in a "hellship" outrage ten years later. At the southwest corner of Vallejo and Front streets, just to the south of the Gibbs' Warehouse's roof, the top story of the Sailor's Home in 1863 is visible. Boardinghouses faced Vallejo, where Heustis & Co. ship chandlery sold provisions.

Courtesy San Francisco Maritime N.H.P.

Four Years Later, One Block Up Vallejo . . . Battery Street crosses Vallejo, directly below the three-story brick rooming house with the laundry on the roof. The Essex House, a boardinghouse, is across the puddle-filled street, with a wooden awning over the entrance to Henry Winkle's Bakery.

The block of Broadway between Front and Davis streets, in the left center of the photograph, was near Clark's Point, one of San Francisco's first landing sites for deepwater ships. The building at the southwest corner of Davis and Broadway was Grosbauer & Co., liquor retailers. Next door is John T. Callender's saloon. Callender, from the West Indies, also ran a "colored" boardinghouse in this building. Callender's had a very lively history. James Douglass, a famed boardinghouse master and one-time partner of "Frenchy" Franklin, resided two doors down, at 9 Broadway. Further down is the Contra Costa Laundry, with laundry strung along a clothes line.

The north waterfront saw the city's earliest commercial development, with massive brick warehouses close to wharves. North waterfront property, even unfilled waterlots, sold for $35,000 to $40,000 per lot in the early 1850s.

Gold (1947), Richard Graham and George Roeben separately ran two of the early sailors' boardinghouses. Roeben ran a lodging establishment at 50 Commercial Street in 1852, but by 1856 he operated Charley's Rancho boardinghouse at the corner of Drumm and Jackson streets. In 1861 Roeben's boardinghouse was at 37-39 Pacific Street, a location he would maintain for nearly 30 years. [7]

One of the most famous crimps was a man who began in the profession early—James Laflin. Born about 1831 in Ireland, he came to America in 1847 and shipped as a cabin boy on the *Arkansas,* which sailed for the California Gold Rush around Cape Horn from New York June 26, 1849. It arrived in San Francisco in December of that year, and the captain, unfamiliar with the tides of San Francisco Bay, ran her up on the rocks of Alcatraz Island. Passengers and crew manned the pumps all night to keep her afloat until two passing whale boats were persuaded, after a hefty payment, to pull the *Arkansas* off the rocks. She was towed next to the Pacific Street wharf near the corner of what would become Battery Street. There she stayed, as did many such vessels that were beached in the growing metropolis. A hole was cut in her bow "to admit the thirsty" and Laflin tended bar at the Old Ship Saloon in her forecastle. The U.S. Hotel was built over the ship and although the ship was sold for scrap and disassembled in 1857, the Old Ship Saloon continued in another building for decades (in the 1990s it was still operating as a restaurant at 298 Pacific Street at the corner of Battery). Dick Ahlers was one of a long line of men who shanghaied sailors at the Old Ship Saloon. [8]

Laflin went into business as a boatman in 1850, as did Patrick Crowley, the city's future Chief of Police, ferrying passengers and goods in the familiar Whitehall boats to and from ships in the harbor. Laflin worked from Cunningham's Wharf, a T-shaped pier north of the area known as Clark's Point. As a bartender to seamen and a ferrying boatman, he was in an ideal position to become a shanghaier. An article on Whitehall boatmen in the *Daily Alta California* in 1882 credited Laflin with rising to a comfortable position in the city through "perseverance and industry." [9]

He earned the nickname "Jimmy the Drummer," drummer being the word for salesman in the 19th century. The origin of his nickname was not explained, but Laflin was selling sailors to shipping masters. In 1859 he was a "solicitor" for the Sailor's Home located at Front and Pacific streets. There he performed the skills of his trade. Solicitor in fact was a polite word for runner. Laflin for decades was well known for shipping crews on whalers. He also ran his own saloon on Pacific Street in 1855 and, according to the 1860 census, operated the Vallejo Boarding House at 30 Vallejo Street near the water's edge. [10]

The shipping articles which sailors signed or put their mark to provide an indication of other early shanghaiers in San Francisco. The ship *Kate Hooper*, which sailed from San Francisco in 1856, paid advance money to Laflin and to a Crowley. This may or may not have been the future police chief—only last names were used, so positive proof does not exist; however it can not be ruled out that Patrick Crowley was shanghaiing sailors. Other names on shipping articles from 1856 are Kelly—James "Shanghai" Kelly—John Peter Sanders, John C. Price, Richard Graham and George Roeben's Charley's Rancho boardinghouse. [11]

After a 30 year career as a saloon keeper and boardinghouse master on San Francisco's waterfront, Laflin became a shipping master in 1881. He moved to 46 Spear in 1890 and 104 Mission Street by 1894; he advertised himself as a shipping agent. In 1886, Laflin commenced annual publication of a *List of Officers Composing the Whaling Fleet of San Francisco*. The listing was helpful to those who wanted to supply whalers with crew; it identified captains and officers.

A successful entrepreneur at his trade, Laflin had a ship built for the sealing fleet in 1886, the *Annie*. The 54-foot vessel, however, was ill-fated. On an expedition off Alaska, two crimp associates of Laflin who were aboard as crew, Harry "Horseshoe" Brown and Nils "Shanghai" Nelson, were shot and wounded while raiding seal rookeries in an area leased to the Alaska Commercial Company. "Shanghai" Nelson barely escaped with his life when the guards for one rookery discovered him and his fellow pirates. As Nelson was picking up an oar to row to safety, a bullet struck him in the arm. Before he and his friends could row away from danger, another bullet hit him in the back of the neck, exiting the side of the neck. Knocked unconscious, Nelson almost bled to death by time he came to. His mates tried to patch up the holes, but he choked on the blood streaming down his throat. In desperation the crew of the small boat put his neck in a chock on the gunwale of the boat, where Nelson's weight compressed the wound. Together they endured several hours at sea before the *Annie* rescued them. [12]

The following year, the *Annie* was seized in the Bering Straits for taking seals illegally, forcing Laflin to post a bond for the ship's release. Saddest of all, the *Annie* did not make it to the sealing grounds in 1889: she was lost, along with her crew of eleven men. Men from Norway, Finland, Portugal, Holland, the West Indies, Sweden, Scotland and California went for a share of the profits but wound up in Davy Jones' locker, entombed in the *Annie*.

Laflin also enjoyed racing his sloop in the annual Master Mariners' Regatta on San Francisco Bay. In 1880 he chartered her out for a fishing trip, this time to a man named Marvin M. Staples, who said he planned to sail down the California coast to Santa Barbara. Four months later he returned to San Francisco and offered Laflin $200 to buy the sloop. In fact, Staples had sailed to Guayaquil, Ecuador; Laflin resorted to the legal system and had Staples arrested for piracy. Two friends made bail for Staples after he was indicted for barratry, a fraudulent act on the part of the captain or crew of a vessel against its owners or underwriters, but when a warrant for his arrest was issued, Staples was long gone, reported last seen on or near the Galapagos Islands. Laflin sued to recover the bail-bond money and court costs. [13]

Another early crimp was James "Shanghai" Kelly (1820-1868), one of those who gave San Francisco international notoriety as the worst shanghaiing port in the world. In 1856 he ran the Boston House at the corner of Davis and Chambers streets. Most sailors' boardinghouses were on Davis, Jackson, Pacific, Front, Broadway, Steuart or Mission, the last two south of Market Street. Kelly's establishment may have been part of the Old Ship Saloon which was advertised in 1856 as having a branch at the same corner as the Boston House. Likely the saloon was a branch of the shanghaiing trade. [14]

Kelly's reputation as the most dreaded perpetrator of drugged liquor and the blackjack was well deserved, and a bar that carries the name "Shanghai" Kelly's keeps the legend alive today. Born in Ireland, Kelly became an American citizen in Philadelphia in 1848 and shortly afterwards left for San Francisco. Like Patrick Crowley, Kelly may have started as a Whitehall boatman. A John Kelly, age 32, was identified in the 1852 census as living in the same quarters that Crowley occupied while plying the trade of boatman in 1852. By 1854 Kelly ran a boardinghouse at 33 Broadway, and in 1867, a James Kelly, age 48—no doubt the same man—was listed as operating another sailors' boardinghouse. A short, heavy man with a red beard and fiery temper, according to author Richard Dillon's *Shanghaiing Days* (1961), Kelly preferred real sailors to greenhorns because they were easier to manipulate. His favorite shanghai cocktail consisted of schnapps, beer and sleep-inducing drugs. Chinatown cigarmakers produced special brands for Kelly—laced with opium. [15]

Legend holds that Kelly's defining moment came in October, 1854, when the boardinghouse master found three ships, including the hellship *Reefer*, badly in need of crews. He chartered a paddle wheel steamer, the *Goliah*, to throw a birthday bash for himself with free drinks for all the guests. According to a nostalgic account years later by Edward Morphy (in 1919-20) and others, Kelly's invitation quickly spread through the Barbary Coast, the city's wildest section, and 90 celebrants soon joined the shipboard party. Kelly, the story went, first ordered the boat south toward Alviso. But as the merrymakers drained the barrels of booze and grew more intoxicated, the steamer turned around and headed out the Golden Gate into the Pacific Ocean. By that time, the partygoers were in a stupor, drugged by the liquor's knock-out potions. By coincidence, a ship, the *Yankee Blade*, had wrecked shortly before and it was believed Kelly picked up some of the shipwrecked survivors. In the excitement when the boat returned to dock, no one questioned what had become of his original revelers. The legend said they were spirited aboard waiting ships including the *Reefer*, which had a reputation as a hellship. [16] (A hellship was one where the crew was driven physically and mentally by the officers to the point where life was a living hell. Suicides on such ships, frequently by jumping overboard to a watery death, were not uncommon).

   "Shanghai" Kelly would have made a fortune supplying 90 men to ships, and his audacity and ingenuity, a source of awe if the story had been true. But the facts suggest otherwise. The *Goliah* was a steam packet with a regularly-scheduled run from San Francisco to San Diego in 1854. On September 30 the ship left San Francisco with more than 100 passengers. Newspaper accounts reported that she came upon the shipwrecked *Yankee Blade* off Point Conception, some 300 miles south of San Francisco, rescued most of the clipper's 800 passengers and continued on to San Diego. There is no report of a ship named *Reefer* having sailed from San Francisco at the time of Kelly's alleged shanghaiing party. For the record, the captain of the *Yankee Blade* was

Courtesy of Henry Klee's Great-Granddaughter, Mrs. Stanley Copel

The Old Ship Saloon, at Battery & Pacific streets, may be the only drinking establishment in the city remaining from the days of shanghaiing . . . Built in New York in 1833, the ship *Arkansas* arrived in San Francisco in 1849. Damaged when the tide ran her into Alcatraz Island, the crew abandoned her for the gold-fields and she was sold. Landlocked on Pacific Street, a door was cut in the bluff of her bow to serve the thirsty. She became a saloon and the cabin boy on her passage from New York, James Laflin, returned to act as bartender on what became known as the Old Ship Saloon. Laflin began his career as a crimp here, when he was not rowing a Whitehall boat at nearby Cunningham's Wharf. By 1859, the hulk was cut up and sold for scrap wood. A two-story brick building, sleeping 22 seafaring men, was built in its place and its saloon continued the Old Ship Saloon name. Warren P. Herman, a crimp of note, operated from the brick building in the 1890s. The building was partially destroyed in 1906, and rebuilt by 1907; seen here with boardinghouse keeper Henry Klee, standing next to the post, sporting a walrus mustache, he is surrounded by helpers and patrons. Ironically, Klee occasionally collected a fee for shipping a sailor through James Laflin's son, Peter J. Laflin.

tried and condemned for abandoning ship shortly after it was wrecked. "Shanghai" Kelly met his own untimely end some years later. [17]

The most sensational case of 1868 was the disappearance of James "Shanghai" Kelly and John Parker. John Parker, a runner born in North Carolina, was seventeen years younger than Kelly's forty-eight years. In late January, the two had $1,500 in their possession. The sum (equivalent to about $30,000 today) was received as advances for sailors supplied to the ship *Intrepid* and other vessels by Kelly, Parker and others. Then the pair disappeared. Rumor had it they were shanghaied.

Whether Kelly and Parker were shanghaied or simply absconded with the money, four months later a story went around the waterfront that Kelly and Parker were in Peru. If shanghaied, they probably jumped ship at Callao, a port on the South American coast. The exciting news, however, was that Parker and Kelly had a shoot-out in Peru and that Kelly died. [18]

From the realm of fact-based legend to pure myth was sometimes a short step when it came to shanghaiing. An oft repeated story was that of a Chileno called "Calico Jim" who made the mistake of shanghaiing six plain-clothes policemen. The cops, after making their way back to San Francisco, vowed revenge and drew straws to determine who would track down the villain, who had fled to Valpariso, Chile. When the avenger found the shanghaier, he shot him once for each cop shanghaied. The story became a popular legend on the San Francisco waterfront. But it is unlikely that six policemen could have been off their beat for long without being missed, and no records indicate that such was the case at the time of the alleged incident. "Calico Jim," though, made his way into several published books about shanghaiing. [19]

Another story is that of an English cockney called Hurley who recounted tales of a Yankee ship on which the captain enjoyed firing from the deck at his crew on the yardarms above with a six-shooter. Hurley, who claimed to have abandoned alcohol, found himself drugged by a cup of coffee and wakened at sea by a mate with a belaying pin aboard a reputed hell-ship, the *Andrew Jackson*.

Another shanghai victim was the young Englishman Frank H. Shaw who sailed on the British ship *Dovenby* in the 1890s. In port at San Francisco, he and a friend found a gambling room at the back of a cabaret where Shaw caught a dealer cheating. Other sailors sprung to Shaw's defense when bouncers were summoned. The two Englishmen tossed the owner through a window, cleaned out the bank and demolished the bar, exiting through the shanghaiing trap door just as police arrived. Shaw told of a former mayor and boardinghouse master shanghaied onto a whaler bound for a three-year cruise. Another of Shaw's tall tales was the one about a leading businessman shanghaied as an act of revenge on the part of a ship captain who had been forced to enter the man's home through the servants' entrance. [20] Such tales were gross fabrications.

An account written in 1937 told of a harrowing voyage in 1875 ending in San Francisco with the vessel's having been boarded by "hundreds" of runners. The author, if he actually experienced the events that he recorded, would have been in his 80s when the article was written. San Francisco's waterfront never supported "hundreds" of crimps. The tale, however, fed the British imagination for romantic seagoing stories.

> Going through the Golden Gate up 'Frisco Bay, we were boarded by hundreds of crimps and boardinghouse runners who swarmed aboard . . . They were just about at the height of their fame then, and a greater crowd of ruffians you wouldn't find in the whole seven seas. We were all aloft putting a harbour stow on the sails, and they followed us out on the yards, trying to get the sailors off to the boardinghouses. They had bottles of rotten whiskey with them, and the noise they made was awful. They got some of the sailors off—poor wretches. Little they knew what was in front of them; given a night's

spree and then shanghaied aboard some ship, to face Cape Horn with a suit of oilskins that wouldn't keep a shower of rain out, and a donkey's breakfast [a mattress filled with straw], and two months' advance on their wages in the crimp's pocket. As a rule they didn't come aboard the ships once they were tied up to the wharf, but the next morning one arrived on the quarter-deck with a big cigar in his mouth, a well-known character on the waterfront. The old man [captain] promptly got him by the back of the neck and ran him over the gangway and then stepped back on deck.

The crimp fairly howled with rage, and dared the skipper to come on to the wharf and fight him. The old man promptly accepted the challenge, but the tough backed down completely and walked off, cursing the ship and everything connected with it —good and hearty—as long as we could hear him. [21]

A more factual story is that of a Swede, Erik Olaf Lindblom. Born in 1857, he was a tailor by trade who sailed for America in 1886, eventually finding his way to San Francisco. In 1898, he was approached one day by two men on the waterfront asking if he was a sailor. Mistaking the word for "tailor," Lindblom replied, "Yah, sure," whereupon the men said, "Come along with us. We have a job for you." Lindblom was taken to a saloon, drugged and shanghaied to a whaling bark, *Alaska*, headed for the Arctic Ocean. He jumped ship at Port Clarence, Alaska, when sent ashore for fresh water. Meeting a prospector, Lindblom headed for gold fields near Golovin Bay. He joined forces with two other Scandinavians—dubbed the "Three Lucky Swedes," although one was Norwegian—and found gold near Nome. Lindblom returned to California in 1899, invested his money successfully in real estate, and co-founded the Swedish-American Bank in 1908. The former tailor had turned his shanghaiing into a fortune—a great result for a tailor thought to be a sailor shanghaied on a whaler. [22]

Returning to facts, "Shanghai" Kelly was typical of boardinghouse owners of the period. Most were immigrants, unlike shipowners and merchants who were largely American-born. Immigrants opened businesses like boardinghouses and saloons, laundries and houses of prostitution to make a living with minimal capital outlay. City directories identify many boardinghouses from the 1850s to 1890s. William Paupitz, who operated the Minerva House saloon, was born in Prussia in 1820 and became an American citizen in 1860. He ran a sailors' boardinghouse at 59 Jackson Street beginning in 1860; he moved to 123 Jackson in 1864. Around the corner, Englishman Thomas Murray (30 years old in 1873) started out as a bartender at 504 Davis for another crimp, Henry "Shanghai" Brown. Murray acquired, through marriage, his own establishment, the Golden Gate House at 510 Davis, which he ran for more than 30 years. When early boardinghouse operator Richard Graham, another Englishman, died in 1863, Murray married his widow Elizabeth, six years his senior and the mother of five children, aged four to sixteen. Together they owned $25,000 worth of real estate. Brown's establishment on Davis Street was taken over about 1871 by his former runner, Thomas Chandler. The Norwegian-born Brown moved his boardinghouse to 810 Battery Street where he lived with his wife Mary and four children. The 11 lodgers in the building remained for short durations, however.

Robert Pinner (1830-1880), an Englishman, was Laflin's business partner in the 1860s. Pinner resided with his wife and five children in a boardinghouse at 35 Pacific—George Roeben was next door—from which crimps supplied crew to whaling ships. Laflin's home at the time was at Francisco and Stockton streets and later, in 1880, at 41 Vallejo where he lived with his five children (daughters Mary, 18, and Ann, 14, and sons Lawrence, 16, Peter, 12 and William, 10), along with a boarder.

Other crimps and their houses were located in the same vicinity. John Gately catered to sailors at 217 Broadway in 1860, Joseph "Frenchy" Franklin at 215 Broadway as late as the

Eric Lindblom . . . Born in Sweden, Lindblom became a tailor by profession. He sailed for America and eventually found his way to San Francisco. In 1898, Lindblom was drugged and shanghaied, and came to on the whaling bark *Alaska*, bound for the Arctic Ocean. He was sent ashore for fresh water near Port Clarence, Alaska and decided to keep going.

He joined with a Swede and a Norwegian and they soon discovery gold near Nome. The next year, Lindblom returned to California and invested in real estate and banking. A great result for a former tailor thought to be a sailor, shanghaied on a whaler.

1890s. Billy Maitland operated a house at 17 Vallejo in the late 1870s, Edwin Charles Lewis on the same street between Front and Battery. Crimps John Hart and John Rogers had houses nearby where a police sergeant, Thomas Langford, resided in the early 1870s. Langford had run a sailors' boardinghouse, the Blue Wing at 8 Washington Street, in 1861, and later on Clay Street before he joined the police force in 1871. Billy Maitland ran the Blue Wing in 1868, when John Devine paid him a famous visit.

The California State Legislature first acknowledged the problem of shanghaiing in 1853 when it enacted a law making it a misdemeanor to entice crew to desert a ship or to harbor deserters. The law was largely ignored, however, and had little effect in curbing the problem. Although the city's legislative delegation exercised a great deal of control over the state in the 1850s and '60s, few efforts were made to regulate or eliminate shanghaiing. Not until 1864 was another law enacted to deal with the matter. It prohibited runners from boarding inbound vessels before they docked at a wharf without first getting permission from ship masters or owners and from enticing crew to desert (San Francisco Consolidation Act of 1856, Amendment 18). The law was aimed at controlling boardinghouse runners but violations were only a misdemeanor with a fine of $100 and/or 50 days in jail. It, too, had little impact on crimping. Harbor police were not effective in catching runners and police officials like two-time chief Patrick Crowley (1866 to 1873 and 1879 to 1897), himself a former boatman, claimed understaffing prevented them from effectively enforcing the law.

Two news stories in 1867 told of Oakland men who had disappeared in two separate incidents, leaving grieving wives to declare them dead after a year. But a dispatch from New York announced to the "widows" that their husbands had been shanghaied. One wife cheerfully sent her husband travel money to return home; the other had to make his way at his own expense. A carpenter who disappeared in 1889 was not so lucky. His family had given him up for dead and returned to Lincoln, Nebraska, when two years later news reached San Francisco that the man, James Mitchell, had been discovered in Alaska. He had escaped constant abuse on a whaler and made his way up the Yukon River, living with natives who were tending his frozen feet. [23]

Runner Edmund Gilbert, described as a "hanger-on around Pacific Street doggeries," was caught inducing several sailors to desert the French ship *Limousin,* taking them directly to another ship in the harbor. If the French sailors were rescued from the humiliation of shanghaiing, William Bray had less luck. From a boardinghouse on Steuart Street he had gotten a position as a hand on a coastal schooner. When he asked his landlord for his sea chest, the man demanded payment in gold for his bill. Bray offered greenbacks and police allowed the boardinghouse keeper to hold the chest until the debt was paid. [24]

Crime among crimps was a common pastime, and a special Harbor Police was established in 1867 at Davis near Pacific Street, a few doors up from Thomas Murray's Golden Gate House. The officers' beat included the waterfront, Barbary Coast and North Beach region around Telegraph Hill, home to Italian, Irish and other immigrant families. Although shanghaiing was a common activity in the area, few of its perpetrators were arrested. That August, for example, 14 sailors were arrested for desertion but only one arrest was made of a runner or crimp for illegally enticing sailors to desert. One other arrest was made for the crime of boarding a vessel without permission although Harbor Police, at the request of ships' officers, boarded twenty-five vessels that month to keep sailors from deserting and prevent runners from enticing away crewmen.

The famous clipper *Flying Cloud* was the target of a shanghaiing attempt in 1868. When she arrived from Australia, she was boarded by a boat-load of five crimps and runners including James McCann, "Frenchy" Franklin and James Douglass. A Harbor Policeman had seen the Whitehall and followed them onto the vessel. He and the ship's mate ordered the crimps off but they refused and the officer, who knew them by reputation, placed them all under arrest. What happened to the other four is not known but "Frenchy" was convicted of a misdemeanor and fined $20. [25]

Crimps, runners and boardinghouse masters alike were often in trouble for other offenses than shanghaiing. McCann was arrested in 1867 for assault and battery. An elderly man, James Devlin, was charged with grand larceny for stealing a coat from a sailors' boardinghouse maintained by a Hawaiian on Clark Street. It was not the coat that was valuable but what it held: four promissory notes, each for $40, drawn by Mason & Company shipping agents, payable to "Mike," B. Irish, John Adams and "Napoleon"—two days after they shipped out on the whaling bark *Jeanette*. [26]

By late 1867, anti-shanghaiing pressure grew, and for a few years under Chief Patrick Crowley more arrests were made of runners illegally boarding ships than of prostitutes. Throughout San Francisco's early years, under the Vigilance Committee of 1856 and its successor, the People's Party, which ran San Francisco until 1865 and again in 1870-71, the only effort to stop shanghaiing was the amendment to the Consolidation Act of 1856 to prevent illegal boarding of vessels by runners. The city fathers were influenced by its merchants and shipowners, who wielded powerful influence on the city's economic and political life and had little interest in controlling or eliminating shanghaiing. [27]

Shipowners and their captains felt the situation in the city was out of control in August 1867. As the British ship *Blackwall* lay in the harbor, a fire was set in the focsle apparently by disgruntled members of the crew. The flames spread through most of the vessel, damaging the cargo and destroying half the ship. Outraged, sixteen ship captains and Matthew Turner, a noted San Francisco shipbuilder, met at the Merchants' Exchange to discuss

Shipping articles from 1856 . . . Warning "No Grog Allowed" and "No Profane Language," these shipping articles from the *Kate Hooper* formed a legal contract. At the right hand side, the names of James Laflin and Crowley, who received $30 advances per sailor, give credence to rumors that Patrick Crowley, later Police Chief, and Laflin were partners as boatmen.

what they considered the serious threat posed to shipping in San Francisco. Washington C. Bartlett acted as secretary and prepared a memo which the captains directed to the city's Chamber of Commerce. The agenda strayed from arson on board the *Blackwall* to a wider discontent with the sailors' boardinghouse system. Sailors' wages shipping from this port were $25 per month, 50 percent higher than any other U.S. port, but the sailor saw none of the benefit because the boardinghouse keepers took two months advance wages, while the shipping master took $20. It cost $70 per man to obtain a sailor. The captains termed sailors' boardinghouses "sinks of iniquity" and also complained that two ships were punished in 1866 for not cooperating completely with the boardinghouses: the *California* had been fined $500 for preventing runners from boarding the ship, although the law supposedly stopped runners from doing so without the ships' permission; and the *Cormorant's* captain had been punished for obtaining three sailors outside boardinghouse channels. Captains worried that the port itself would get a bad name—but it already had done so worldwide. But there the affair ended. [28]

The leading merchants of San Francisco started something called the Labor Exchange in 1868. Intended to place unemployed men and women in jobs, it was an early effort at a social program for those down and out. *The Daily Alta* and *San Francisco Newsletter* were enthusiastic supporters of the Labor Exchange. The sailors' boardinghouse masters adamantly opposed the Labor Exchange as a threat to their power. If the Labor Exchange could ship sailors, it would pose a very serious economic threat. The sailors' advances which went to the boardinghouse masters would be gone. *The Daily Alta* editorialized against the brutal system sailors faced. "Instead of being an intelligent freeman, the sailor is a slave, not only to his purposely excited passions, but to a race of beings known as landlords, or boardinghouse keepers." Ship captains wrote letters of support for the Exchange. They thought it encouraged sobriety among and dignity toward sailors by eliminating crimps with their foul liquor and false promises from enticing away sailors from their ships, then forcing these sailors to ship out sometimes the same day. Despite persistent efforts to ship sailors through the Labor Exchange, the boardinghouse masters exerted a combination of political pressure and threats of violence to prevent shipping through the Exchange. [29]

At the state level, a bill to protect sailors from the abuses of crimps, boardinghouse keepers, shipping masters and unscrupulous captains passed the state Senate but failed in the Assembly. The *San Francisco Newsletter* reported sailors' boardinghouses were operating "full blast" three weeks after the defeat of the sailors' boardinghouse bill. [30]

The Daily Alta called for national legislation to regulate shipping agents (usually in league with boardinghouse masters) and the wages and contracts of sailors. Local laws would always be inadequate, the *Daily Alta* observed. The local shanghaiing combines had the requisite political pull to circumvent such laws. It would not be until 1872 that Congress began to deal with the issue at the national level.

Footnotes

1 *Daily Alta*, November 28, 1853, p.2, col.4

2 Ibid, January 8, 1854, p.2, col.2

3 *The Oxford Companion To Ships and The Sea,* ed. by Peter Kemp, 1976, p.213

4 *The California Star*, September 25, 1847, p.2, col.3; T.H. Watkins and R.R. Olmsted, *Mirror of the Dream: An Illustrated History of San Francisco* (San Francisco: Scrimshaw Press, 1976), pp.14-17; *Daily Alta*, March 25, 1850, p.2, col.1

5 Kevin J. Mullen, *Let Justice Be Done* (Reno: University of Nevada Press, 1989), p.56

6 The English were far less tolerant of cruelty to sailors by ships' officers; at least one captain was hung for less than what Robert "Bully" Waterman did.

7 Coversation with Kevin Mullen

8 *San Francisco Daily Sun*, June 30, 1856; H.H. Bancroft, *History of California*, vol. VI (San Francisco: History Co., 1888), p.173; Jerry F. Schimmel, *An Old Ship From the Gold Rush* (San Francisco: Prepared for the Token and Medal Society Journal, 1992), p.18. The numbering system for buildings along Pacific Street, and much of San Francisco, changed after 1906—before 1906, the Old Ship Saloon's address was given as 228 and/or 230 Pacific Street. Later it became 268 Pacific Street.

9 *San Francisco Daily Alta*, May 8, 1882, p.1, col.2

10 See "Whitehall Boatman" pamphlet file, J. Porter Shaw Library; *Men and Memories on San Francisco in the Spring of '50*, Barry and Patten, p.80; "San Francisco City Licenses 1850-1856," microfilm Roll No. 2-86

11 "Ship's Articles and Crew Lists, 1854-1892," Record Group 36, Roll No. 106, National Archives, San Bruno, California

12 *San Francisco Daily Alta*, Sept. 18, 1886, p.8, col. 1-2

13 *Daily Alta*, October 4, 1874, p.1, col.3; October 9, 1874, p.1, col.4 and p.2, col.3; October 10, 1874, p.1, col.3; Compiled by D.M. Bishop & Co., *San Francisco City Directory, 1876,* (San Francisco: B.C. Vandall, 1876), p.23; *Daily Alta*, July 4, 1875, p.1, col.1; July 6, 1875, p.1, col.9; July 17, 1876, p.1, col.7; August 4, 1880, p.1, col.2 and August 17, 1880, p.1, col.3; November 20, 1880, p.1, col.2; July 21, 1881, p.1, col.3; *The Oxford Companion To Ships and The Sea*, ed. Peter Kemp, p.62; United States Criminal Court Case No. 1210, California District; *Daily Alta,* October 12, 1887, p.2, col.5; July 25, 1889, p.2, col.1; and WPA Ship Registery and Enrollments; San Francisco City Directories 1859, 1860, 1861,

1862, 1890-95, Great Register of Voters, 1873; *Morning Call*, May 25, 1886, p.3, col.5

14 *San Francisco Bulletin*, May 1, 1856 and *San Francisco City Directory, 1859*. One day in 1866, Kelly became angry with a young man working for him, Warren Frize, and proceeded to beat his employee quite severely. Frize was resourceful, and pulled out a razor sharp pocket knife, cutting Kelly on the arm. The *Daily Alta* took note of James Kelly's reputation, saying he was "sometimes known by the sobriquet of 'Shanghai Kelly.'" See *Daily Alta*, June 10, 1866, p.1, col.1 and June 13, 1866, p.1, col.1

15 Richard H. Dillon, *Shanghaiing Days* (New York: Coward-McCann, 1961), p.190

16 Edward Morphy,"San Francisco Thoroughfares," San Francisco *Chronicle*, May 2, 1920, p.8F, cols. 2-3

17 *Daily Alta California*, October 10, 1854, p.2, col.2; October 11, 1854, p.2, col.2; October 16, 1854, p.2, col.2; October 22, 1854, p.2, col.3; The *Daily Alta California* also includes several articles on the trial of Captain Randall in January 1855.

18 Ibid, January 29, 1868, p.1, col.3 and *San Francisco Newsletter*, June 13, 1868, p.16, col.1

19 Dillon, pp. 187-8

20 Ibid, pp. 209-10

21 Sackville Smyth, "Liverpool To Melbourne and 'Frisco About The Year 1875," *Sea Breezes*, vol. 22, July 1937, pp.41-2

22 Dillon, pp. 211-2 and *Press Reference Library. Notables of the West, vol. I* (New York: International News Service, 1913), p.511

23 *Daily Alta*, October 3, 1867, p.1, col.2; December 13, 1867, p.1, col.2 and *Mroning Call*, May 26, 1891, p.4, col.3

24 *Daily Alta*, February 13, 1868, p.1, col.2 and April 9, 1868, p.1, col.2

25 Ibid, June 18, 1868, p.1, col.2 and August 18, 1868, p.1, col.4

26 Ibid, October 18, 1867, p.1, col.2

27 *San Francisco Municipal Reports, 1875-6*, pp.819-21

28 *The Daily Alta*, August 25, 1867, p.1, col.2; August 27, 1867, p.i, col.3; and August 28, 1867, p.1, col.3

29 Ibid, October 16, 1868, p.1, col.2; October 16, 1868, p.2, col.1 and November 27, 1868, p.2, col.1

30 *San Francisco Newsletter*, May 9, 1868, p.16, col.1

California Historical Society

Thomas Chandler, circa 1868 . . . Already a famous boxer, Thomas Chandler poses in ring togs. Born in Ireland, Tommy moved to San Francisco before 1860. At the time of this photograph, Chandler was Henry "Shanghai" Brown's partner in a sailor's boardinghouse on Davis Street.

The Boardinghouse Masters Organize

O sweet Jesus, into thy hands I commend my spirit.
The last words of crimp John "Shanghai
Chicken" Devine before his execution for
murder.

Daily Alta, 1873

To contemporaries, sailors' boardinghouse masters were well
known and included police, businessmen, bare-knuckle boxers,
powerful politicians and a number of women. Among the latter
were legends like Mother Bronson, Chloroform Kate Johnson and
Miss Piggott, who employed a runner called Nikko. Nikko was a
Laplander who may have deserted a Swedish naval vessel, *Eugenia*, in 1852 to begin a new life on shore. Nikko became famous
for selling ship captains dummies who twitched in a life-like
manner because of the rats sewn into their sawdust-filled coat-
sleeves which made the dummies appear as drunks. Real female
crimps (who received payments for delivery of victims) included
Dorothy Paupitz, Mrs. Edgar, Anna Gomes who always signed
her "x" when she received her due bill and Mrs. Sheehan.

"The great majority of sailors, even those who were not
shanghaied," wrote historian Herbert Asbury in *The Barbary
Coast* (1933), "were shipped through the boardinghouse masters.
When a man signed his name, or put his mark to a ship's articles,

29

he received, in theory at least, two month's pay in advance so that he might outfit himself and not have to depend upon what he could purchase from the captain's slopchest." Advances, which were sometimes legal and other times, again theoretically, highly restricted, went to pay bills to boardinghouse masters who inflated the bills with overpriced whiskey, food and other little extras. According to Asbury and other accounts, boardinghouse victims often reached such establishments not on their own but after being removed from ships drunk or drugged, kept stupified while ashore under the vigilant escort of their Barbary Coast hosts and frequently shipped out again within 24 hours. Crimps sometimes hired someone to sign the legally-binding contracts for sailors who were beaten or otherwise tricked into signing on to a vessel's crew. "God help the poor sailor!" Asbury wrote. [1]

A *San Francisco Chronicle* newspaper report in 1899 described how a sailor's $40 advance was allocated. A shipping master, the middle man between ship captain and boardinghouse crimp, received $7.50 for placing the sailor; the boardinghouse operator got the balance, $32.50, of which $5 was paid to a runner. The rest was absorbed in boardinghouse costs, with a healthy profit for the boardinghouse keeper. [2]

The shipping master's role was crucial to shanghaiing. Typically a crimp of long-standing reputation, a shipping master obtained contracts from agents of shipowners to supply the ships with crewmen. When a ship was ready to sail, usually a new crew had to be recruited, as the old crew deserted or was run off by the ship's captain. (As British sailors, for example, were not paid unless they returned to a British port, the captain saw their desertion as money saved for the owners and/or himself.) The agents told the shipping master how many men and what qualification they needed—ordinary or able bodied seamen, a mate, carpenter, blacksmith and, especially on whaling voyages, a

"A Typical Crimp" . . . The Klondike Gold Rush caused a shortage of men in San Francisco and the old institution of shanghaiing had new life breathed into it with that shortage. The *San Francisco Chronicle* ran a full page story on shanghaiing in 1903, including drawings of "a typical crimp" and kidnapping of a non-sailor for a new life at sea.

San Francisco Public Library

San Francisco Public Library

"Sometimes force is necessary" . . . So said the *San Francisco Chronicle* when it devoted a full-page to the shanghaiing phenomenon in 1903. The article gave a fairly complete rundown of the leading figures in San Francisco's shanghaiing community, some of the tricks runners used to get a crew to leave a ship and follow them to a boardinghouse and a breakdown of the advance money between runner, shipping master and sailors' boardinghouse master—money that should have gone to the seamen fattened the shanghaiers of San Francisco for over sixty years.

31

cooper. The cooper built barrels to hold whale oil. The shipping master let his contacts among the boardinghouse masters and saloon keepers know what was needed, and boardinghouse residents, or men who were slipped a "Shanghai" concoction, were mustered, signed shipping articles and shipped out. The man or woman who presented the sailor, experienced or not on the sea, would receive a due bill, payable one or two days after the ship sailed, for the first two months of the sailor's wages.

A favorite tactic of runners was to stir up trouble among the crew if they found sailors reluctant to leave. One trick was to put a bar of soap in the soup. When sailors tasted it, they were in such a rage that an entire crew might follow a crimp off the ship.

Another lure for gullible or desperate men onto whalers was the potential of making large sums of money. Sailors were paid a percentage of whalers' profits from each voyage's haul. In 1892, the *San Francisco Examiner* ran a story about a Pacific Whaling Company captain who earned $7,000, and the third mate, $3,500. Another whaler's captain made $25,000. The story attempted to be evenhanded, though. An unidentified veteran seaman on whaling ships disputed the captain's version, saying that whaling-fleet sailors were left penniless at the end of voyages in the autumn when ships returned to port, or were paid a token $1 to $5 to comply with the legal requirement that they be compensated, and that whale-bone prices were purposely devalued below the actual market price (from $5 or $6.50 a pound to $1.50) in order to reduce on paper the amount of a ship's profit and thus, the sailors' share of earnings. Whale oil, too, was artificially marked down in market rules drawn up by whaling business interests. In addition, crew were charged five to fifteen percent on their advance notes, and deductions made for purchases from a ship's slopchest of clothing and tobacco, further reducing sailors' earnings. On one ship, the *Hunter*, which recorded a big catch worth $150,000 in 1892, ordinary seamen, who should have made $1,000, received less than $400. [3]

A whale oil refinery was constructed in the Potrero district, at the foot of Center Street—later to become 16th Street—by the Arctic Whaling and Oil Refining Company. The complex, sporting four large tanks, became known as the Arctic Oil Works and introduced a new manufacturing enterprise to the west coast, that of whale oil refining, manufacture of sperm oil candles and other products. The Arctic Oil Works, with its T-shaped wharf, presented a unique landmark on San Francisco's southern skyline for four decades. [4]

If all sailors were not drugged or stupefied with drink by crimps anxious to reap profits on human flesh, many genuinely were attracted by promises of jobs on coastal rather than deepwater vessels for three or four times the pay they had been making on long-distance voyages that lasted months or years. Images of frequent shore leaves, with drinking and women, were enough to make many men follow their new "friends." It is unlikely that many were kept under guard during their time ashore, normally several days or weeks, although there were severe shortages of sailors during the gold rushes in California (1848-9) and the Alaska Klondike (1897-98), the Spanish-American War (1898) and the days of the British grain fleet in the 1870s and '80s.

Boardinghouse masters, though, wielded enormous control over sailors, determining when and on what ships they worked, especially if they were unable to pay their hotel bills. The crimps' influence was enhanced in 1889 when the California legislature made it a criminal offense to renege on hotel accounts, and sailors often found themselves obligated to boardinghouse masters for their lives; they could not ship out unless they stayed in a sailors' boardinghouse. Their advance became, as it had for years, property of the boardinghouse master. [5]

A well-known boardinghouse owner was Irishman James McCann, whose place was at 11 Front Street in the early 1860s.

John "Shanghai Chicken" Devine stayed at McCann's when he arrived in San Francisco in 1861, but McCann soon shipped him out. James McCann was frequently in the news. In 1869 he was arrested after biting off a man's nose. By the 1870s, McCann's boardinghouse was located at 896 Front Street, known as the National Sailor's Home.

In October 1869 the wild spirit of McCann's boardinghouse continued on Front Street. William Taylor and John Kelly, two sailors, had a disagreement in front of McCann's and Kelly proceeded to put nine severe wounds in Taylor's body with his sheath knife. The capper was the shooting of James McCann himself at the corner of Montgomery and Washington streets. Edward B. Dugan inflicted a "dangerous" wound, but McCann managed to live.

The next month news broke that a man named Frank Jessen had been shanghaied from McCann's boardinghouse in February of that year. Jessen's case was atypical in that he was able to leave his ship in the port of destination, Manila, see the American Consul and return home to his wife and family. Jessen had arrived in San Francisco and was taken by a runner to McCann's place. He was not well and immediately went to bed. At breakfast the next morning Jessen was told by McCann that he would ship out on the *Southern Cross* to Manila. Jessen refused and McCann and three of his runners forced the reluctant sailor-to-be into the backyard, where McCann continually struck Jessen in the face until he signed shipping articles. He was taken to the ship and told the captain the situation but the captain told him it was too late to find a replacement. Jessen was so ill he could not work during the voyage. Attempts to prosecute McCann came to nothing.

Life caught up with James McCann in early 1875. He attempted to act on a grudge he held against another sailors' boardinghouse keeper named John McLean while he, McCann, was drunk. In that state, McCann went to McLean's boardinghouse and picked a fight. McLean responded by hitting McCann

San Francisco Maritime Museum N.H.P.

The Arctic Oil Wharf (center, with coal loaded onto the dock) was the center of Pacific Coast whaling in 1900 . . . Whaling vessels brought their oil and bone into the Arctic Oil's T-shaped wharf at the foot of today's 16th Street. The storage warehouses of Mission Rock are at the upper right. Smoke spews from the Union Iron Works, at the bottom left, whose factories built the first steel hulled ship on the Pacific Coast in 1885. Gleaming new cable cars sit in the foreground, outside the office of the Atlas Iron Works.

San Francisco Maritime Museum N.H.P.

Crimp James McCann forced Frank Jessen to ship on the *Southern Cross* to Manila in 1868 . . . Jessen was taken to McCann's boardinghouse by a runner. Jessen was ill, but McCann and three others struck Jessen in the face until he agreed to ship out. He was too sick to work on the voyage, and reported his plight to the American Consul when he arrived in Manila. McCann was not prosecuted when Frank Jessen returned to San Francisco—what the boardinghouse keeper had done, other than the assault, was not against the law at the time.

McCann was one of the most troublesome sailors' boardinghouse masters along the waterfront. In addition to beating Jessen, he bit part of an Italian's nose off, illegally boarded vessels and shipped out the "Shanghai Chicken." McCann was ultimately killed when he went to a rival boardinghouse while drunk and picked a fight with the operator. Hit in the head with an iron bar, McCann died a few days later.

with an iron bar over his left eye, knocking him out. Taken to the surgeon at the City Jail, McCann was later released. The surgeon thought the wound insignificant. McCann stayed in bed at home and "within a few days fever set in—induced, no doubt, in a great measure by dissipation as much as any other cause. Sunday night he died at his hotel and McLean was charged with murder." The charge was later reduced to manslaughter. [6]

The *Daily Alta* reported the wreck of the North Pacific Transportation Company's steamer *Continental* in the Gulf of California 30 miles off Cape St. Lucas in its October 17, 1870, edition. Included in its report was the account of the ship's carpenter's survival at sea.

> I was ship's carpenter on the vessel for about seven months . . . . In the hurricane the vessel rolled and pitched terribly . . . . The Captain placed me in charge of the second lifeboat that left the ship . . . . I had on board eight passengers, among whom were two women and three children, and ten of the ship's crew. A Mexican women fell overboard from my boat. I seized her by her clothes, but was unable to haul her into the boat. She had on a life-preserver, and it caught in the gunwale of the boat. We came near having our boat smashed against the side of the ship. We were obliged to pull away and leave the poor woman to her fate . . . .
>
> While we were around the vessel, and during the whole time we were out, the sea was alive with sharks. Their fins could be seen sticking up on all hands. This is probably the reason why those who were left on board the ship refused to leave. When we approached the shore, the water was fairly black with sharks, and most of us became alarmed for fear we capsized in beaching the boat and be devoured by them. . . . The bow of the boat grounded, when a large wave receded, and in a moment after, a wave raised the stern of the boat and turned it clear over. It fell bottom side up, and spilled us all

out . . . . The water was only waist deep, we succeeded in reaching shore in safety . . . . [7]

Thus was San Francisco introduced to John Curtin. Not long thereafter, Curtin lost an eye working as a ship's carpenter, and became known as One-Eyed Curtin. Curtin decided to emulate the sharks who haunted him in 1870, and opened a sailors' boardinghouse, living by selling sailors' flesh. He started the Fulton House, in the growing South of Market area, around 1875.

In 1880 Frank Roney held a meeting of his Seamens' Protective Association in front of Curtin's boardinghouse on Steuart Street. As Roney describes the scene, "I was assaulted with a volley of antiquated eggs, one of which struck me squarely on the breast. I jumped off the hay wagon I was using as a platform and dashed at the crowd before Curtin's. They immediately sought protection within the house, where they remained during the rest of our meeting." On another occasion, in 1885, Curtin's house was set afire. Curtin exemplified everything that sailors hated—bold and defiant exploitation of them by stealing their advances and cheating them on their wages. He was attacked and badly beaten at least twice in 1886 but a judge dismissed charges against his sailor attackers.

John Curtin had his problems with boarders from time to time. Because he shipped non-union sailors on coastal vessels he was bitterly despised by union sailors. One fine day in September 1889 three union sailors arrived in San Francisco and went to Curtin's Fulton House with their duffel bags. One-Eyed Curtin was very pleased to see them as they owed him $20, $36 and $31 for a previous stay at his establishment. The sailors left their gear in Curtin's baggage room, slept the night, had breakfast and went to be paid off. The Tars did not return, however, so One-Eye, exercising his legal right, went to the police and had the missing sailors' bags opened. A crowd gathered and all had a big laugh at

Curtin's expense as it was revealed the contents of the bags consisted of pieces of canvas, beat-up tomato cans, worn out buckets and frayed rope. Curtin marched down to the headquarters of the Coast Seamen's Union, but he did not obtain satisfaction. [8]

Curtin showed considerable resourcefulness when faced with the hostility of the union. In October, 1887, the captain of the bark *Cowlitz,* reluctant to pay the union rate of $45 per month per sailor, contacted Curtin who vowed to supply a crew of sailors at no more than $40 per month. One o'clock one morning Curtin gathered the men from his boardinghouse and attempted to drive them down to the *Cowlitz.* Union men were on the lookout, and headed John off. He and his men returned to the boardinghouse to avoid trouble. The union men went to bed, thinking they had stymied their arch enemy. At 2 a.m. John set forth once again and this time had no trouble loading his men onto the bark.

On September 24, 1893 a huge explosion rocked Steuart Street. Six men had arrived at Curtin's New Fulton boardinghouse at 334 Main Street about midnight and found a black valise outside the front door. Curtin's son picked up the valise and suddenly yelled out "There is dynamite in it." Dropping the bag, he ran off. His friends laughed and started to inspect the bag, when BOOM! Young Curtin was right. The valise was, indeed, full of dynamite and four men were killed outright when it exploded. A fifth died later. Curtin's boardinghouse was wrecked. Public reaction was one of outrage. Politicians and newspapers picked up the public sentiment. The Coast Seamen's Union denied any responsibility and expressed its indignation. The Governor, Shipowners' Association and Coast Seamen's Union all offered a reward. Three ex-union men were arrested and tried but there was no conviction. No new arrests were ever made in the case. [9]

Crimps along the north waterfront, where boardinghouses which supplied sailors for deepwater voyages were located, felt it necessary to form a protective trade organization in response to the 1864 law which tried to regulate runners. They also wanted to

Sutro Library

John Curtin was thoroughly despised by the Coast Seamen's Union .
. . John Curtin was a ship's carpenter and lost an eye in that capacity. He
opened the Fulton House, a sailors' boardinghouse South of Market in the
mid-1870s. One-Eyed Curtin, as he was known, shipped out non-union men
and did not care what the Coast Seamen's Union thought. Around midnight
one evening in September 1893, a valise full of dynamite exploded outside
Curtin's New Fulton House on Main Street. Five men died and John Curtin's
son was seriously injured. Former members of the CSU were arrested but no
conviction resulted from their trial.

Curtin's attitude toward the CSU caused the union to harrass him almost
continually during the 1880s and '90s. His boardinghouse was set on fire, he
was beaten and ultimately his place dynamited. One-Eyed Curtin continued to
be antagonistic toward the union, shipping non-union coastal sailors at below
the CSU rate.

exercise some control over men like James McCann and John Curtin. The Seamen's Boarding House Masters' Association was chartered on March 27, 1865. It sought to achieve a labor cartel, a monopoly on finding sailors employment. The crimps realized that they would be more effective and profitable working together than against each other. Increasing the political power of its members to protect their interests was also an unwritten goal of the group. The association existed for some 25 years (until at least 1888, although it was not listed in the city directory after 1883) and transformed the chaotic boardinghouse system of the 1850s and early 1860s into a tightly-woven net during the 1870s and '80s. Its constitution and the determination of members gave it control over the market, and its presence increased the political power of members, the deepwater boardinghouse owners.

The association's constitution read, in part, "We will avoid shipping our men, if possible, in any office that takes men from houses who do not belong to the association," article four of its constitution read. "No shipping master will ship any men except from a regular seamens' boardinghouse; and if any applications are made by persons to ship from outside houses not regularly in the business, the shipping master will recommend said party to go to some regular boardinghouse belonging to the association." Men shipped on vessels bound for New York, Boston "or any foreign ports" would have two months' advance pay given to the crimps, payable when the sailor was "rendered on board for duty" and signed on by the commanding officer (article five). Association members who were caught "enticing any boarder" from another member's house were penalized, and all proceedings of meetings were to be kept secret under penalty of expulsion after a third offense (article six). Most of the best-known crimps served as officers in the association at various times. They made certain that ship captains knew about the organization and its power.

The annual officers' installation dinner was widely covered by the press, the *Daily Alta* noting in 1888 that the association's office (at the southwest corner of Front and Jackson streets) hosted "as jolly a lot of good fellows gathered . . . as it is possible to meet in a day's walk . . . A large table was set in the middle of the room, and this actually groaned under the weight of sweetmeats and edibles placed upon it. A huge tub nearby was filled with ice on which were placed innumerable bottles of real *Clicquot* [champagne], the corks of which persisted in cracking as quickly as a platoon fusillade." That year "Frenchy" Franklin was elected president, George Roeben treasurer and Harry "Shanghai" Wilson secretary. Retiring president Al Mordaunt was presented an inscribed gold-handled cane "of exquisite workmanship" for his three-years' service. John Langford was master of ceremonies and Thomas Chandler, its long-time former president, reminded members of the constant threats to their livelihoods that boardinghouse masters continued to face from sailors trying to cheat their landlords. [10]

Norwegian Henry "Shanghai" Brown's own shanghaiing may have been the stuff of which myths were made. Brown was running a boardinghouse at 810 Battery Street in 1887 when he died of a stroke. Stories about his being shanghaied nearly ten years later on a four-masted bark, *Springburn*, were therefore untrue. Harry "Horseshoe" Brown, also known as "Shanghai," could not have been the supposed victim either. "Horseshoe" died in 1895, a year before the alleged incident. "Shanghai" Brown's son Henry who was arrested in 1899 for shanghaiing-related activities could have been involved. Although some said the younger Brown had been stabbed to death in Rio de Janeiro, he nevertheless turned up in San Francisco in 1899 where his name appeared in newspapers. "Shanghai" Kelly had fallen victim to his own profession in 1868. But many accounts of shanghaiing that were passed down through time were improbable or did not match facts, perpetuated by books written in the 20th century that romanticized the brutal trade. [11]

Harry "Horseshoe" Brown's life was that of a passionate man. He had sailed the seas himself, but gave that up when he came to California around 1867. He murdered his mistress in Sacramento and served ten years in prison for the act. After his release, "Horseshoe" opened the Horseshoe Saloon on Battery Street and the saloon lent Brown his nickname. Harry Brown was associated with Nils "Shanghai" Nelson and James Laflin as partners on the sealer *Annie*. Brown may have been wounded in the leg on one of the *Annie's* voyages that almost cost "Shanghai" Nelson his life. Years later, George Maginn, a sailor, recalled "Shanghai" Brown walked with a limp. "Horseshoe" rose to the top of his profession—in 1890, shipping master James Laflin paid Brown $9,310 (equal to $150,00-$200,000 today) for the 182 men brought by Brown for the whaling and sealing fleet alone. Brown received additional payments for men he shipped on deepwater ships. [12]

By 1895, "Horseshoe" Brown's fortunes had deteriorated—he lost interest in his stable of fast horses and brooded over his declining income from shanghaiing. His wife, injured in an accident, suffered from memory loss and deafness, and could not take care of herself. He decided to take her with him in death: one morning he murdered her, then turned the gun on himself in their home on Lombard Street.

The weak laws against shanghaiing allowed crimps and runners to practice their profession openly with little fear of serious punishment when caught. "Shanghai" Brown and John Hart were arrested in 1868 for illegally boarding a vessel and fined $20. Hart was arrested five days later for the same offense. Police began cracking down on crimps that year and four more arrests for illegal boarding were recorded in November, seven the following March. But police resources were limited. While busy on a British bark, they were summoned to the *Cowper*, just arrived from

Australia and besieged by runners. Police could not get to her until she had anchored—and lost most of her crew. [13]

Thomas Murray paid one of the higher prices the law exacted for shanghaiing in 1869. The ship *Hercules* came into San Francisco's port one evening with a load of coal for the U.S. Government and was boarded at Lime Point by Officer Burns. The captain needed his crew to take the ship up to Mare Island and he asked that Burns stay on the ship to keep any runners off. This Burns did successfully until morning. The irrepressible Murray boarded the *Hercules* at 5:30 a.m. the next morning and was promptly arrested and chained to the mast by Officer Burns. Murray was convicted of illegal boarding and sentenced to pay a fine of $50 or spend twenty days in the County Jail. [14]

It was not unusual in those years for youths who committed crimes to be sentenced to go to sea. Such was the case with Samuel Robinson, about 16, when he was found guilty in 1868 of burglary. Robinson was too young to be sent to the state prison at San Quentin and too old for Industrial School so the judge ordered the boy to sea as punishment. [15]

The poorly-constructed boardinghouses were subject to one of the commonest dangers of the day—fire. Murray's Golden Gate House on Davis between Jackson and Clark streets burned in 1868, as did the four-story Franklin House run by Cornelius Maloney on the southwest corner of Sansome and Broadway. Early in the morning flames engulfed the building, fed by its flammable paper and muslin wall coverings, and spread quickly before a fire engine arrived a half hour later. Several horses in the basement perished and two bodies plus an unexplained human hand were discovered in the charred ruins. [16]

The case of Augustus Leonard and the *Alaska* got the attention of ship captains and shipowners alike. The bark *Alaska* shipped a crew from San Francisco's harbor without going through the sailors' boardinghouses. The first mate of the vessel,

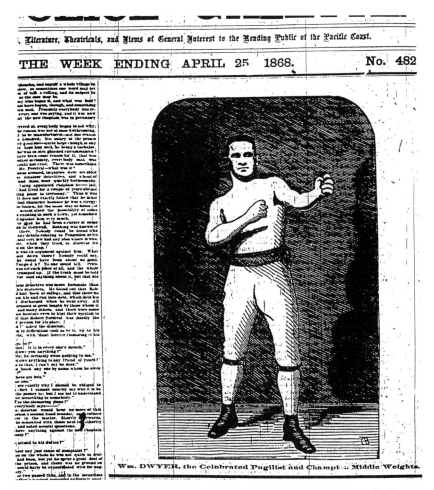

Literature, Theatricals, and Items of General Interest to the Reading Public of the Pacific Coast.

THE WEEK ENDING APRIL 25 1868.   **No. 482**

Wm. DWYER, the Celebrated Pugilist and Champion Middle Weights.

Bancroft Library

William "Billy" Dwyer as drawn by a *California Police Gazette* artist . . . Tommy Chandler fought Billy Dwyer to a draw on Goat Island. Dwyer and his brother, John, were constantly in trouble with the police. Billy continued his belligerent ways and one fall day in 1873 he beat John "Happy Jack" Harrington in the backroom of Denny O'Brien's saloon. "Happy Jack," a much smaller man, pulled out an eight-inch, razor sharp Bowie knife and plunged it into Billy's rib cage. The tip of the knife broke off in the wound and an aorta was severed. Dwyer stumbled to the doorway and fell dead in the street. The common opinion was that Billy's end fit the "troublesome, vindictive" life that he lived.

a Dane named Augustus Leonard, did not appear when the vessel departed and foul play was suspected. Leonard was described as a steady, sober and reliable man, for two years the first mate of the *Mameluke*. He also had two hundred dollars in gold when he left the vessel the day before she sailed. His friends feared he was shanghaied or worse. [17]

Uncooperative sailors fared just as badly at the hands of San Francisco's crimps. A German sailor named Carl Garvey arrived on the brig *Fire Fly* from Tahiti in late April, 1869. He went to a sailors' boardinghouse on Davis Street the next morning. John Anderson and James Ryan violated the Seamen's Boarding House Masters' constitution when they went into Garvey's bedroom and cajoled the German to go to their boardinghouse, known as the Ocean House, at 407 Drumm Street. Garvey finally gave in and went with them. The sharks took Garvey to their bar and asked him to ship out. Garvey declined, as he had made up his mind to sail only in the coastal trade. Anderson and Ryan decided to beat some cooperation into young Carl so they could get his $60 advance money. Garvey was clubbed on the legs, over the left eye and his lips split open. When he tried to call for help, he was gagged, thrown on the floor and kicked in the chest. Garvey fought his way into the dining room and broke a glass pane in the front door. Attracted by the commotion, a large crowd gathered and Garvey called for help. Captain Kentzel and Officer Langan arrived and demanded an explanation. Anderson refused to go to the police station without a warrant but before long he was convinced it was in his best interest to come along peacefully. John Anderson and James Ryan were soon free on $500 bail each. The pair were charged with aggravated assault. [18]

The mysterious disappearance of mates who went outside the boardinghouse channels had a chilling effect on the willingness of ships' officers to resist the cartel. Such was the case in 1870 when the British ship *Royal Allus* was boarded by several crimps who made off with eight men. The second mate recognized James McCann and the captain filed a complaint against him for enticing sailors to desert but, intimidated by threats of retaliation, he withdrew the complaint. Two days later the ship *Van Dieman*, lying in the stream off Meiggs Wharf, was beset by runners. Three of them boarded the ship without permission. Two were arrested the next day. The *Daily Alta* called for vigorous enforcement of the law to prevent repetition of violence. The police judge seemed to take a rather casual attitude toward the infraction, letting them off with a $5 fine each. Arrests for illegal boardings in 1870 were down from the previous few years, as a result of the influence that the boardinghouse association and its politician members had on police, judges and ship captains. As late as 1902 eight crewmen were enticed to desert a British ship standing in the bay while the captain apparently turned a blind eye rather than run up a distress flag to signal Harbor Police for help. [19]

Sailors continued to be shanghaied at unremitting rates. Typical was the case of another German sailor, who had unwillingly signed on to the British *Lotta Maria* in 1869, bound for deepwater ports in the Atlantic. At St. Thomas the ship was condemned as unseaworthy and he was discharged without being paid, forced to work his way via Panama and a Pacific Mail ship up the coast, arriving destitute at San Francisco nine months later. [20]

Fines on runners were nominal for many years—four arrested in two separate incidents in 1870 each were ordered to pay $15—and arrests were rare for shanghaiing activities. As late as November, 1874, runners were arrested for illegally boarding a vessel. That month John Fitzgerald was convicted in the United States Circuit Court of illegally boarding a vessel in San Francisco Harbor. With a fine of only $25 and twenty-four hours in jail, Fitzgerald stood to gain more enticing one sailor off a ship than the amount of his fine. [21]

The year 1873 saw a rise in shanghaiing commensurate with a tight labor market in San Francisco. Crimps were hard at work. One case was that of a young tanner named John Sweeney who had lost his job in the suburb where Mission Dolores was located and "come to town" to find other work. An easy target for crimps, Sweeney was asked if he would like work unloading a ship. Accepting the job offer, he found himself at McCann's boardinghouse, expecting to meet the captain and receive orders. Instead, he was tricked into a signing a paper that the illiterate Sweeney could not understand—shipping articles. On returning to the boardinghouse, he was arrested as a deserter. An understanding judge, seeing no complaint against the young man, dismissed the case. [22]

Few cases exemplified the horror and heartlessness of the business like that of a young man with tuberculosis who was shanghaied that year. A British ship captain had paid the man's advance wages but he refused to sign the shipping articles or to board the ship. Each of his objections was overruled and a physician even provided the boy with a certificate stating that he was in condition for the voyage around Cape Horn to Liverpool. When he continued to refuse to sail, he was charged with desertion and thrown in jail. His case was abandoned five days later and he was released—the press noting that all he could eat while imprisoned was part of a boiled egg. [23]

Sailors' boardinghouse keeper old-timer John C. Price served as vice-president of the Seamen's Boarding House Masters' Association in 1873 and 1874. On the night of September 8, 1874, a battle broke out at Price's sailors' boardinghouse. As Price closed his boardinghouse bar at the foot of Pacific Street, two women evicted from Albert Mordaunt's saloon next door carried on a quarrel. Price told them to leave the neighborhood, but Mordaunt emerged, pistol in hand and shot Price in the left cheek. The bullet exited Price's mouth. A Barbary Coast habitué, Jack

Donahue, was hit by a bottle, and Mordaunt suffered the same fate. The police arrived and carted the three off to jail. [24]

A clothier named Gussie Stein was a crimp as well, supplying gear to sailors whom he in turn supplied to ships. One day in 1889 a policeman noticed a wagon driven toward the waterfront bearing three men holding down a fourth, F. Hackman. The officer diverted the wagon to the station house and could see from the state of Hackman's face that he was a shanghai victim. He had signed shipping articles and wanted more than the $2.50 that Stein had paid him from the sailor's advance. When he refused to sign a note acknowledging receipt of $20, Stein and his runners undertook to persuade the man differently. "You stood at the door while the others were beating me and told them to give it to me until I weakened," he told police, but refused to press for Stein's arrest. The Laflin Record indicates that Hackman reported for duty after the incident. [25]

Stein and two other clothiers, George Fogle and Louis Levy, specialized in finding crew for whalers and worked with Laflin. Laflin recorded paying Levy $5,940 in advance money for supplying ships in 1887 with sixty-eight men. Levy's and Fogle's businesses were located between "Shanghai" Brown's boardinghouse and Thomas Murray's Golden Gate House on Davis Street. Another clothier across the street, William Harris, was also involved with shanghaiing. [26]

By this time San Francisco's reputation for shanghaiing was very much a matter of public awareness. The same month Gussie Stein and his toughs pounded Hackman's face to a pulp, a crowd gathered around two men as they carried a very drunken sailor down the Clay Street boat steps. Officer Donohoe of the North Harbor Station arrested the two shanghaiers. The sailor had come in from New Bedford, Massachusetts on the whaler *John P. West*, signed on as a blacksmith for another whaler, the *Andrew Hicks*, received a $60 advance note, then got wildly drunk and refused to ship out. The two men were released and the sailor booked for drunkenness. [27]

Crimps were men of many talents, not the least of which was a skill at boxing. Harry Maynard had the unlikely combination of talents as a boxer who played the concertina to sailors singing sea chanteys in his Charing Cross Saloon. He claimed to have been lightweight boxing champion of England and liked to take on sailors for bets. He also was proud of his concertina expertise and could play a tin whistle with his nose. Harry had come to San Francisco in the late 1870s from Wales with two brothers, Tom and John, via Australia, and ran a saloon at 425 Pine Street. Maynard lived at 17 Fourth Street across from a shoe store owned by politician John T. Sullivan, an oarsman with the Pioneer Rowing Club, a friend to boatmen and boardinghouse masters who made their living as shanghaiers. Sullivan also was a member of the Board of Supervisors dominated by Democratic Party boss, "Blind" Chris Buckley, and one of the principal stockholders in 1884 of a San Francisco whaling firm, the Arctic Whaling and Trading Company. [28]

A widely-reported event involving Maynard was a boxing match with Patsy Hogan in which crimp Tommy Chandler served as referee. The *Daily Alta* noted that the Board of Supervisors, which it called the "Board of Brokers," was well represented in the enthusiastic audience which also included many prominent politicians, members of the legislature and city and county officials—enough political power, the paper remarked, to override the mayor if the group had been in the business of enacting resolutions. The battle went round after round until the seventh when "the portly form of Police Captain Douglass appeared in the doorway." "Immediately," according to the *Alta*'s account, "there was a scrambling down from elevated positions, and the men who could not get far enough in front at the commencement of the fight vacated their places without a murmur. A well-known politician and an officer of the late Assembly . . . smashed out a window at their back, sash and all, and jumped out on the roof of an adjoining building. The distance was some 10 feet, and as the well-known politician is quite a heavy weight, it was somewhat astonishing that he did not break the roof or his own neck." [29]

Maynard was a showman who gave the competitors from his saloon-side ring catchy names: John L. Herget was "Young Mitchell," Martin Costello the "Buffalo," George Brown "Sailor," Jack Mullen "Liverpool Rat." An African-American boxer, Henry Fields, he dubbed "Black Angel." (Henry Fields would go on to future fame on his own as "Deacon Jones.") [30]

Other crimps whose pugilistic prowess would be useful were Tommy Chandler, Johnny "Shanghai Chicken" Devine and Francis Murray, more commonly known as "Yankee Sullivan." Yankee Sullivan was tied to the Irish-Catholic Democratic workingman's "machine" led by David C. Broderick. (In 1856 Yankee Sullivan was arrested by the Committee of Vigilance for stuffing ballot boxes and other election frauds and died in the custody of the committee. Vigilantes called it suicide but, in an act of disbelief, the Catholic Church authorities permitted him to be buried in consecrated ground at the Mission Dolores cemetery. Four men were hanged by the vigilantes and 28 others banished in an effort to break Broderick's power. Irish were under-represented among the 8,000 vigilantes but over-represented as their victims). [31]

Tommy Chandler (1840-1914) fought in both boxing and political rings. Born in County Wexford, Ireland, he had sailed around Cape Horn to California by 1862 and made a name for himself as a bare-knuckle prize fighter. He was described as five feet, eight inches tall with a "well-knit frame, good countenance, rather gentle eyes, but with a determined expression about his mouth, his lips looking thin when his mouth is closed, a sinewy form, large head and rather confident look in his face."

Chandler was famous for a fight in 1867 against a 40-year-old Englishman, Dooney Harris, which was stopped by the

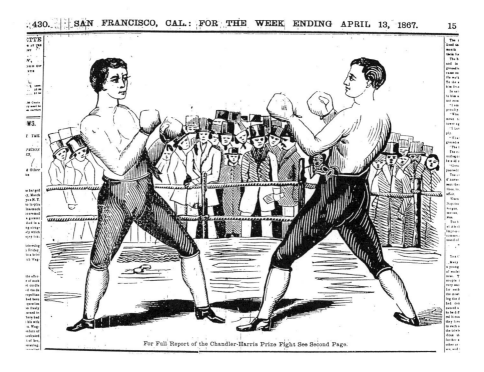

430. SAN FRANCISCO, CAL.: FOR THE WEEK ENDING APRIL 13, 1867. 15

For Full Report of the Chandler-Harris Prize Fight See Second Page.

Bancroft Library

The *California Police Gazette* version of the Tommy Chandler-Dooney Harris Prizefight . . . Originally planned to take place in San Mateo County, south of San Francisco, interference by the sheriff forced the fight to an unannounced location. Excitement among San Francisco's sporting element was intense in April 1867, as the two men were widely respected bare-knuckle boxers. (The combatants are shown with gloves on to protect them from arrest—bare-knuckle bouts were highly illegal). Harris fell to the much younger Chandler when Dooney could not "come to scratch" at the start of the twenty-third round. Tommy Chandler and Dooney Harris followed different paths after the bout—Chandler continued as a successful sailor's boardinghouse master and became a mainstay of the Democratic party for over forty years. The life of a Barbary Coast ranger appealed to Dooney. He was a thief, a drunk, often in fights, and did at least one stretch in San Quentin prison.

San Mateo County sheriff. Through some subterfuge, the combatants managed to meet two days later. It was announced that the fight would be held at Sausalito, but shortly after the ferry and tug boats left San Francisco for Sausalito, their course suddenly changed in Racoon Straits and they set off for Point Isabel on the Contra Costa shore (not Goat Island, now known as Yerba Buena Island, as reported by Tommy Crowley. Chandler had fought Billy Dwyer on Goat Island). Point Isabel, some 20 miles from the county seat of Martinez, was far enough away from the Contra Costa sheriff to allow completion of the bout. After 23 rounds of tough boxing, Dooney Harris fell to the much younger Tommy Chandler. Tommy also carried off $2,000 as the victor's share. Chandler at the time shared a partnership in a saloon at 116 Pacific with Thomas Kirby, a noted oarsman, and the following year was listed as a partner in the boardinghouse at 504 Davis Street with "Shanghai" Brown. In the 1870s he ran an establishment known as the Mariners' Home located at the same Davis Street address. [32]

The connection between bare-knuckle boxers and sailors' boardinghouse keepers was made very clearly in a bare-knuckle bout which went ninety-two rounds and resulted in the arrest of the principals. Two pugilists, Cannon and William P. Riley, fought in Marin County in October, 1869, and testimony was taken in the city to determine whether or not to send the men to Marin County to stand trial, as they were San Francisco residents.

Although Cannon stayed at Edwin Charles Lewis' sailors' boardinghouse for four weeks, Lewis seems not to have realized a prizefight was to take place when he testified. Lewis was very-forgetful on specifics. Tommy Chandler took the stand and was even more forgetful than Lewis. A set-to (sparring match) had taken place at Platt's Hall to build up the bout; Chandler's name

San Francisco Public Library, San Francisco History Room

Behind the gaslights is the entrance to the Lick House, a popular hotel on the west side of Montgomery Street, between Post and Sutter streets . . . Men like Tommy Chandler liked to rub shoulders with the powerful men of San Francisco in the saloon of the Lick House. One evening in 1871, a violent quarrel broke out between M.H. De Young of the *San Francisco Chronicle* and Bill T. Higgins, San Francisco's Republican boss. As Higgins drew a revolver to finish de Young, Chandler disarmed him. Higgins had killed a man during an argument over a boxing match Chandler had competed in five years before. Higgins' saloon at 709 Davis Street was in the midst of the sailors' boardinghouses of the north waterfront.

The meeting place for crimps and commercial interests moved to the Bank Exchange Saloon later on. As Duncan Nichol quenched his guests' thirst with Pisco Punch, John Langford murdered James Hayes and Tommy Crowley, Sr., met the leaders who would help him become a millionaire by 1917—and a billionaire by the 1960s.

Courtesy William B. Secrest Collection

John "Shanghai Chicken" Devine . . . Born in Waterford, Ireland, Devine came to San Francisco in 1861. He worked for fellow Irishman James "Shanghai" Kelly as a boardinghouse runner until Kelly fled the country with $1,500 in advances—or the "Chicken" shanghaied him. This photograph is the Chicken's official mug shot from the San Francisco Police mug book.

was on the flyer, but he disclaimed any responsibility for giving permission to use his name. Chandler did say that what a man needs when he is training for a fight is "plenty of room, a good bed and eating, and nothing to annoy him." Another boarding-house keeper, Billy Jordan, offered more absent-minded testimony. Jordan said he always acted as master-of-ceremonies, as he did during the sparring match at Platt's Hall. He did not know who asked him to serve as master-of-ceremonies or how his name got on the bill.

The principles were transported to Marin County, along with their trainers and seconds. The local Justice of the Peace set them free on bail and the affair died. [33]

In August, 1868, newspapers reported that Chandler and "two friends" had capsized in a Whitehall boat late at night off Broadway wharf. Presumably they were not out for the night air but on a delivery mission to a waiting ship. Chandler reputedly specialized in supplying Germans, called "Square Heads," as crew. A celebrity due to his boxing prowess, he attracted publicity for his personal escapades if not for his shanghaiing. In February of 1869 he was attacked by three men on his way to his boardinghouse on Davis Street. The would-be muggers quickly recognized their error for Chandler knocked one of them to the ground and the other two fled to avoid a beating. Chandler decided to carry a firearm after that but a month later was arrested and convicted of carrying a concealed weapon. He was fined $20. [34]

Chandler and Devine were well acquainted as bare-knuckle boxers and their revelries were duly reported in the local press. One morning at two o'clock the two were reeling through the Barbary Coast in a drunken state when they heard a whistle. A police officer, thinking an alarm had been sounded by Harbor Police, rushed to the source of the sound and found the crimps.

Chandler, when asked by the police officer who had blown the whistle, retorted, "How do you know *I* didn't blow it?" and gave the officer a shove. Whereupon the officer struck Chandler with his club and arrested him for "using bad language." Chandler lodged a complaint against the police officer but when he appeared in court, he had trouble remembering exactly what he had said. [35]

His pugilistic fame preceded him and continued to be a source of trouble. On one occasion in 1870 at the bar in the elegant Lick House hotel, a man by the name of Ned Fairman spoke to Chandler, apparently provoking him. Instantly, fists flew but friends intervened and took Fairman outside. He realized that he had left his hat at the bar and returned to retrieve it. Chandler went for him again and this time the two were allowed to continue the fight, leaving Fairman the worst for it and covered in blood. On another occasion at the Lick House, Chandler turned out to be a hero. Michael H. de Young, editor and publisher of the *San Francisco Chronicle* newspaper and a man with political ambitions, was playing pool. As he was about to shoot, the city's Republican Party boss, Bill Higgins, walked in, angry about an offensive article that had appeared in the *San Francisco Chronicle*. Higgins, who had killed a man in an argument surrounding a Chandler boxing match in 1866, swung at de Young with a heavy cane. De Young blocked the blow with his pool cue, which shattered, leaving him with a large piece to defend himself. As the two men scuffled, Higgins drew a revolver but before he could fire, Chandler lunged forward and grabbed the pistol as bystanders separated the men. Eight years later, Michael's brother Charles de Young was assassinated in another political controversy in which the de Youngs managed to become embroiled.

At one point in 1870 rumors circulated that Chandler would fight a local man, Billy Dwyer, for a $5,000 purse. But Chandler scotched the idea, announcing he would have nothing more to do with boxing. [36]

The popular Chandler even had a horse named after him and in 1872 he was selected to help the prestigious citizens' committee plan the annual Fourth of July celebration. But in April, 1873, his career was put on hold when he accidentally shot himself in the hand while playing with a derringer in bed. Tradition held that Chandler once had punched Devine when he caught Devine stealing a sailor whom Chandler already had shanghaied and Devine shot Chandler in the hand, crippling him. But Devine was locked in chains at the county jail at the time of Chandler's self-inflicted hand wound. The ball had to be dislodged from the shattered palm; a resulting infection jeopardized Chandler's life for a time, and the shooting ended Chandler's boxing career. Years later Tommy Crowley, Sr., recalled that Chandler did not have use of his right hand. [37]

Chandler did not entirely give up the ring, however. He served as referee in the boxing match between Charley Mitchell and Mike Cleary on May 23, 1885, along with referee/crimp Billy Jordan. The two referees could not decide on a winner, so the match was declared a draw. [38]

By 1874 Chandler had taken another partner in his business ventures, Billy Maitland, who had defeated fellow shanghaier Devine in a different sort of a fight six years earlier. An account in the *Daily Evening Bulletin* of June 14, 1868, gives us the particulars, under the headline, "Pugilism on the Rampage— Comes to Grief.

> Some months ago, an able negotiator for crews, shipped after the fashion called after the Chinese port where the practice is supposed to have originated, left for foreign parts in so great a hurry that he forgot to bid good-bye to some friends who had been engaged with him in shipping a crew for a large vessel for the East. John Devine, otherwise popularly known as the "Chicken," a man who, in his humble way as a lightweight and a member of the California Pugilistic Ring, is an unfailing contributor to local items; and his bosom friend, Johnny

Nyland, the man who boasts that he is the champion of light-weights, and therefore able to wop his friend the "Chicken," took the unexpected departure of their friend very much to heart.

Devine and Nyland learned that their pal had died abroad "and made no sign of requiting them for their kind interest in his welfare," the story went on, so the bereft friends decided to console themselves.

They drank the cup of grief together, they drank many cups, they went on drinking cups for many hours. As they wept and drank, and poured spirits down, their spirits rose. At length, this morning early, when the night birds were going to bed and the early birds were stirring in search of the proverbial worm, these two gentle ones determined to celebrate the occurrence by a grand feat of arms. They lived by Jacks [sailors]— by selling Jacks with money to sailor boardinghouse keepers, and selling Jacks who had no money to shipping masters who would buy them drunk or sober. They had long come to the conclusion that Jacks were made for the natural prey of boardinghouse keepers, and also that Jacks liked being licked.

They had come to this conclusion by close attention to sailors' testimony in the United States Courts. So out these two men went for pastime to lick Jack. They entered a boardinghouse, and found Jacks of various nationalities, ages and weights, hanging about the benches of a sailors' bar room. They sailed into Jack, and Jack fled. The two lightweights were left masters of the situation; but they did not sleep on the field. They marched upon the castles of other boardinghouse keepers and cleared them of Jacks. At length they came to one Lewis' place on Vallejo Street [Edwin Lewis' at 41 Vallejo]. Jack at Lewis' was unwilling to go when told by a couple of half mad "lightweights," and showed fight.

Johnny Nyland has the credit of capturing the enemy's weapons, that is, he entered the kitchen and seized the cook's knife, a great French carving-knife, only less heavy than the sword with which Richelieu slew the Englishman at Rochelle.

Brandishing the knife, he attacked the resisting Jacks and cut at them from all directions; two of them dodged behind the liquor counter. While the "Chicken" used such weapons as belong to a pugilist, Nyland relied . . . on the "sabre." He made a cut at one of the besieged—a little more, and half the fellow's head would have fallen a trophy to the prowess of his arm . . . there is an excellent case for needle and plaster work in the hands of some surgeon, but the counter got the worst of it.

Anyone who wants to see what the champion of the light-weights can do in the way of cutting through . . . planks, let him go to Lewis' place and see the track of the knife. Many a man who considers himself no tyro [novice] in woodcraft could not equal the stroke . . . Suffice it the besieged garrison, sorely wounded, and fearing another assault upon their wounded rampart, made a desperate sortie and escaped into the street, joining the fleeing army of their comrades.

The victorious twain, full of potvaliant glory and elated by victory, then made for the house of one Maitland, another place where Jacks do freely congregate. Maitland was in bed. Hearing a terrible row break out amongst his people, he came down in time to see blood flowing from his boarders' heads and fingers, drawn by Johnny Nyland's knife. Maitland objected to his place being cleared of customers in this summary fashion, and remonstrated with Nyland. He remonstrated so forcibly, and used his arguments so skillfully, that in spite of the champion's struggles Maitland got the knife. The champion was struggling . . . and "Chicken" came to his aid, striking, so says Maitland, the owner of the house, a smart blow.

What occurred next must be left for a court to decide. We only know that the "Chicken" put out his left arm with a hard fist at the end of it, and when he drew it back, his severed hand was hanging to his arm by a shred of skin. The supposition is that it came in contact with the knife, but how is the question. Johnny Nyland, appalled by the sight, fled so far that the police have not been able to overtake him. Devine, sobered, was taken to the hospital, where he was placed under chloroform and the doctors dressed his wound. Maitland

WILLIAM MAITLAND chopping off the hand of John Devine, in an affray at the house of the former, 13th of June last.

Courtesy of the Bancroft Library

Billy Maitland Ends the Boxing Career of John "Shanghai Chicken" Devine . . . Into the early hours of the morning of June 13, 1868, "Shanghai Chicken" and his pal Johnny Nyland celebrated the news that "Shanghai" Kelly had died in Peru. The drunken pair decided to stage impromptu boxing matches with the sailors of various boardinghouses. Winning these fights handily, Nyland carried off a large carving knife from Edwin Lewis' boardinghouse on Vallejo Street. Boardinghouse keeper Billy Maitland objected to his residents being treated in a rough manner; he seized the knife from Nyland, and when the "Chicken" tried to strike Maitland, Billy put up the blade in self-defense. Once again, the *California Police Gazette* captures the gruesome moment of the drama for its readers: Devine's hand hangs by a thread, blood spurting from the stump of his arm.

went to the Harbor Police station and gave himself up.

> The present state of affairs is the indomitable "Chicken" is lying between life and death in the surgical ward of the San Francisco City and County Hospital. Maitland is out on $3,000 bail. The champion Nyland, for all the police know, is still running. The man who escaped death by . . . planks getting between his head and the French carving knife is in bed at Lewis;' the cases of the slightly wounded are convalescent; and the district inhabited by Jacks has relapsed into its normal state of peace and quiet. [39]

John "Shanghai Chicken" Devine had a nice hook installed where his hand had been.

The beginning of this tale speaks of the death of a "loved one" abroad, someone who had been shanghaied while supplying the crew for a vessel some months before. "Shanghai" Kelly and Parker disappeared in late January; the news of Kelly's death came just as Nyland and Devine were drowning their sorrows—or celebrating. Dillon states that Devine worked for "Shanghai" Kelly for some time. The logical conclusion is that Devine shanghaied his old boss.

Chandler continued to assume the role of respectable businessman, listed, with his son, as shipping masters in the 1901 edition of *The Men of California.* He died, "a grizzled and crippled old man," in a Sixth Street hotel at the age of 74 in 1914. His crimping and politics were not mentioned in his obituary, only his fistic prowess. A Southern Pacific special agent who saw Chandler fight, said of him, "Chandler was a small-boned man, so delicately constructed he appeared almost effeminate. But, my, how he could punch. He was a straight puncher, never swung, and beat his men as scientifically as did any champion before or after his time." Billy Jordan, Tommy Chandler's contemporary as a crimp and boxer, exclaimed "we never had a more wonderful fighter than Tommy Chandler." [40]

John "Shanghai Chicken" Devine's (1840-1873) career was more shrouded in myth than Chandler's. Devine managed to attain the status of folk-villain during his short life. The *Daily Alta*, *Evening Bulletin*, and, especially, the *California Police Gazette*, reported the latest exploits of the "Chicken" prominently. Devine was recognized early as someone to avoid, a dangerous character on a waterfront that hosted a large number of men on the run or hiding out for previous crimes. Devine was born in Waterford, Ireland, June 19, 1840, and came by way of China to San Francisco in 1861 aboard an English ship. He stayed at James McCann's boardinghouse, but McCann soon shipped him out again, this time on an American vessel to New York. When he returned to San Francisco in 1863, according to Dillon, he vowed never to go to sea again and became a boardinghouse runner for a crimp named Johnny Walker. He gained a well-deserved reputation for readily undertaking criminal jobs on his own or for hire.[41]

Walker was said to have given Devine the moniker "Shanghai Chicken" when referring to a proposed fight between Walker and Billy Dwyer. "You may talk as much as you want, but I have a little shanghai chicken that none of you fellers know of who can clean Paddy [Irish fighter Paddy West] out in no time," Walker said, pointing to Devine. The bout was arranged for a pot of $100 and Devine, barely 130 pounds, carried the day at Minturn's Corral on Vallejo Street. Devine's new nickname stuck, according to legend, not because he was a coward or a shanghaier but because he resembled a Shanghai rooster, considered the bravest, most foolhardy fighter.[42]

If Devine's first fight fell into the category of myth, another was easier to corroborate. He met Hugh Marlow in a bareknuckle bout at Black Point. The "Chicken" underwent training for several weeks before the match, which ended in a draw. Dillon describes the "Shanghai Chicken's" next fight as taking place in 1864 at Point Isabel, lasting three hours and called because of darkness. Dillon sounds confused with the side attraction to the Harris-Chandler fight three years later at Point Isabel, when Thomas "Soapy" McAlpine and James "Steuart Street Pet" McElroy fought one-hundred and eight-rounds until darkness fell. The fight was called a draw. Devine had his last ring bout in 1866 at San Bruno in San Mateo County, battling "Soapy" McAlpine for 116 rounds until, "the 'Chicken' was so badly 'soaped' that he couldn't crow." [43] (Bare-knuckle bouts were fought under London Prize Ring Rules. The rounds ended when one or both parties were knocked down, or fell down to rest).

After his boxing career was over, the "Shanghai Chicken" went on a crime spree which lasted several years. He was arrested for assault and battery after being paid $50 to rough up a man whom he beat so severely that he was heavily fined. He was caught trying to steal a sailor's sea chest after having enticed the man off an English ship to a nearby wharf. The sailor refused to go any farther so Devine demanded the chest. The sailor summoned police and the "Shanghai Chicken" was arrested and convicted of petty larceny. He invited Mary Martin, a German woman, to join him at a coffee stand on Merchant Street one June day in 1867 but when she reached for her purse, Devine grabbed the pocket of her dress that held it and its contents—$25 in cash and a check for $85. Again, police arrested him but the woman disappeared and Devine was let go, three days later assaulting and robbing a man. Another man, struck on the head near Front and Jackson streets, sounded an alarm in time for police to catch the assailant—Devine. A pair of brass knuckles was found in his coat lining. During one of his forays in jail, he met Mary Dolan, "a notorious woman," with whom he set up housekeeping as a married couple. He reportedly had seven other prostitutes working for him at the time and in August, 1867, Dolan was arrested for robbing a gold watch and chain from one of her clients, a Frenchman named Ailert Frels. When Frels demanded his watch back, Devine stepped in and punched him in the eye. For that he received 50 days in jail while Mary Dolan went to state prison for 18 months. [44]

The stories about Devine's wild behavior propelled the "Chicken" to the level of a living legend. One account in the *San Francisco Call* told of a revival meeting a Yankee preacher from Cape Cod started at two o'clock in the morning at Three-Finger Jack's saloon. "British Bill" thought it was a good joke and let him go on. "When the preacher got going good, 'Chicken Devine' dropped on his knees and said he was saved. He cried and sobbed and said he would never sin again. Everybody cheered and the drinks were on the house. Then the 'Chicken' said to the preacher it was a shame that all those sinful men out on the ships couldn't find salvation. He would take him out in a boat and they would board the big clipper ship yonder and save all those poor souls. They drew alongside the ship just at dawn. 'Throw down a bow line; I've got a good man for you,' the 'Chicken' called out. Down went the line and up went the preacher—sold for $60." [45]

Dillon reports that the "Shanghai Chicken" attempted to attack Tommy Chandler as Chandler entered Shanghai Kelly's boardinghouse on Pacific near Drumm street. Devine was Kelly's runner at the time. Chandler avoided the iron bar Devine wielded, but the two were wary of each other for awhile. This time the Chicken's luck held, but Billy Maitland's knife ended the Chicken's lucky streak.

In another episode in 1867, Devine and two other men were arrested for raping and tossing a young Scottish woman, Martha McDonald, off a bridge at Mission and 16th streets into Mission Creek. McDonald testified that it was Devine's voice that she heard saying, "Kill her! Kill her!" Devine claimed to have the perfect alibi: he was locked up in the County Jail for a different crime. As it turned out, he had been a trustee at the jail and was out on an errand at the time of the incident. That put an end to the practice of trustees at the jail. Soon afterward a harbor policeman was quoted as telling Devine that he had been arrested for every crime in the book except murder, predicting that "Shanghai Chicken" would one day swing at the end of a rope if he continued his present career. [46]

The Chicken was not about to learn his lesson, though. In October 1868 he was convicted of assault and battery and fined $30. Early the next year, the Chicken and another man were arrested at 2 o'clock in the morning at the residence of Mary Sullivan. The Chicken and his accomplice entered the front door of her building on Spofford Alley as she slept in a first-floor room. Hearing a noise, Sullivan went upstairs and found Devine about to steal some valuables from a bureau. Sullivan screamed, Officer Miles heard her and arrived in time to take the pair into custody.

The Chicken was arrested once again in January 1870, this time for mugging W.B. Cantin on Pacific Street. Devine was apprehended for the theft of Cantin's gold watch and chain. The "Chicken" tried to explain that he had taken the watch as security for a loan. The police discovered the watch in question at a pawnshop. Allowed to produce witnesses to verify his story, the Chicken was unable to do so. The judge set bail at a very high $1,000, recognizing the "Shanghai Chicken's" dangerous reputation. Devine was convicted of petty larceny and got six months in the County Jail. The judge, on pronouncing sentence, said, "It was the merest accident you were not convicted of grand larceny. I am satisfied you are depraved." [47]

On May 15, 1871, the "Shanghai Chicken" turned the policeman's comment about swinging at the end of a rope into a prophecy. A young German named August Kamp met Devine, and the Chicken touched him up for a loan of $20. Devine evaded paying back the loan but Kamp persistently asked Devine for the money. Finally Devine told Kamp if he would come with him to Devine's mother's ranch, near Bay View, Devine would repay him. They took the Bay View and Potrero Railroad to the end of the line. Walking toward a field, the German stooped to go through the rails of a fence. The "Shanghai Chicken" pulled out a pistol and shot Kamp in the head. Devine left hurriedly, but three people had observed him fire the bullet into Kamp's skull.

The shot did not kill Kamp immediately. The Chicken was arrested and placed in a police lineup. Kamp pointed out Devine but Captain William Douglass was not able to tell who Kamp was pointing at. August Kamp walked up to Devine in the lineup and very deliberately laid his hand on the Chicken's shoulder, saying "This is the man that shot me." Chicken was charged with attempted murder. Unfortunately for Kamp and Devine, Kamp's wound became gangrenous. The German died ten days after Devine's attack.

During the coroner's inquest into Kamp's death, it came out that the Shanghai Chicken was trying to shanghai August Kamp the day he shot him. Devine had worked as a runner for Alexander Phillips' sailors' boardinghouse at 919 Battery Street only a short time before killing the young man. The Chicken told Kamp that he was mate of a fishing vessel, and would take Kamp with him on a fishing voyage. Devine probably received Kamp's advance, then decided to kill Kamp instead of shipping him out.

Police officer John Colter testified that he arrested Devine on the morning of May 16 at Meiggs Wharf on the steamer *Wilson G. Hunt*. Colter testified the Chicken said to him, "'You are a God damned son of a bitch, but I think you are a friend of mine; you will be the means of having me hung.'" When Officer Colter protested he would not like to see anyone hung, the Chicken confessed he shot a man the night before. The Chicken, heavily under the influence of alcohol, started to cry. Colter found a revolver in the Chicken's back pocket. Two chambers had been fired. [48]

At the trial, the cases of each counsel were very spirited. The

British Columbia Archives

Police officer John Colter arrested Devine at Meiggs Wharf as the "Chicken" tried to board the paddle wheel steamer *Wilson G. Hunt*. . . The morning after shooting August Kamp in the head, the "Chicken" attempted to flee San Francisco on the *Wilson G. Hunt*. John Colter, a Harbor policeman, picked up the drunken Chicken. As the Chicken started to cry, Colter found a revolver in the Chicken's back pocket.

After the *Wilson G. Hunt* left service on San Francisco Bay, she went to British Columbia. She is shown here near Victoria, British Columbia.

San Francisco Public Library, San Francisco History Room

"O sweet Jesus, into thy hands I commend my spirit" . . . John "Shanghai Chicken" Devine uttered these, his last earthly words, on Thursday morning, May 14, 1873. The prior Tuesday evening his son had been brought to him; Devine "warned the youth by the example of his life." At one p.m. the sentence was executed in the building on the right, off Portsmouth Square. Hundreds of people crowded San Francisco's City and County Jail to witness the "Chicken's" death by hanging.

John Devine had titillated all California with his crime wave and generally low life. Publications like the *California Police Gazette* could never find one person to supply the colorful copy the "Shanghai Chicken" had provided during his short life in San Francisco. As his coffin was carried from the scene of his execution, the cover was removed to satisfy the morbid curiosity of the crowd.

jury found the "Shanghai Chicken" guilty of murder in the first degree on February 28, 1872; a week later he was sentenced to hang for Kamp's murder. His counsel obtained another trial for Devine, but the verdict remained unchanged. When interviewed by the press in May, 1873, in his jail cell off Portsmouth Square, the Chicken appeared cool, defiant and sure of a new trial. He stubbornly insisted on his innocence. But the State Supreme Court refused a new trial. Governor Newton Booth delayed the Chicken's execution for five days to allow him to prepare for his end. But Booth would not grant a pardon.

Devine softened as he finally accepted the inevitability of his fate. His son came to him on Tuesday evening; Devine wept and "warned the youth by the example of his life." On Thursday morning, May 14, 1873, Devine took his last walk, in the company of a priest. The four hundred lucky persons who had received invitations to witness the execution of the "Shanghai Chicken's" death sentence crowded the City and County Jail. Devine's last words were, "O sweet Jesus, into thy hands I commend my spirit." At one p.m. the sentence was executed.

Devine's last wish was that his body not be dissected but that it be turned over to his spiritual adviser for a Christian burial. The doctors in attendance, however, desired to ascertain how the neck had been broken. Devine's body was placed face down and the neck dissected. Three neck bones were dislocated; the judgment held that the "Chicken" must have died instantly, therefore he felt no pain. As his coffin was taken to a local undertaker, a large crowd gathered. The cover was removed from the coffin to satisfy the morbid curiosity of the crowd. [49]

The Chicken was arrested eighty-eight times—eleven times for fighting, thirteen cases of assault and battery, thirty charges of drunkenness and one of murder. All San Francisco could breath a little easier with the wringing of the Chicken's neck.

Footnotes

1 Herbert Asbury, *The Barbary Coast: An Informal History of the San Francisco Underworld* (New York: Alfred A. Knopf, 1933), pp. 201-2

2 *San Francisco Chronicle,* June 18, 1899, p.2, col.1

3 Ibid, May 17, 1903, p.3, col.1; and *San Francisco Examiner*, December 3, 1892, p.4, col.5

4 *Daily Alta*, December 30, 1883, P.12, col.2. Prior to the early 1880s, all the whale oil, bone and other materials gathered by the Pacific whaling fleet was taken to New Bedford, Massachusetts. In 1883 Millen Griffith, Charles Goodall, Captain F.N. Knowles, George C. Perkins, A.K.P. Harmon and Edwin Goodall subscribed $500,000 in capital stock for the Arctic Whaling and Oil Refining Company.

5 *Coast Seamen's Journal*, Vol. 2, no. 19, March 6, 1889 and Vol. 3, no. 18, p.1, February 12, 1890

6 Ibid, September 23, 1869, p.1, col.5; October 2, 1869, p.1, col.2; October 28, 1869, p.1, col.3 and *San Francisco Examiner*, January 3, 1870, p.3, col.4; *Daily Alta*, January 26, 1875, p.1, col.1 and January 27, 1875, p.1, col.1

7 *The Daily Alta*, October 17, 1870, p.1, col.1

8 Ira B. Cross (ed.), *Frank B. Roney: Irish Rebel and California Labor Leader* (Berkeley, Ca.: University of California Press, 1931), p.330 and *Daily Alta,* September 16, 1889, p.2, col.2

9 Cross, p.330; *The Daily Alta*, August 12, 1886, p.1, col.4; August 29, 1886, p.8, col.1; October 22, 1887, p.1, col.7; *San Francisco Call*, September 25, 1893, p.2, col.2 and September 26, 1893, p.3, col.1

10 *Daily Alta*, September 1, 1889, p.7, col.4 and December 2, 1888, p.1, col.6

11 Frederic Cecil Rhodes, *Pageant Of The Pacific Being The Maritime History Of Australasia*, 2 volumes (Sydney, N.S.W.: F.J. Thwaites, 1937); interview of Captain McKenzie by Jack McNairn, San Francisco Maritime Museum Library. *Daily Alta*, May 12, 1887, p.1, col.4

12 Interview of George Maginn by Jack McNairn, San Francisco Maritime Museum Library; *The Laflin Record, 1886-1890*

13 *The Daily Alta*, August 25, 1868, p.1, col.4, August 30, 1868, p.1, col.4 and September 1, 1868, p.1, col.4; March 4, 1869, p.1, col. 3

14 Ibid, March 5, 1869, p.1, col.2 and March 7, 1869, p.1, col.2

15 Ibid, April 17, 1868, p.1, col.2

16 Ibid, October 9, 1868, p.1, col.2 and December 12, 1868, p.1, col.1

17 Ibid, October 13, 1868, p.1, col.2 and October 14, 1868, p.1, col.2

18 Ibid, May 4, 1869, p.1, col.4. Ryan was involved in another bloody crime in 1873 during a drinking binge with two other men, a steamboat fireman named Owen Gillen and one Lloyd Bell. In the fracas Gillen nearly lost his head from an axe but the other two were too drunk to tell police and inquiring reporters what had happened. At his trial for manslaughter, Bell was observed to be suffering from delirium tremors. During subsequent trials (in 1876-77), he was free and staying at a boardinghouse whose owner was in prison for receiving stolen goods. When Bell was confronted by the owner's wife demanding the rent, he cut her throat, then stabbed himself several times in the chest. The woman died within minutes but Bell survived his self-inflicted wounds. See *Daily Alta*, October 18, 1873, p.1, col.3; August 26, 1874, p.1, col.3; January 8, 1876, p.1, col.1 and September 15, 1877, p.1, cols. 1 and 3

19 Ibid, March 2, 1870, p.1, col.1; July 20, 1870, p.1, col.3; July 22, 1870, p.1, col.2 and July 23, 1870, p.1, col.2

20 Ibid, April 16, 1870, p.1, col.2

21 Ibid, August 11, 1870, p.1, col.2; August 12, 1870, p.1, col.4; August 28, 1870, p.1, col.4; September 15, 1870, p.1, col.3 and November 12, 1874, p.1, col.1

22 *Daily Evening Bulletin*, March 13, 1873, p.3, col.6

23 Ibid, October 20, 1873, p.1, col.1

24 *Daily Alta*, September 9, 1874, p.1, col.3

25 Ibid, December 1, 1889, p.4, col.4

26 *San Francisco City Directory* (Langley, 1867)

27 *Daily Alta*, December 4, 1889, p.2, col.3

28 When Sullivan's shoe business declared bankruptcy in 1887, he assigned his assets to fellow oarsman, former Board of Supervisor member John D. Griffin. William Camp Martin, *San Francisco: Port of Gold* (Garden City, New York: Doubleday & Company, Inc., 1947), p. 215; Dillon, p. 216; *San Francisco City Directory*, 1884; *Daily Alta*, October 25, 1884, p.1, col.1 and July 8, 1887, p.8, col.3

29 *Daily Alta*, April 13, 1878, p.1, col.3

30 *South of Market Journal*, February 1933, p.10, col.2. Fields gained future fame under the ring name "Deacon Jones," and during a fixed fight with a Jewish boxer, Gus Brown, nee Issacson, was supposed to go down in the fourth round. Jones knew that he could beat Brown, however, and refused to drop as arranged. Brown reportedly leaned over and whispered that if he didn't go down, Jones wouldn't "get a cent." The Deacon dropped to the mat and the crowd roared approval. Another crowd-pleaser was the Chinese boxer, Ah Wing, a porter by occupation from Sacramento. He wore his hair in a queue and displayed a "rare gameness," according to accounts. He and Deacon Jones fought at the San Francisco Athletic Club with Buckley's bodyguard, Alex Greggains as referee. If fans treated the fight as a

laughable affair, the protagonists were in earnest. The Deacon would get his glove tangled in Wing's queue, and the two sparred verbally over the pigtail which occasionally wrapped itself around the Deacon's neck, forcing Greggains to intervene and unravel the two, to the delight of the crowd. The two fought with in earnest until Greggains called it a draw.

31 Richard Maxwell Brown, *Strain of Violence* (New York: Oxford University Press, 1975) and James P. Walsh, *The San Francisco Irish, 1850-1976* (San Francisco: The Society, 1978), pp. 14-23

32 *Daily Alta*, April 12, 1867, p.1, col.2. Harris' life was plagued by trouble like an incident 10 years later when he reeled drunkenly into an eatery on Kearny Street wielding a cocked pistol and followed by a man waving a knife. The two were headed to a back room to settle their differences when a police officer interfered and hauled Harris to jail. See *Daily Alta*, September 11, 1877, p.1, col.1

33 Ibid, July 11, 1870, p.1, col.2

34 Dillon, p. 189; *Daily* Alta, August 11, 1868, p.1, col.3 and March 12, 1869, p.1, col.3. Thomas Kirby lost a rowing match and $500 side bet to Henry C. Hoyt on February 28, 1864—the earliest recorded rowing race in San Francisco's history.

35 *Daily Evening Bulletin*, June 1, 1868, p.3, col.4

36 *Daily Alta*, Aug. 11, 1870, p. 1, col. 2; October 8, 1870, p.1, col.3 and October 9, 1870, .1, col.3; May 8, 1871, p.1, col.2

37 Derringers were very popular in San Francisco among men who had reasons to carry concealed weapons. They were small but deadly—as Chandler discovered.

38 *The New York Clipper*, May 30, 1885, p.174, col.4

39 *Daily Evening Bulletin*, June 14, 1868, p.4, col.4

40 ed. Wellington C. Wolfe, *Men of California, 1900-02* (San Francisco: The Pacific Art Company), p. 196; *San Francisco Examiner*, August 11, 1914, p.4, col.8 and *San Francisco Bulletin*, August 12, 1914, p.6, cols. 1-8. After defeating Dooney Harris, who had come all the way from England to meet Chandler, after twenty-three rounds in 1867, Chandler refereed the one-hundred-and-eight round undercard fight between McAlpine and McElroy.

41 *Daily Alta*, May 8, 1873, p.1, col.3 and Dillon, p. 217

42 Dillon, p.217

43 *Daily Alta*, May 8, 1873, p.1, col.3 and *San Mateo Gazette*, June 23, 1866

44 Ibid, June 9, 1867, p.1, col.3; June 12, 1867, p.1, col.1; May 8, 1873, p.1 col.3; August 30, 1867, p.1, col.3. For a more colorful account see Dillon, p.220.

45 *San Francisco Call*, September 18, 1937

46 Dillon, p.219 and *Daily Alta*, May 8, 1873, p.1, col.3

47 *Daily Alta,* October 21, 1868, p.1, col.2; February 15, 1869, p.1, col.3; March 27, 1870, p.1, col.1, March 22, 1870, p.1, col.1 and March 24, 1870, p.1, col.3; October 21, 1868, p.1, col.2 and February 15, 1869, p.1, col.3; February 1, 1870, p.1, col.4 and February 3, 1870, p.1, col.3 and *Daily Evening Bulletin*, p.3, col.3

48 *Daily Alta*, March 27, 1870, p.1, col.1 and June 2, 1871, p.1, col.4

49 Ibid, June 2, 1871, p. 1, col.4; February 29, 1872, p.1, col.2; May 15, 1873, p.1, col.4

San Francisco Maritime Museum N.H.P.

Downeasters and British ships off Vallejo Street, circa 1890—These deepwater ships rest after their long voyages inbound to San Francisco, with Telegraph Hill in the background. The first wharves along San Francisco's waterfront were built at the foot of Broadway, Pacific and Vallejo streets, respectively. Sailors' boardinghouse sprang up on these streets quickly after construction of the wharves. The term "shanghaiing" probably was coined very near here in the early 1850s. The castle on the top of Telegraph Hill existed from 1885 until consumed by fire in 1903.

The Latter Days of the
Boardinghouse Gang

As William Holland lay near death . . . the *San Francisco Examiner* divulged that he had become notorious by placing the body of a dead man on the old bark *California* when one of the crew could not be found. When the *California* returned to San Francisco, an entry in the log read: "James O'Brien died of alcoholism on the first day out from port. Body buried at sea."

San Francisco Examiner, July 31, 1894

The early 1880s saw San Francisco's crimps come into their own politically. Two members of the crimping community served as state legislators during the 1880s. And Chris "Blind Boss" Buckley, a friend of the shanghaiers, ran the Democratic machine in the city. By the 1890s, however, the political and economic star of many of the crimps was on the wane.

The political fortunes of boardinghouse keeper Joseph "Frenchy" Franklin (1844-1896) dramatically improved under Democratic boss Chris Buckley. Franklin was born in southern France of Italian parents in 1844 and became a well-known figure on San Francisco's waterfront as proprietor of boardinghouses beginning in the late 1860s (first at 105 Clark Street and in the 1880s at 215 Broadway). Buckley saw to it that Franklin was appointed city dogcatcher for which he was paid $900 a year plus whatever fees he could collect for dog licenses, running to several thousand dollars a year. In 1884, one unhappy dog owner, angry that his animal had been impounded, petitioned the Board of Supervisors to investigate Franklin's heavy handling of the job, asking compensation for the loss of his pet and action to "require the Poundkeeper to treat citizens more civilly." [1]

Franklin's personal life did not fare as well as his political activities. He divorced his wife, accusing her of drunkenness, a charge substantiated by another leading citizen, Benjamin F. Napthaly, a newspaper reporter, writer and member of the Bohemian Club who claimed that Mrs. Franklin had led Napthaly's wife into the same state of debauchery. [2]

Franklin continued in the boardinghouse business and used his political connections whenever he needed help, like the time one of his boarders took his Whitehall boat for an unauthorized trip on the Bay, smashing it against the rocks of Alcatraz Island in the night. The young man immediately was offered as crew on the *Hospodar,* a ship with a reputation as unlucky (its watchman reportedly had been murdered on the incoming voyage). When the shanghaied sailor balked, Franklin and his runner, Thomas Coyne, beat him unmercifully. The captain refused to accept the boy and police arrested Franklin and Coyne. In court the sailor, afraid for his life, refused to say who had attacked him, and the police court judge, Hale Rix, a colleague of Franklin's on the Republican County Committee, dismissed the charge against him. Franklin continued as a crimp until he died of tuberculosis in 1896. [3]

Another of Buckley's cabal was Whitehall boatman "Big" John Rogers who got a position as the city's hangman. A well-known Whitehall boatman and shanghaier, he once posed as a ship captain and married a young couple offshore. After a few drinks one night, Rogers decided to demonstrate his hanging technique by putting a noose around his own neck, when an

San Francisco Public Library

Billy Jordan (at right) was a sailors' boardinghouse keeper, former pugilist and well-known boxing referee . . . Due to his fame as a boxing referee, Jordan's name was rarely mentioned in a negative way in public. Nor was his connection to shanghaiing, even though he received sailors' advances from James Laflin. Active in Democratic politics, Billy was appointed state meat inspector by Governor James Budd in 1894—a job Jordan held for many years. Photo circa 1907.

Joseph "Frenchy" Franklin had a fascinating career in California . . . "Frenchy" was born in Nice, France, of Italian parents. He took up the profession of sailors' boardinghouse keeper in the late 1860s. "Frenchy" was active in Republican politics, and was elected state assemblyman in 1884. In 1890 he became a Democrat. He died in his early 50s. *Photo Courtesy Sutro Library*

unexpected wave struck the stern of the launch. Rogers was thrown overboard, still attached to the rope. Fellow boatmen Tommy Crowley, Sr., and Jimmy Sinnott pulled him back, but Rogers was dead. "Them that lives by the rope dies by the rope," Sinnott was quoted as his pal was laid to rest. [4]

Another crimp who built a reputation in the boxing ring was Boston-born Billy Jordan (1833-1916) who arrived in San Francisco in 1853 at the age of 20. After a hitch in the Union Army during the Civil War (in which he lost four brothers, two on each side), Jordan refereed title matches for more than forty years. He, too, enjoyed political patronage and in 1894 was appointed state meat inspector by Democratic Governor James Herbert Budd, a post that he held until his 80th birthday. Neither his shanghaiing nor the fact that he had left his wife in 1873 to travel to Peru with another woman (his wife, an alcoholic, tried to kill herself without success with laudanum) were mentioned in Billy Jordan's obituary in 1916.

One of the most colorful women in the trade was the widow of William Paupitz, Dorothy, who, in 1892 at the age of 78, married a Swede, Peter Olsen, 20 years her junior. If he had married for money, he was disappointed. Soon after they wed, he learned that the new Mrs. Olsen had been a widow twice and a third husband was declared insane. Misconstruing something that his wife said, Olsen screamed, "You've got two husbands in hell and one in Napa's insane asylum, and I'll be damned if I'll go on the list!" He grabbed a pistol to shoot his bride but she had removed the bullets. He then attacked her with a knife but her steel corset stopped the thrusts. He then seized her by the hair and was pulling out handfuls of ringlets when Officer Callahan came to her rescue. Olsen was arraigned on a charge of assault with a deadly weapon but the charge was dismissed. Sarah Windt, another wife of a boardinghouse keeper was attacked by her husband with four soup plates as she was packing to leave. [5]

Duncan Nichol (far left) dispenses Pisco Punch at the Bank Exchange Saloon . . . Nichol, a Scottish immigrant, took over the Bank Exchange Saloon in the late 1870s and ran it until Prohibition closed its doors forever in 1918. This photo dates from around 1914.

The Bank Exchange Saloon was one of those San Francisco places that continually crop up in the annals of shanghaiing in this town. Tom Maguire started a bar called The Snug at the corner of Montgomery and Washington streets and sold Pisco Punch to thirsty San Franciscans and visitors to the city. Chris Buckley met the city's elite as he worked behind the bar of The Snug. In 1888, John Langford murdered fellow sailors' boardinghouse keeper Jack Hayes as Duncan Nichol looked on—but Nichol swore he did not see anything from his vantage point at the bar. Tommy Crowley said all the sailors' boardinghouse masters used to come to the Bank Exchange Saloon to rub elbows with San Francisco's leaders and act like they were big shots.

One of the ingredients of Pisco Punch was Pisco brandy from Peru. When Duncan Nichol died in 1926, he took the recipe with him to the grave. Others have imitated Pisco Punch, but no one has duplicated its success.

The most sensational case of the 1880s involving San Francisco's shanghaiing community was the murder of Joseph Hayes, son-in-law of the late Henry "Shanghai" Brown, by John Langford, brother of police sergeant Thomas R. Langford. Hayes, usually peaceful when sober, was drunk by 7:30 p.m. one December evening in 1888 at the Bank Exchange Saloon on Montgomery and Washington streets. When Hayes became drunk he also became abusive. Hayes and Tom McEnerney started to quarrel in the presence of several other men. A shot rang out and Hayes fell to the floor, a bullet entering under his right eye and lodging in his brain. He died later.

Sergeant Tom Langford stated he went to the Bank Exchange Saloon when he went off duty with his brother John, boarding-house keeper James Douglass and contractor Tom McEnerney. Hayes and McEnerney started to argue and Tom Langford advised both men to go home, to which Hayes responded by calling the officer a god damned loafer. The policeman struck Hayes in the face with his fist and Douglass grabbed Langford's arms before he could strike him again. Then the shot rang out. But no one seemed to see who fired the shot.

The bartender, Duncan Nichol, famed dispenser of Pisco Punch, testified at the coroner's inquest, that Hayes, Tom Langford and John Langford stood in a triangular relationship to each other and that smoke rose between the three after the fatal shot was fired. Other witnesses testified the shot came from outside. Jane Lane, proprietress of a cigar store outside the Bank Exchange, said she heard the shot but that it positively did not come from outside the saloon.

None of the men at the bar was found carrying a pistol. The police, however, discovered a pistol behind the bar. Duncan Nichol, the bartender, claimed he did not know how the pistol came to be behind his bar. And through a coroner's inquest which ran several days, no one recalled anyone firing the shot which brought Joseph Hayes to his doom, but John Langford was charged with the murder.

Selecting a jury was an arduous task. Then forgetfulness struck all the witnesses in epidemic proportions. No one saw who fired the shot; no one heard anything of consequence; everyone seemed confused, even Sergeant Langford, who would have been trained to keep his head under trying circumstances. Predictably enough, John Langford was acquitted after a brief trial. [6]

A conspiracy probably existed between John Langford and Duncan Nichol. Langford either went for the pistol he knew was behind the bar or Nichol handed the weapon to him. After disposing of Hayes, John Langford handed the pistol back to Nichol, or threw it on the bar (one witness reported hearing a loud thump on the bar after the pistol was fired). And everyone quickly agreed they would protect the police sergeant's brother, who had killed a man with numerous enemies.

John Langford, slayer of Joseph Hayes, managed to make the news in late 1890 when he quarreled with a miner at a Battery Street boardinghouse. Langford asked Daniel Reddy to ship as a sailor, then bought him several drinks. Reddy decided not to ship so Langford grabbed the miner and, in the ensuing struggle Langford bit off part of Reddy's right ear. "He wasn't satisfied then, so he blew it back into my face." The attending doctor, noting that Reddy was short a bit on his left ear as well, commented that at least Langford had an artistic eye. [7]

Police Sergeant Tom Langford's son, also named John Langford, ran a sailors' boardinghouse at 724 Front Street in 1892. He shared his uncle's knack for attracting trouble—to others. The young Langford and John Ashton, master of a boardinghouse at 816 Front Street known as the Portland House, were on a pub crawl in the Barbary Coast one evening and stopped at 807 Kearny Street. They met a prostitute named Lizzie Valentine and

P.G. Sabatie & Co.'s letter to the whaling firm of Wright, Bowne & Co. . . . . Sabatie, a French liquor importer, sent this letter to the company Henry Jobet shipped with as steward on the *Little Ohio*. The letter asks for information on behalf of a "lady of good standing in France" concerning her nephew, Jobet. "A good result would very likely occur" for the young man.

Henry Jobet was shipped by James Laflin. He never reentered Laflin's shipping offices: the *Little Ohio* was lost in October 1888. The captain and all but eight of her thirty-one hands were lost.

82

Mrs. Brown.
[*From a photograph.*].

Harry Brown.
[*From a photograph.*]

San Francisco Public Library

Harry "Horseshoe" Brown murdered his wife and committed suicide
. . . In 1895, Harry Brown became despondent over the decline of his fortunes in the shanghaiing business and decided to end his life. Brown was known as "Shanghai" or "Horseshoe" Brown, for the saloon of that name he ran for years. He felt his wife could not manage on her own due to an accident which affected her memory and hearing, so took her with him in death. A long-time associate of Nils "Shanghai" Nelson and James Laflin, Brown shot his wife, then himself at their home at 611 Lombard Street on March 12, 1895.

A lover of fast horses and easy money, "Shanghai" had served ten years in San Quentin for murdering his mistress in Sacramento years before. His wealth had stood at $150,000 in earlier times (equivalent to about $3,000,000 today). "Shanghai" Brown wanted the good life and when he could not have it anymore, he left the world behind.

Ashton decided to spend some time with her. He went to her room, drank some beer she had spiked with morphine and soon passed out. Valentine, who had done four stretches in the state prison, disappeared along with the $170 Ashton had in a coat pocket. Three days later he died of a morphine overdose. Police found her and charged her with murder. [8]

A letter slipped in the pages of the Laflin Record from the French concern P.G. Sabatie & Company to the whaling firm Wright, Bowne & Company requested news of a young man named Henry Jobet. A Frenchwoman "of good standing" sought to find Jobet, her nephew, who had shipped as a steward on the whaling bark *Little Ohio*. Jobet stood to inherit a goodly sum of money; as Sabatie wrote, "Some good result will very likely occur in the welfare of the young man if he is still alive." The Laflin Record shows that Jobet had perished, however, along with all but eight hands on the *Little Ohio*, when the vessel was lost.

African-Americans, too, figured in the shanghaiing trade, both as victim and victimizer. One black boardinghouse keeper, John T. Callender, who specialized in supplying "colored" sailors, had a sideline business purchasing coal pilfered by boys from waterfront coalyards for which Callender paid 25 or 50 cents a bag. The R. D. Chandler coalyard in 1873 reported losing 30 to 50 tons a month because of theft. Police found three and a half tons in Callender's basement.

Callender was born in Barbados in 1832 and worked as a ship steward, arriving in California on the ship *Lookout* in June 1865. He married Mary Pointer and opened his sailors' boardinghouse at 5 Broadway in May, 1866. [9]

John T. Callender's black sailors' boardinghouse on Broadway was a lively place in the late 1880s. One evening, as Thanksgiving grew near, Callender's cook, Thomas Arnold, took umbrage at an order from sailor John McFay to get McFay's supper ready. Confusing McFay for a Thanksgiving turkey,

Arnold grabbed a large knife and fork, knocked McFay down and started to slice the sailor's throat and body with the knife, while jabbing the fork into McFay's face. Thinking McFay was dead, Arnold ran away. McFay was taken to the Police Surgeon. Arnold's knife had come within an eighth inch of McFay's jugular vein and he had 20 puncture wounds in his scalp. McFay recovered. [10]

Callender's woes continued two years later when Peter Lopez, foreman of Callender's stevedore and ship repair business, fell and drown as he was hanging a rudder. About that time a sailor named John Griffiths ran up a boarding bill at Callender's house. When Callender requested the sailor pay his bill, Griffiths hit Callender, then broke every window in Callender's boardinghouse by throwing bricks through them. [11]

John T. Callender's saddest tale happened in 1888 when his boardinghouse was filled with sailors returning from the whaling fleet. Two of his boarders, Mariano Torres and Manuel Jo, Mexican and Portuguese respectively, ran up a bill of about $60 between them, then failed to appear for breakfast one morning. Callender, "nearly wild with grief," received a note which advised that his missing men were about to be shipped on a whaler in a very drunken condition. Callender hurried to the Harbor Police Station and went aboard the whaler where he and the two policemen in attendance found that Captain Wing had mustered his crew that morning and found four men who did not fit the description of the men who had signed articles at the shipping office. Captain Wing dismissed these very drunk men, two of whom were Callender's and two of whom belonged to Joe Gomez, a.k.a. Portuguese Joe. Portuguese Joe had taken his men and Callender's men, shipped them all on another whaler and pocketed the proceeds. Even though Callender had recently won $15,000 on a 75-cent lottery ticket, he was so upset that he began to make threats against Gomez' life. Callender was arrested but soon released. [12]

The press did make light of Callender's troubles in large part, no doubt, because he was black, although San Francisco's newspapers generally had fun with the troubles of all sailors' boardinghouse masters. The *San Francisco Examiner*, however, highlighted prominent blacks of the city in 1889 and called Callender "the most prominent businessman in the colored community." His fortune was estimated at a minimum of $75,000— equal to $750,000 to $1,500,000 in 1996 dollars. Perhaps members of the white establishment press were jealous of John Callender's financial success. [13]

One of the most controversial boardinghouses was the Sailor's Home, founded in 1856 by the Ladies' Aid and Protection Society for the Benefit of Seamen (its name was later changed to Ladies' Seamen's Friend Society). In 1863 the Home moved from a dilapidated building on Davis Street to one at the southwest corner of Battery and Vallejo Streets, and in 1875 to the former U. S. Marine Hospital near Rincon Hill which the federal government had abandoned after it was damaged by an earthquake in 1868. The imposing building, unoccupied since the earthquake and turned over to the city, was leased to the ladies' society for the nominal sum of one dollar a year and turned into the Sailor's Home. The state legislature paid for many of the improvements in 1878—the initial lease term was twelve years. The Sailor's Home would have a checkered history.

In 1863, Jack F. Stewart was appointed superintendent of the Sailor's Home. Stewart had been in partnership with James Anderson as shipping masters before the ladies hired him as superintendent. They should have checked his background. He was, however, president of an organization which sought sobriety among sailors, which fit in well with the ladies' goal of abstinence from drink on the part of sailors. In 1871 Stewart left the city and immediately a number of complaints were lodged with the police to the effect that he had made off with money

Fred J. Hunt, a shipping master who specialized in supplying crews to British ships . . . At the turn of the century, three men controlled shipping of crews on British ships—Tommy Chandler, Fred J. Hunt and James Douglass. Hunt had a photograph of himself published in *Men of California, 1902*

San Francisco Public Library

Police Sergeant Thomas R. Langford kept a sailors' boardinghouse on Clay Street before becoming a San Francisco police officer in 1871 . . . Langford worked at the harbor police station, but his ability to enforce the laws prohibiting shanghaiing against his old business associates is suspect. In 1867 Langford lived in the sailors' boardinghouse at 894 Front Street presided over by John Rogers and John Hart. Rogers later served as city hangman under "Blind Boss' Chris Buckley. Thomas' brother, John, ran a sailors' boardinghouse.

SERGEANT THOMAS R. LANGFORD.

Sutro Library

placed in his safekeeping. Chief Patrick Crowley had Stewart arrested in Reno and brought down to San Francisco. Stewart had commingled money placed by individual sailors for safekeeping with the funds of the Sailor's Home and there were some shortages among individual sailor's funds but Jack F. Stewart was allowed to stay on at the Home until 1875. He would be but one in a long line of suspect superintendents. [14]

The Home was intended to serve destitute sailors at low cost, and its name in other ports implied a safe haven for seamen in a foreign port. But in San Francisco the Home became a haven for the operation of crimping. Its management was continuously criticized and investigated for inadequately providing for and outright abuse of sailors. The Sailor's Home continued operating until after the turn of the century, despite its unsavory reputation.

The boardinghouse masters success occasionally turned against them. In 1891, the boardinghouse masters tried to reduce payments to runners from a reported $15 per sailor to $10. The runners formed a "union" of their own and began to steer incoming sailors to scab boardinghouses, i.e., boardinghouses that did not belong to the boardinghouse masters' association. The boardinghouse masters had no choice but to give in, and reinstate the "blood-money" payments to runners. [15]

As late as 1903, shanghaiing was so prevalent that the *San Francisco Chronicle* ran a full-page story on the crimping problem, declaring it to be in full swing. Twenty-five hundred men shipped each year, according to the article, many of them shanghaied for $55 to $75 per sailor. British flagships were particularly hard hit: 43 percent of crew on British vessels from Europe deserted in San Francisco, 27 percent left ships from Australia. [16]

Sailors who were wanted out of the way as witnesses of crimes also had a way of disappearing. John Wilson, who had witnessed a murder at Curtin's boardinghouse on Steuart Street in 1882, was shanghaied to the *Mary Glover*. It returned to San Francisco sooner than Wilson's antagonists expected and he was about to be shipped on another vessel when police learned of his whereabouts and put him in protective custody to ensure his presence at the murder trial. [17]

The stories of sailors who disappeared were legion in the 1880s. A man's disappearance for a day or two led to speculation that the obvious had happened but in at least one case the rumors were exaggerated. A 70-year-old boardinghouse master, George O'Brien, vanished, a suspected shanghai victim of a rival crimp. O'Brien turned up a day later at the *Daily Alta* newspaper office to prove that he had not been a victim of his colleagues.

William Holland's name comes down to us for an activity occasionally rumored along the waterfront but rarely credited to a specific individual. As Holland lay near death at the San Francisco City and County Hospital in 1894, the *San Francisco Examiner* divulged that he had become notorious by placing the body of a dead man on the old bark *California* when one of the crew could not be found. When the *California* returned to San Francisco, an entry in the log read: "'James O'Brien died of alcoholism on the first day out from port. Body buried at sea.'" [18]

William R. Anderson, another black sailors' boardinghouse keeper, ran afoul of the law when Hugh Brodigan visited Anderson's house while drunk. Anderson and Brodigan argued and Anderson grabbed a potato masher and "proceeded to convert it into a skull breaker. Brodigan's head looked as if it went through the rollers of a sugar mill." Brodigan's head was sewed up, while Anderson faced charges of assault with a deadly weapon. [19]

Runners were ever on the alert for sailors who had just been paid off. Victor Cameron was such a victim when a runner employed by Charles McCarthy took him into a saloon soon after he had left the Australian ship *J. B. Brown* in 1883. The runner, Ed Mordaunt, knocked Cameron out while he was having a drink and fled with $17. Although unconscious for several hours,

Cameron gave a description of his attacker and Mordaunt was apprehended.

A scarcity of sailors developed in early 1887. Predictably, a boardinghouse made the news when its runner attempted to shanghai a sailor in a rather clumsy manner. "Shanghai" Brown's runner, Charles Ashton, tried to trick a sailor named William Kennedy into serving on the *Benjamin F. Packer*. Ashton took Kennedy on a tour of waterfront saloons and, when Kennedy became good and drunk, proceeded to drag the sailor down the boat steps at the foot of Washington Street, toss him into Ashton's Whitehall boat and make their way to the *Benjamin F. Packer*. Kennedy protested to the captain and Ashton was arrested. [21]

Cyrus Errington, a young man from the California farm community of Petaluma, was persuaded by a runner to stay at the Sailor's Home and to sign on to a British ship. Errington already had found a job with a store soon after arriving in San Francisco. The resourceful Errington had heard that deepwater ship captains rejected men subject to seizures so when he found himself on the deck of a ship, he chewed on a small piece of soap and soon went into convulsions. He was ordered ashore and returned to his previous place of employment, keeping a wary eye out for runners after that. [22]

Control of shipment of seamen was still very much in the hands of crimps in 1902, as the skipper of the British ship *Rahane* found. He decided to recruit a crew on his own rather than pay $40 advance money for each man to the shanghaiers. When the captain set out to execute his plan, he found all available sailors had mysteriously disappeared. Scott then approached the boardinghouse keepers, who demonstrated to the Lime-Juicer (British sea captain) what a corner on shipping sailors means. Their conversation was reported along these lines:

> "Of course . . . I'd like to have a crew; some good men, my boys, for I'll be wantin' to send the ol' gal home in good time. No idlers or stragglers, mind you."

The southeast corner of "Lime-Juice Corner" was a collection of ramshackle buildings by 1905 . . . Lime-Juice Corner was named for the British sea captains, or Lime-Juicers, who came there to recruit crews for their ships. Men who signed on British ships had to sign articles of agreement before the British Consul, who presided at 520 Battery Street. Tommy Chandler also had his office at 520 Battery. Lime-Juice Corner was not just a corner—it ran the entire length of Battery between Washington and Jackson streets.

At the southeast corner of Battery and Jackson rested a collection of forlorn buildings. S. Giancoli and R.D. Pogetto (Pocal), liquors, sits at the corner, 227 Jackson. Thomas Meherin, seedman, is at 552 Battery, while the shack about to tumble into Battery Street was the location of Patrick J. Helen's commission merchant business. It could not have been very lucrative. These buildings may have been owned by the estate of James G. Fair.

A water trough at the corner, while providing water for the horse slowly making its way up the street, is suggestive of the passing of an era—shanghaiing would end in a few years, and the fire after the earthquake of 1906 incinerated this whole scene.

"Can't be did, skipper," says Tommy Lyons, spokesman for the gang.

"Eh? What's that you say?" snorted the Britisher.

"Can't be did," says Tommy, "the price has taken a rise."

"Forty dollars and no more," growled the captain.

Tommy shook his head. "See here skipper," he says, "when you wants sailors you comes to us. When we wants a ship we goes to you. See? Ain't that right? Well, we got the sailors, and any bloke from salt water what thinks he can run sailors on dry land better than we can, why, the price goes up. See?"

And that's why the *Rahane* is in the stream tugging on her cable and anxious to put her nose in deepwater. She will get a crew some time this week probably, and Captain Scott will pay more that $20 blood-money and $20 advance for them. [23]

In 1905 Alfred J. Austin, a house painter from Pennsylvania, was walking down Market Street, when he was stopped by a man who asked if he was looking for work. "'Bet I am,'" Austin told the man, Warren P. Herman. Herman invited Austin into a saloon, where he bought the Pennsylvanian a drink. Herman insisted Austin have another. The next thing Austin realized, he was being shaken and a voice said "'Get out of this, you bloody stiff. Get on deck and sign articles. Look lively now.'" [24]

Austin was on the forecastle of the British ship *Battle Abbey*. His throat burned, eyes throbbed and his head pounded. But he refused to sign shipping articles, saying he was not a sailor and had no interest in learning how to become one. Captain Davidson was not due to ship immediately so the captain told Herman to take Austin away and fetch another sailor. Herman left the *Battle Abbey* and contacted a policeman. His story to the policeman was that Austin was a deserter from the United States Army. Austin

San Francisco Maritime Museum N.H.P.

Alfred J. Austin was walking down Market Street when crimp Warren P. Herman asked if he were looking for work . . ."'Bet I am,'" Austin told Herman. Herman invited Austin into a saloon, where he bought him a drink. The next thing Austin knew, he was on the British ship *Battle Abbey*.

His throat burned and his head pounded. But he refused to sign articles. The captain let him go, and Austin vowed to leave San Francisco as soon as he raised enough money.

John T. Callender ran a "colored" sailors' boardinghouse on Broadway for over twenty years . . . Callender arrived in San Francisco after spending his youth sailing and started a successful boardinghouse. The press took particular glee in pointing out John's problems, although they enjoyed ridiculing the difficulties of all crimps. The press was probably jealous of his success—by 1889, Callender was estimated to be worth over $75,000—a goodly sum in those days. He was involved in his church and in Republican politics.

unfortunately wore a set of khakis. The policeman and non-sailor went off to the Harbor Police Station where the officer in charge, Captain Martin, found Austin's story believable but wanted to check with the military authorities. Three hours later the word came from the Presidio that as far as they were concerned Austin was not a deserter.

Warren P. Herman had quite a varied career supplying sailors—for a price. From 1891 until 1897, Herman continued the old tradition of the Old Ship Saloon by shanghaiing sailors from the saloon at 228 Pacific Street. The San Francisco City Directories during this period describe Warren P. Herman as in the liquor, boarding or brewing businesses. Nils "Shanghai" Nelson's Chicago Hotel was next door. In 1898 Herman hung up his shingle at 26 Steuart Street as a shipping master. From 1906 until at least 1908 he supplied crews (mainly greenhands—non-sailors) to whalers. Herman's successor at the Old Ship Saloon, Henry Klee, occasionally placed a sailor on a whaler. The Old Ship Saloon building still exists, at 298 Pacific Street, as Bricks Restaurant.

An inventive shanghai victim was soldier James McGuire, stationed at the U. S. Army's Presidio garrison in 1882. While on leave in town, a stranger approached McGuire and asked if he would like a drink, which the soldier accepted. The next thing he remembered was waking up on a British ship in a sailor's uniform. He wrote a letter to a saloonkeeper whom he knew, weighted it down and tossed it onto a passing ferry boat en route from Sausalito to San Francisco. The Presidio's commanding officer was notified and the soldier retrieved from the ship. [25]

Alcohol abuse was a common enemy not only of sailors but of shanghaiers. Billy Maitland died of kidney disease in 1884 at the age of 49, and alcoholism claimed 28-year-old Jack Gately on Christmas Day, 1885. Many of the crimes in which crimps and their cohorts were involved were triggered by drink. [26]

Shipping crews through shipping offices, the market makers between the demand for a crew from a ship's captain and the supply of men from sailors' boardinghouses, continued until passage of the La Follette Act in 1915. Crew members from Third Mate down to seaman, "greenhand" and cabin boy all shipped through shipping offices. The J. Porter Shaw Library, part of the National Maritime Museum of San Francisco, has a list of names of all members of all crews who shipped on whaling vessels from San Francisco from 1906 until 1928. In addition to the name of the crewman and ship sailed on, his position in the crew, agreed portion of the "lay," or profits and the shipping office he went through, comprise this very important set of documents. Whether men asked to ship, were dispatched by their boardinghouse keeper or "shanghaied" is not recorded. Familiar crimps are listed such as Henry Brown, son of "Shanghai" Brown, Billy Cane, Warren P. Herman, Thomas Murray, Jack O'Brien, Walter W. Lane, George Webb, Johnny Cane, Harry Lewis, Andrew Peterson and men mentioned by Tom Crowley, Sr., such as Stan Friedman and his partner Morris Stabens, Louis Levy, Luis Gomes, Harry Klee or an occasional woman: Mary Duarte, Mrs. Chiragino and Mrs. Muheim. Money was made peddling sailor flesh until the last moment legally and economically feasible. [27]

The business of shanghaiing in San Francisco thrived into the 20th century, affecting unknown thousands of sailors. The practice did not end until the death of sail.

Footnotes

1 *Daily Alta*, November 13, 1884, p.1, col.4

2 Ibid, August 5, 1875, p.1, col.4; August 13, 1875, p.1, col.2; July 25, 1876, p.1, col.1; September 8, 1876, p.1, col.3; July 27, 1879, p.1, col.3; and July 29, 1879, p.1, col.4; July 28, 1880, p.1, col.2 and October 5, 1880, p.1, col.3; July 14, 1882, p.1, col.2; July 25, 1882, p.1, col.2; October 25, 1882, p.1, col.2; September 10, 1882, p.1, col.4; and December 30, 1882, p.1, col.2; December 9, 1886, p.1, col.3; "Martin Kelly's Story," by Martin Kelly, ed. by James H. Wilkins, *San Francisco Bulletin*, September 4, 1917, p.9, col.2; *Daily Alta*, July 14, 1882, p.1, col.2; July 25, 1882, p.1, col.2; October 25, 1882, p.1, col.2; September 10, 1882, p.1, col.4; and December 30, 1882, p.1, col.2; December 9, 1886, p.1, col.3; *Morning Call*, June 1, 1882, p.3, col.2. Franklin also failed in business and was forced to declare bankruptcy twice, in 1882 (when he reported liabilities totaling $1,318 and assets of $100) and again in 1886.

3 Winfield J. Davis, *The History of Political Conventions in California, 1849-1892*, (Sacramento, Ca.: California State Library, 1893), p.624; *San Francisco Municipal Reports, 1884-85*, p.70; *Morning Call*, April 20, 1896, p.7, col.1

4 Dillon, p.183

5 *San Francisco Examiner*, August 25, 1892, p.3, col.5; August 27, 1892, p.3, col.6 and *Daily Alta*, December 3, 1887, p.1, col.5

6 *Daily Alta*, December 4, 1888, p.2, col.4; December 5, 1888, p.1, col.4-5; December 8, 1888, p.1, col.4 and December 10, 1888, p.1, col.5; September 24, 1889, p.1, col.3; September 25, 1889, p.8, col.3 and September 26, 1889, p.1, col.4

7 *San Francisco Examiner*, December 12, 1890, p.3, col.2

8 Ibid, December 12, 1890, p.3, col.2; November 4, 1892, p.8, col.4; November 5, 1892, p.3, col.6; November 7, 1892, p.9, col.4 and November 29, 1892, p.5, col.2

9 *San Francisco Examiner*, June 16, 1889, p.16, col.7 and Delilah Leontine Beasley, *The Negro Trailblazers of California* (New York: Negro Universities Press, 1919), p.122

10 *Daily Alta*, November 10, 1887, p.1, col.5

11 Ibid, October 26, 1889, p.2, col.1 and October 5, 1889, p.1, col.6

12 Ibid, November 29, 1888, p.1, col.6 and December 7, 1888, p.2, col.5

13 *San Francisco Examiner*, June 16, 1889, p.16, col.7. Callender was actively involved in his community as a member of the West Indian Benevolent Society, on the Sunday School committee of the Epsicopal Mission, organizing picnics for both groups, and marched in the parade to celebrate ratification of the Fifteenth Amendment to the United States Constitution, extending equal rights to black citizens. In 1872 he was elected as a vice-president at a meeting of black and white San Francisco Republicans to consider voting for Horace Greeley, rather than

Ulysses S. Grant for President. See San Francisco's *The Elevator*, January 22, 1869, p.3, col.3; March 25, 1870, p.3, col.2; June 13, 1874, p.3, col.4 and July 11, 1874, p.3, col.6 and San Francisco *Pacific Appeal*, August 17, 1872, p.1, col.1. Callender, however, did shanghai men for over twenty years.

14 Ibid, January 18, 1871, p.1, col.2; January 22, 1871, p.1, col.2; January 24, 1871, p.1, col.4; February 26, 1878 and Dillon, p. 197

15 *San Francisco Examiner*, August 16, 1891, p.4, col.5

16 *San Francisco Examiner*, May 27, 1902, p.7, col.6; *San Francisco Chronicle*, May 17, 1903, p.3, col.1 and *San Francisco Call*, November 24, 1903, p.5, col.6

17 Ibid, August 19, 1882, p.1, col.5

18 Ibid, July 22, 1890, p.2, col.1; July 23, 1890, p.6, col.3 and *San Francisco Examiner*, July 31, 1894, p.7, col.4

19 Ibid, February 19, 1875, p.1, col.3

21 Ibid, April 17, 1887, p.1, col.4

22 Ibid, August 18, 1892, p.4, col.5

23 Charles Page scrapbook, vol.1, p.33

24 *San Francisco Call*, July 30, 1905, p.50, col.1

25 *Daily Alta*, September 13, 1882, p.1, col.5

26 Ibid, December 9, 1883, p.1, col.5; August 19, 1884, p.1, col.5; November 3, 1884, p.1, col.5; October 21, 1884, p.1, col.4; December 26, 1885, p.8, col.2

27 Manuscript of crews of whaling vessels from the J. Porter Shaw Library

Bad Whiskey & Blood Money

Gordon Grant, Greasy Luck! 1932

Crimps had crews of inbound ships half-drunk before the ship came near a wharf . . . Crimps would carry whiskey with them, described as terrible rotgut, when they boarded an incoming ship. The crew were supplied with ample doses of the stuff, along with the promises by the crimps of high paying jobs on coastal vessels or tempted with friendly women. Many of the sailors followed the crimps, who acted as runners for particular boardinghouses, to stay at that boardinghouse. For British sailors, any wages due were forfeited when they deserted their ship.

First Hand Accounts of Shanghaied Sailors

Yeah, I was shanghaied in San Francisco in 1902.
Oral history of seaman Johann Carlson.

First-person accounts of the shanghaiing trade vividly corroborate much of what newspapers reported over the years. Men such as Alexander McKenzie, among several people whose oral histories were recorded in 1959 and 1960, well remembered the boardinghouses run by men such as One-Eyed Curtin and "Shanghai" Brown. "Two sailors placed a bomb there, thinking they'd blow the place up," McKenzie recalled of Curtin's establishment.

Another man, Alfred C. Hansen, recounted his own shanghaiing from a bar in Astoria, Oregon. "I went down to take a look at the girls and I woke up aboard a German ship," he remembered. "I didn't even stop to find out what the name was. I jumped overboard and swam ashore," seeking out shipowner George Nelson to come with him to the saloon on a mission of revenge. "The same bartender was behind the bar. I ordered a stein of beer" as did Nelson, whereupon Hansen "picked up my glass and cracked the bartender across the head with it. He dropped behind the bar and I turned around and walked out." [1]

Captain Edward Connors, who sailed aboard whalers and served as a Whitehall boatman for a time, also had the names of shanghaiers impressed in his memory. "'Shanghai' Brown, he was the worst of the bunch. His place was on Steuart Street most of the time [Connors confused Brown with Curtin]. He got most of his men out of traps in saloons, drop them down the wharf, slip them out that way. But he'd take them any way. I can't remember any of the saloons he'd hang [out] in but he had a trap-door there. He'd knock them on the head and let them through a trap, take a Whitehall boat and row them out. That was all there was to it. Oh, yes, I knew them. Kane was another but he was good. He had a boardinghouse; he treated the men right. Anybody that come in, especially a seafarin' man, he liked to cater to real seafaring men. He'd go to work and he'd allow them a month or so, maybe longer it they couldn't get nothin.' But he'd have the honor of signing them on and getting a month [advance money] out of it, you see."

Connors was modest about his own role in shanghaiing as a Whitehall boatman. "I pulled for 'Shanghai' Brown one time, only a short time, but I pulled oars for old Crowley. Not for that purpose at all; used to bring them out once in a while, those that were shanghaied . . . Brown was a pretty tough sort of a scout. As I say, I didn't associate with him much, I didn't know much about him. I only have a very faint recollection of Tommy Chandler. Dammit, that was a long time ago. 'Shanghai' Nelson [the Norwegian who started out with 'Horseshoe' Brown] was an old man then. Once I got scow schoonering [sailing scow boats on the Bay and coast], I got clear of that crowd."

Connors told of the long, arduous voyages on whalers that he later joined—sometimes for two or more years at sea—the tough discipline and poor pay that crew received.

> Whalers as a rule didn't want anybody who was a sailor; if he knew the blue book—rights of a sailor—they knowed he'd cause a mutiny right away. I was so young they didn't

"The Men Behind Crowley's Fleet," 1909 . . . These young men ran motor launches and fought for towing jobs for Tom Crowley, Sr.

know what to make of me, but to get a full crew they took me. After they got out and, hell, they seen I had my sea legs on me, they didn't know what to make of that. I got to be a boat-steerer right off. My last trip [of seven] in the *Alice Knowles* was in 1904 . . . We jumped ship in the islands; that's why I didn't like to talk about this.

On a whaler they didn't draw no wages. It was by percentage. "By the lay," we called it. You got so much percent of whatever the ship took in. Ordinarily speakin,' you never got nothing. The idea was if you was a big, green, husky guy, wanted to go to sea in the worst way, they'd bull you how you was going on an excursion trip on some multi-millionaire's boat to the South Seas and so forth. They'd go the South Seas all right.

What they wanted was a bunch of big farmers and over-grown lumberjacks. They could break them in their way and they'd be damn good men. There was one that I knew of, he died over there. He was so sick that he couldn't stand it. [2]

In practice, whaling crews rarely saw any of the ship's profits but because maritime law required that they be paid something, they were often given one dollar at the end of a voyage. Their pleasures were few and far between, but exotic. "In the whaler we always used to stop at Hakodate [Japan]. Oh, that was a prize," Captain Connors recalled. "I could tell you stuff about that. Well, we used to love to get those oriental women. The Japanese are very . . . funny people, a rich man especially. He will not marry until he is sure she is broken in, and they'd get the sailors to break them in, we'd get that for only four or five yen. They didn't run it like in the South Seas where the women came on board; Hakodate is a big city."

John K. Bray recalled how the gullible might be shanghaied if they were not careful:

"The *Roanoke* was laying at Howard Street . . . . A Hollander and I were looking at it . . . . A big husky guy, Murray, the son of the boardinghouse master, came up . . . 'Fine ship!'

'Yes!' 'She's going to New York, how would you like a job on a ship like that?' 'Fine.' 'I can get you a job in her.' 'You big so and so, you go in her, we're too wise for the likes of you.'" [3]

Captain John E. Johnson had pleasant memories of "Shanghai" Nelson.

It was around six o'clock in the morning we got to 'Frisco. We went up to the waterfront and there was a place, coffee and doughnuts, five cents. We were dirty and we hadn't washed for three days and look tough, you know. That was our last dime, and from then on we were on our own. We came out of there and there was a surrey out there [this was in 1902], a two-seater tied out at the water trough outside of this place. This man tied up his horse and came up on the sidewalk.

"What are you, sailors?"

"Yes."

"You have a ship? You want a ship?"

"Yes, but not deepwater; we don't want any deepwater."

"Well, come to the house; I have a house. Talk to the boys. We have deepwater, on the coast, any place you want."

"I don't want to get tied down to a house, I want to be on my own," said Johnson's friend. Charlie, he got kind of cold feet and I guess, so did I. He said, "Let's go and see."

So we got into the buggy with him. That was "Shanghai" Nelson, they called him. He had three runners in the house there, [for] deepwater ships. He lived in an old hotel on Pacific Street between Battery and Davis [the Chicago Hotel] . . . "Shanghai" Nelson was an old man then, past 60. He ran a sailors' boardinghouse there. There was a saloon. He took us up and showed us the bar.

"Do you want a drink, on the house?"

He opened the door to the dining room and said, "Here, all this for five dollars a week." That was OK, you know. So we stayed there.

"When you get your clothes, I'll go down to the Sailors' Union and get a 'Temp' [temporary] card for you and you can ship on the coast." Which he did . . . We got our clothes and he took us right down to Furuseth and we shipped in Pope and Talbot lumber schooners.

This Norwegian Nelson had worked for "Shanghai" [actually Harry "Horseshoe"] Brown in the early days. But that was years before; he was an old man now . . . The food at the boardinghouse was good, too; we got plenty to eat. They had a cook there and waiters, men waiters. There must have been about 25 or 30 sailors who stayed there. Some of them were shanghaied; they come in one night and the next thing they were gone. The boardinghouse got a month's advance on each man they shipped out again. Some of these sailors would come along and start to drink; they would get drunk, and then they got abusive, too. Those were the fellows; the next morning they were gone. In those days whole crews deserted their ship and Nelson supplied new crew with these fellows. [4]

When one crimp tried to pass a corpse off on a ship, Captain F. N. Lyons remembered, he was foiled by a sharp-eyed mate. "That shanghaiing was dirty business. By God, they actually brought a corpse out there, they really did. The mate saw it before they got it aboard and he shouted out; that's the reason I heard it. The captain said, 'Don't let it come aboard, don't let it come aboard.' They sailed one man short." [5]

Hans Hansen relates his experience:

There was one time, in an American ship, the *Yankee* . . . every ship was hard at that time. It was laid up in Buenos Aires a long time. It shanghaied a crew, picked up anybody . . . . One night two men came in a boat and the mate says

"What you got there?"

"A good man, a colored man, but he's dead drunk." The mate says to the crew, "All right, put the block [pulley] up and put it on the main yard and hoist him aboard." So they did and the mate says, "Yes, he's drunk. Take him forward and put

"Lime-Juice Corner" **as it appeared barely two months before the earthquake and fire of April 1906 . . .** The demolition of the old Post Office was the occasion for a cameraman to take a few pictures of the intersection at Battery and Jackson streets. Lime-Juice Corner was actually the entire length of this block of Battery Street. Men were recruited to sail on British ships on this block, since it was also the location of the Customs House. The British Consul signed men to articles of agreement at his office in the Custom House.

The structure at the northwest corner of Jackson and Battery streets was an old aluminum building scarcely able to stand on its own. Rundown commission merchant offices, carpenter and cooper shops and, of course, the obligatory saloons—very necessary for shanghaiers when sailors were being hired—form the collapsing world of Lime-Juice Corner. Even the trees are barren.

Workingmen (right) and men in bowler hats (left) inspect the ruins of the old Post Office, with a nearby wagon to cart off anything of value.

him in bed there." Crew were summoned at four o'clock each morning and expected to go to work promptly. If you were too slow to get to that door and if you was a young fellow, the mate would kick you around. "Get up there on the focsle head and get hold of a bar and heave up the anchor." So in the morning the mate comes to the door and says, "Turn to." That means, get out on the deck as quick as you can, clothes or no clothes on. You just have a black cup of coffee and start to heave anchor.

"Where's the colored man?" [the mate asked].

"Oh, he's still in bed sleeping."

"Sleeping! he's supposed to work now."

The mate went and he grabbed that fellow and he turned him over on the doorstep and dumped him on the deck. Then he kicked him.

"Get up. You get to work." He didn't get up so one of them said, "Wait a minute, mate." They felt him. "He's dead." So the mate says, "Throw him overboard; we have no use for a dead man here. Throw him to the sharks.

That was his only funeral—no funeral. This is the truth. [6]

Johann Carlson left his native Norway in the 1890s and started sailing in Baltic schooners at the age of twelve or thirteen. He graduated to ships sailing out of England and Germany and if he did not like a ship, "runned away."

I runned away at Honolulu, that's how I got here—an old four-masted bark by the name of *Norma*. She was an English ship . . . Yeah, I was shanghaied in San Francisco in 1902. I was shanghaied in "Shanghai" Nelson's on Pacific Street. That's where I was shanghaied out of . . . I went up to "Shanghai" Nelson's and I got in the boardinghouse there. I didn't have much money, they didn't pay much then . . . He had a bar but you had to have money to get anything. We used to get an eye-opener in the morning but that was all you used to get. They didn't keep you any longer than they had to because, you see, they was getting a month's advance. So that's when I was shanghaied. They had bunks in all the rooms, two or three rooms. They were feeding pretty good, two meals a day. You know, in the ships I sailed in, we didn't get very much to eat. Nelson didn't shanghai me. No. The God-damned saloon keeper that I used to go a little farther up on the [Barbary] Coast. There used to be a saloon, a pretty nice bartender; he always used to give me a drink now and again. So I went up there again and as far as I can remember, I started to get dizzy, feel funny. So I says, "Gee, I feel rotten."

"Why don't you go in on the couch, there's a couch in there, go and lay down on the couch and you'll be all right."

But I didn't know . . . I went in here, laid down on the couch and that's all I remember. Then I was a hundred miles off shore in the old *Jeanette*. Of course, I had been in whalers out of home, see, so I could smell the God-damned whale oil as soon as I woke up. I knew what it was all about. I went aft to see the skipper and tell him I wanted to get back ashore. I said I wasn't hired aboard there. I couldn't speak English very well, you know. It was all black Portugees; there were only two white men, me and a Swede. They [told me], "You go back where you belong." "I want to see the captain." Well, they wouldn't let me and blocked the door. I was tough, and finally the captain came out.

"What does he want?"

"I want to get ashore. I don't belong here."

Here come the funny part of it. They took hold of me and chased me forward, packed me forward and then they throwed me down in . . . the hold. And there I was, laying a whole God-damned week down there; they sent me some water and some biscuits down there a couple of times a day. They opened up the hatches and said, "Have you had enough of it now? Do you want to behave yourself?"

I said, "No, God-damned no." I was mad and hungry. So they closed the hatch down on me again and I was there for another four or five hours. Finally they opened it up and let me out. They sent me down in the focsle and I stood there four or five days . . . getting very little to eat . . . Finally I thought to myself, what the hell, I'm here, I might as well stay with it so I got up. They were fixing the boats up at that time, whale boats, so they gave me one of the boats to go into . . . the boatsteerer's boat . . . they had six boatsteerers . . . We had to . . . splice things, fix up things . . .

Another "funny part," Carlson recalled, was his effort to change into dry clothes after getting wet from sea spray while dumping ashes overboard. Carlson went below deck to change when "here comes the God-damned skipper. 'What are you doing down there? You're supposed to be on deck!'" Carlson remained below and when he came up a companionway, the skipper waited. 'They make their own brooms up there, you know, out of bamboo strips. Here came the God-damned broom; he tried to swag me. But I was quick on my feet, I got away. I swung around and I hit the son-of-a-gun in the jaw and there he was lying down on the deck. Then the Portugees came and grab a hold of me and started to bang at me." Carlson retreated below where he stayed for four or five days before going top-side. "We was out and we got three whales," he next remembered. "They didn't take the whales then, the only thing they took was the lower jaw, see? The rest of the crap they let it go. They just wanted the whale bone; they was gettin' eight dollars a pound for the whale bone at that time." [7]

Another shanghai victim was Max DeVeer and a friend. DeVeer recounted their experiences in San Francisco when the Barbary Coast era still operated.

In San Francisco, as far as culinary work is concerned, it was easy to get. You go around the street and you see a sign in the window Dishwater wanted or Cook wanted, see? So I had quite a bit of experience along that line so I went up on Kearny Street and there used to be a White Lunch Room on Kearny Street and I got a job there. I stayed there for a little while and then—they used to have a big hot cake griddle in the window, and they put a white uniform on me, and I was making hot-cakes in the window there.

My pal, he wasn't as lucky as I am, you know, because he was more on the huskier side and he was doing the laboring type and I had to keep him up. He went to work and wanted to go to Alaska, fishing. As long as I had a job I liked in San Francisco I wasn't going to go to Alaska. So he did go. At this time of the year, they signed them up for Alaska. About three months later he came back, and he had a roll that big. And I worked all that time too.

Well that old honky-tonky outfit out here, the Barbary Coast, they were still in existence; they were going full swing; mostly they showed moving pictures and a bunch of dames down there, hustling for drinks, and you sit down and you see a moving picture or some kind of vaudeville sketch, you know. We went down there and were enjoying ourselves, see? We made an acquaintance with another fellow; he was sitting down with us; and he mentioned something about, "Like to go out with some girls?"

Well, naturally at that age we were raring to go any-where—females were far and wide between.

"We wouldn't mind."

"You fellows got money? I know the girls but you can't—their finances are limited—you got to show them a good time." Hell, my partner showed them the big roll.

The results of it was we woke up on a three-mast barken-tine going through the Golden Gate—shanghaied. He bought drinks, and we went up to his room, and we had some more drinks, and that was the last I remember. The vessel's name was the *Albatross*, a Danish boat. They were all Danes, but they all spoke English. Besides my partner and myself, there was three other guys. One of then was a city fireman, and one was a store clerk and the other one was a wino, I guess. I don't remember their names. That was before the fire, in about 1905 or 1906. I was about nineteen then; I'm seventy-five now. [8]

Courtesy San Francisco Maritime Museum N.H.P.

Whaler *Jeanette* at Hay and Wright Yard, Alameda, California . . . Norwegian Johann Carlson found himself aboard the *Jeanette* one morning in 1902, courtesy of a bartender in the Barbary Coast. "'Shanghai' Nelson did't shanghai me. No. The God-damned saloon keeper . . . . As far as I can remember, I started to feel dizzy, feel funny. So I says, 'Gee, I feel rotten.' 'Why don't you lie down on the couch? Lay down and you'll be alright' . . . . I went in there, laid on the couch and that's all I remember.

"Then I was a hundred miles off shore in the old *Jeanette*. Of course, I had been in whalers out of home, see, so I could smell the God-damned whale oil, as soon as I woke up."

Carlson refused to serve for several days on the ship. The crew chased him down into the hold, where he stayed for five days. "They sent me water and some biscuits down there, a couple times a day." Finally Carlson decided as long as he was on the whaler, he might as well work.

Whalers had a very hard time finding crewmen, due to low pay, awful conditions and long voyages. A "greenhand," a man who had no experience on a vessel, frequently formed a large part of crews on San Francisco's whaling fleet.

San Francisco Maritime Museum N.H.P.

The steam whaler *Narwhal* in San Francisco . . . George W. Kimble was shanghaied onto the *Narwhal* while he worked for Tommy Crowley in 1903. Ironically, Kimble sometimes took shanghaied men on the Crowley launch out to waiting ships. Fourteen years old at the time, he did duty as wiper in the engine room part of the time, and washed dishes the rest of his time. Kimble said he made pretty good money on the trip—in contrast to most whalers, who were paid off with $1 at the end of a one-year voyage.

San Francisco Maritime Museum N.H.P.

John R. Savory, as measurer at a the San Francisco Bay Yacht Club . . . On the waterfront, Savory was called "Scab Johnny," a nickname he earned while shipping non-union crews in the 1890s. "Scab Johnny" was proprietor of a boardinghouse, where the board sidewalk formed the roof for many a man down-and-out in post-earthquake San Francisco. Said Jack Shickell, a one time resident, "It was quite a sight to look down that sidewalk of a morning, seeing the planks tipped up and heads appearing like so many Lazaruses."

George W. Kimble ran a launch for boat operator Tom Crowley, Sr. "Every once in a while we'd get a call, and I'd go up to the dock and they'd bring somebody down there and I'd take them out to these ships anchored in the harbor—and then come in, that was all there was to it." But Kimble himself became a shanghai victim and found himself headed north on the whaler, *Narwhal*. He was gone eight months on that trip. "We had a lot of trouble on the way up [to Seattle]. About three-quarters of the crew was shanghaied and they were fighting all the time. We got a new master up there and from Seattle we went up into the northern waters . . . whaling . . . On a whaler we didn't fare so bad, not as bad as you did on a sailing vessel. She was both sail and steam . . . In those days, we didn't have the harpoons like they had later with guns . . . on the *Narwhal* you was an all-around man. They need you here, and they need you there; they used you. I made a good percentage on the catch. In fact, I was kind of glad after the trip was over that I made [it]—outside of the smell. It was a terrible smell, although it wasn't any worse than the old guano boat that we used to go out to the Farallones [Islands off San Francisco coast] later on. Boy was that stinking, worse than a whaler . . . The only trouble was in the beginning, and after that everybody quieted down and a lot depend upon your officers. If they [didn't] get overbearing with the crew, generally it [was] pretty good.

> I don't remember anything about the boardinghouse runners, I was too young. I was about 14 when I was shanghaied on the *Narwhal*. I was on the dock . . . They came over and said they wanted to see me . . . I used to like to get in to the free-lunch counters that they don't have today—five-cent beer and all you could eat. Those were the days. There was a big goat on the waterfront and they used to paint his horns green. He spent many a night in the Harbor Police station. He got drunk. If you didn't treat him to a glass of beer when you had yours, he'd butt you out of the saloon. [9]

Bill Coffman was a young man in 1902 when he worked at a Barbary Coast dive called the Cave. His description of being shanghaied in his autobiography, *American in the Rough* (1955), graphically depicted the experience.

One night, just before closing, I had drinks with two men who looked like foreign seamen, ashore for a good time. They claimed to have seen everything on Pacific Street and wondered if that was all the town had to offer . . . I accepted an invitation to guide the party and we made the rounds: the [Hotel] Nymphia [a brothel] on Stockton Street, the Bella Union at Washington and Kearny, and Purcell's Negro dive, the So Different. After that, I remember walking the length of Jackson Street toward East Street just as day was breaking.

My last recollection was of standing before the bar in a waterfront saloon. My knees were sagging and wobbly, despite every effort of will to straighten them out. I remember crumpling to the floor in a heap, a feeling of utter irresponsibility sweeping over me as I lapsed into a state of blissful unconsciousness. I never did discover what happened after I passed out, or how much time had elapsed before I became conscious again. My awakening was accompanied by all the elements of a tormented soul atoning for past misdeeds—a horrible nightmare coming true. I was lying on a cot, face down, with my head hanging over the edge while I retched violently, striving to empty my stomach of every single thing fastened down. My head ached, creaked and cracked, and seemed swollen to such proportions that I put up a shaky hand to make sure it would not pull loose and float upward toward an overhead skylight where a ghostly light just barely broke the darkness of the dingy room. I must have lapsed into unconsciousness again because when I came to, it was so dark that not even the skylight was visible. Painfully struggling to my feet, I located a door and beat on it, making a terrible racket.

Suddenly the door opened and two pairs of hands grabbed me and threw me violently on the cot, which collapsed to the floor. Then a voice shouted, "Keep quiet, you bum, or I'll blast you again." I subsided and the door was slammed shut. For a long time I lay in a sort of a coma, my head feverish and throbbing, my throat parched and my stomach in severe cramps. Sometime after daylight a man came into the room and, without even asking how I felt, told me to open my mouth, then poured steaming hot coffee and rum down my throat until my insides almost sizzled. As soon as I was able to speak, I asked for a doctor and demanded to know where I was and what had happened. He replied that a doctor had seen me the day before and had said I would be all right, that I was at Mr. Brewer's boardinghouse on Steuart Street, that I had been there for two days and owed more than $12 for medicine, food, lodging and the doctor—and that I had better pay up.

Without even searching my pockets, I groaned that I had no money and no prospects of getting any soon. "We'll see about that," he said. "Mr. Brewer says you'll pay or work it out." Coming back later with more hot coffee and rum, he pointed to a bucket of water and a washbowl and told me to clean up; we were going visiting. He led me down a flight of stairs, and through a saloon, past several bleary-eyed men lounging at the bar. Out on the street I was hoisted into a horse-drawn delivery wagon. Dizzy and miserable, I lay on the bottom of the wagon while the driver flapped the reins and we started off. The jolting ride over several blocks of cobblestones almost finished me. At our destination I managed to get to my feet long enough to be pushed into a room and to a counter, where my keeper volunteered my name and nationality. He handed me a pen with which I scratched my name feebly. Afterward I was handed back into the wagon, and given a shot of rum which put me out . . .

On the return trip I was so far gone that I only remember being carried bodily upstairs and dumped into the room. In the late afternoon food was brought in and I tried to eat, but my stomach was still upset and rebelled so badly that my jailers

San Francisco Maritime Museum N.H.P.

The Bells of Shandon on Howard Street, near Steuart, about 1912 . . . A young man in the foreground shows off his new hat as the decrepit Bells of Shandon forms a backdrop. The Bells of Shandon was a sailors' boarding-house for years. It was also known as Brewers' Hotel, for its proprietor, Richard Brewer. Ten years before, Bill Coffman had been drugged and kept at Brewers' Hotel on Howard Street until he recovered enough to be shanghaied onto the British ship *Belfast*.

finally gave me a mug of hot coffee and rum which put me to sleep again. I awoke several times but it was always pitch-dark in the room. Remembering the manhandling I had received before, I decided to wait until morning before making a move. Daylight came and with it the same men.

"Get going," one of them said. "Get going where?" I groaned. "Put your shoes on and start moving. You'll find out soon enough," was the reply. The same wagon was waiting outside but this time there were six of us besides the driver and the two men in charge who carried heavy sticks as persuaders. We were driven to the foot of Howard Street and hustled out of the wagon to a rowboat tied up at the dock. Four of us were shoved down the ladder and the other two, both drunk, were swung over the wharf and dropped like sacks of wheat into the arms of the boat crew. The boardinghouse runners dropped into the boat and shoved off . . . We were heading for a cluster of three large sailing ships, swinging at anchor. As we came close, I saw that two flew the British flag. Rowing close to the nearest ship, one of the men at the oars shouted, "Ahoy, the *Belfast*." A dozen heads showed over the rail; a line was thrown down and made fast and then a rope ladder came hurtling down. My heart was beating like a trip hammer as I climbed the rope ladder, stepped on a broad rail, missed my footing, and fell about four feet to the deck. The fall almost knocked the breath from my body. I struggled to my feet, confused and bewildered, just as an officer (whom I later learned was the second mate) grabbed my arm and demanded to know if I were a sailor. "I've sailed on a schooner," I answered.

"Then if you've sailed before," he shouted at me, "why don't you say 'Sir?'" And with that, he plunged his fist into my midriff with such force that my breath left me completely. I caved in, rolling over and over in the scuppers, gasping like a dying man. [10]

Coffman survived 153 days on the *Belfast* until arriving at Cork, Ireland, where he was paid, after deductions for his advance and slopchest purchases, $36. He returned to San Francisco and pursued a successful business career, noted for founding the East-West Shrine college football game.

(The Hotel Nymphia that Coffman remembered was a brothel at 739 Pacific Street that opened in 1899. Three hundred prostitutes worked from an equal number of "cribs" for which each paid $5 a day rent. The owners planned to call it the "Nymphomania" but that was too much for the San Francisco police commission, which vetoed the name. One floor was devoted to women billed as nymphomaniacs. The hotel was operated by two German-Americans, Emil and Valentine Kehrlein, sons of a devout Catholic immigrant. Emil was one of 25 founders in 1877 of the Dolphin Swimming and Boating Club; he was part of a winning rowing crew for the club in 1879 and ran for the Board of Supervisors as a Democrat in 1896. [11])

The quality of the boardinghouses depended on their keepers. Captain Jack Shickell described one that he knew in 1910.

> Scab Johnny's lodgings on Steuart Street probably characterized the lowest ebb a sailor could reach on the waterfront and still survive. [It] was just a shack and there wasn't much room in it. He had a unique way of accommodating the overflow, a condition that set in when things were slow along the [water]front and jobs were hard to find. I remember the first time I made application to him; he was standing on the board sidewalk out in front, whittling with a long knife.
>
> "Can you put me up, Johnny?" "Are you one of my boys?" "No." "Say 'No, Sir.'" "No, Sir." I was just a kid and he didn't want any impertinence.
>
> He gave me 15 cents (that was in lieu of meal tickets for the three meals a day he was supposed to supply—at a nickel for coffee and——, it theoretically kept us fed). Then he showed me where I was to sleep. He walked down the sidewalk, scanning chalk marks and then leaned over and lifted a couple of boards. Underneath was a "donkey's breakfast" on the ground—there were a couple of feet of clearance under the board sidewalk . . . a whole row of straw mattresses, side by

VAL. KEHRLEIN

Brothers Emil and Valentine Kehrlein started the biggest brothel in San Francisco in 1899 . . . The Hotel Nymphia was created by the Twinkling Star Improvement Company. Their signatures are at the lower left, with those of their partners. Emil and Val were members of the Dolphin Swimming and Boating Club in the late 1870s. Emil dabbled in politics, was a jeweler and then went into entertainment—first in an opera house, then as a brothel owner and later as owner of a string of silent movie theaters. He is credited with being the first person to accompany silent movies with music. The talented Emil had problems with partner Abe Ruef in a business they ran—some money in Emil's possession disappeared while he was secretary.

The Hotel Nymphia advertised that the women on its ground floor were nymphomaniacs. 300 women served the customers in the three story building on Pacific Street. A coin operated slot in each doorway allowed anyone with a dime to inspect the goings-on of the inhabitants. Do-gooders spoiled the fun, mounting a successful campaign to drive the Nymphia out of business. *Dolphin Swimming and Boating Club*

Courtesy Walt Schneebeli

Emil Kehrlein

side, their confines defined by chalk marks on the planks above. Johnny issued blankets at the shack and every night there were a number of us making use of this out-of-doors dormitory. In the morning you had to be careful not to rise too abruptly and bump your head. It was quite a sight to look down that sidewalk of a morning, seeing the planks tipped up and heads appearing like so many Lazaruses. [12]

Shickell soon moved to other lodgings, the Humboldt House on Broadway run by Billy Cane. Like Johnny,

Billy always did his business out on the sidewalk, back to the wall, and always whittling away on a stick with a seven- or eight-inch bladed knife as a safety measure against aggrieved seamen who occasionally returned to San Francisco thinking they had paid too much for the last job and who sometimes got rough about it. I had a brief talk and was told to join the circle indoors. This place had a roof, the only advantage over Johnny's. Otherwise, the mattresses were on the floor and pretty dirty at that. I slept on a bench with an old *Examiner* for mattress and a *Chronicle* for blanket. The waiting room was much more spacious than the shack on Steuart Street and besides the benches around the walls, boasted a table . . .

Grub . . . was taken care of by an organizational genius, a man with rare executive ability and leadership known as Bosun, a downeaster who had served as second mate on several hard-case ships, and looked it. He had drifted into the place, sized it up and took charge naturally. If there was any opposition, it didn't appear while I was there, but I would have enjoyed seeing him deal with anyone having the temerity to dispute his authority.

After the wake-up can of coffee and smoke by all hands, the Bosun lined up the crowd and sang out, "You there, Dirty, and you, Wingy, take the crab nets and a coupla gunny sacks. Put the big 'uns in one sack and keep the runts in the other out of sight under the pier in case the cops come around. Bring 'em in after dark. Take a bag o' cookies with you." Another pair, young and able to sprint when necessary, would be given a sack each and dispatched to the produce district, there to pick up what they could—a spud, a bunch of carrots, onions or a head of cabbage, etc. In that way they got enough vegetables in one morning to last "Doc," the cook, for a few days.

At that period of my life I was a pink-cheeked lad who wore a still decent-looking blue serge suit, and was able to put on a guileless expression when necessary. I'd had some experience in begging a meal or making a touch. The Bosun sized me up as too good to waste on the more menial tasks and coached me in the role I was to play. After getting the others equipped and started out on their missions, he took me down to the 'front and stopped near the Colchester Hotel, a waterfront flophouse. There he gave me my first orders. "Go aloft," he said, pointing to the stairs, "and see if the purser's on watch in the office. If he ain't, dash down to the head, the washroom." He explained where it was situated. "And scrub your mug until it shines. Comb your hair so it don't look so much like a bag o' wrinkles [chafing gear used on ships] and brush your shoes. Don't let him catch you coming out either if you can help it. Get going and make it snappy." And he gave me a gentle push that made me take the first three steps in one hop.

Returning and glowing like a kid going to school on his first day, I rejoined the impatient man on the sidewalk. "Took you long enough," he growled. We then headed toward Market Street, but at Clay he paused and pointed to the butchershop halfway up the block. He gave me a dime. "Go into Gaffney's, the ships' butcher up there, and tell the guy your mom is sick and you want a beef bone with a bit o'meat on it to make her a cup o'broth. Make it real, and *bring the dime back*!" the emphasis on the last four words implied that it would be unhealthy to return without it.

I must have put on a convincing act as the few times I tried it, in different shops of course, I got away with it, usually getting a marrow bone or fistful of stew meat. All of this was added to the contents of the five-gallon can in which "Doc" made the mulligan stew. But after the first day, I took the precaution of having a dime of my own as insurance against the chance of losing the one Bosun provided.

The butcher being disposed of, I was next sent to a bakery on lower Market. "Your mom's still sick and you want a stale donut or a cinnamon bun for her breakfast, see? And if there's a black-haired old bat on watch, come right out again. The bitch has a heart smaller than the dime. But *bring the dime anyway!*" I found out that the cake or whatever I got was for his own breakfast—too good for the gang, although if I got three or four portions, he would generously hand one to me.

Evenings at the Humboldt were usually merry. The bucket would be full of "Dago Red" [wine] and the dipper made the rounds like a pipe at Sioux pow-wow. Smokers helped themselves from the heap of tobacco on the table and cigarettes were rolled, the papers coming from packs found attached to Bull Durham sacks, thrown away by discriminating smokers who used another brand of paper. Talk would be wonderful to a youngster whose head was full of romantic ideas and usually the Bosun did most of the talking. After hearing some of his yarns, getting wilder and more thrilling after each round of the dipper, I had occasional doubts about his veracity. [13]

Such was the life of a boardinghouse resident in San Francisco in the late 19th and early 20th century.

Footnotes

1 Captain Alfred C. Hansen ms., J. Porter Shaw Library

2 Captain Edward Connors ms., J. Porter Shaw Library

3 Captain John K. Bray ms., J. Porter Shaw Library

4 Captain John E. Johnson ms., J. Porter Shaw Library

5 Captain F. N. Lyons ms., J. Porter Shaw Library

6 Hans Hansen ms., J. Porter Shaw Library

7 Johann Carlson ms., J. Porter Shaw Library

8 Max DeVeer ms., J. Porter Shaw Library

9 George W. Kimble ms., J. Porter Shaw Library

10 William Milo Coffman, *American in the Rough* (New York: Simon and Schuster, 1955), pp. 68-71

11 Asbury, pp. 262-6

12 Roger R. and Nancy L. Olmsted, *San Francisco Waterfront* (San Francisco, 1977), pp. 384-5

13 *San Francisco*, December 1968, pp. 60-2

Dave Crowley, Sr., at Meiggs Wharf . . . His Whitehall boat propped at his side, Dave Crowley stands on Meiggs Wharf, Alcatraz in the background. Crowley started his career as a boatman in 1873.

Tom Crowley, Sr., in 1898— Tom Crowley, Sr., step-son of Dave Crowley, Sr., was well-established as a Whitehall boatman by 1898. Crowley had two gasoline launches taking captains, passengers, cargo and shanghaied sailors at his disposal by then.
Both photographs courtesy Bancroft Library

Whitehall Boatmen

The darkest legend circulated about town was that
knockout drops, a sudden plunge through a trapdoor
into the chilly waters of the bay and a voyage under
brutal mates to some faraway port awaited those who
visited the realm of the devil on the waterfront.

William Martin Camp
San Francisco: Port of Gold (1947)

Shanghaiing required mobility and discretion and boatmen
played an essential role in the business. For ships forced to anchor out in the stream, the use of small boats to move people and
goods from shore to the ships allowed commerce and communi-
cation to continue. The favorite small craft were Whitehall boats,
developed in New York City at the time of the War of 1812 specifically for harbor use. Taking their name from Whitehall Street
in New York, they were sleek, eighteen to twenty-one foot row-
boats with a shallow draft, plumb stem and four-foot beam. They
were constructed of cedar which resisted worms (toredoes) with
oak frames, ash thwarts and mahogany transom. For decades in
San Francisco Bay, such craft served as ferries between the waterfront and ships, and boatmen were indispensable not only to
the mercantile community but to shanghaiers. The boats handled

well in rough water, could be sailed or rowed and could carry five or more people.

Other essential ingredients to shanghaiing were shipowners and ship captains who frequently were in league with crimps they knew could supply immediate crew, particularly during periods when they were in scarce supply. A captain or ship's agent could look under "Shipping Masters" in a San Francisco city directory to find a list of men in intimate contact with the city's boarding-house keepers, ever willing to supply sailors.

The principal device for shanghaiing was the shanghai drink—beer, whiskey or schnapps and opium. Our perception today is frequently that shanghaied men were dropped through trapdoors into a Whitehall boat waiting below. The unsuspecting victim stood at a bar, enjoying his drink (spiked with opium or laudanum) one moment, the next he was plummeting through space into the arms of runners ready to row him to a waiting ship.

Descriptions of trapdoors come from the realm of myth, however. The mythical Miss Piggott's runner Nikko reportedly vowed never to tend a trapdoor again after he left her service and he went to work for an honest saloon keeper. According to Herbert Asbury, who interviewed members of the city police department for his book, *The Barbary Coast* (1933), legend held that Nikko gradually edged a prospective catch toward the trapdoor, Miss Piggott hit the victim on the head, the trap opened and he tumbled onto a waiting mattress in the basement. He was, after all, too valuable a commodity to risk injury in falling. "Shanghai" Kelly reportedly had not one but three trapdoors in his saloon. [1]

"The darkest legend circulated about town," wrote William Martin Camp in *San Francisco: Port of Gold* (1947), was "knockout drops, a sudden plunge through a trapdoor into the chilly waters of the bay and a voyage under brutal mates to some faraway port awaited those who visited the realm of the devil on the waterfront." [2]

" 'Shanghai' Brown, he was the worst one of the bunch," one seaman remembered in an oral history recorded in 1960. "His place was on Steuart Street most of the time. He got most of his men out of traps in saloons. Slip[ped] them out that way. But he'd take them any way. I can't remember any of the saloons he'd hang in, but he had a trapdoor there. He'd knock them on the head and let them down through the trap; take a Whitehall boat and row them out. That was all there was to it." [3]

John Roberts, a ship caulker who plied his trade South of Market from 1869 until at least 1904, remembered that "near Mission Street, on Steuart Street, was Thompson's . . . a sailors' boardinghouse. This place had a bad name as there was a trapdoor in the floor and many a sailor went through this trap into a boat and was rowed to some ship that was waiting for a crew." [4]

The storyteller's memory may have been enhanced or reduced by time. "Shanghai" Brown actually operated from Battery Street and another Brown with the same reputation on Kearny Street. But it was true that boats could move in shallow water beneath buildings until the late 1890s when a seawall was built that protected the north waterfront as far as Powell Street, thus reducing the level of tidal waters that formerly flowed under waterfront structures. Another seawall along the southern waterfront was completed in 1915. Until then, small boats could be taken under wharves south of Market Street as far up as Steuart Street, the site of many sailors' boardinghouses and saloons, lending credibility to the trapdoor legend. The boatmen had to maneuver between pilings, avoid being smashed against them in tidal swells as they glided beneath wharves, streets and buildings to the point beneath a trapdoor where they waited for their cargo.

Thomas Crowley, Sr., ridiculed the trapdoor technique, since wharves in San Francisco were state property beginning in 1863 and the state did not allow saloons on government property.

Courtesy San Francisco Maritime N.H.P.

Robert Gibson, Whitehall Boatman . . . A fixture at the foot of Third Street for years, Robert Gibson started his long career on San Francisco's north waterfront in 1869, as a boatman at the Howard Street Wharf.

By 1875, Gibson's boathouse, seen here with his dog, stood at the foot of Third Street. Gibson sailed for the Corinthian Yacht Club, and rented his sailboat, *Magic* from this site. From his southern waterfront vantage point, next to the Channel and China Basin, he transported crews and officers from the men-of-war anchored off Mission Bay. An experienced boatman like Gibson could pick up a lot of work helping bulk cargo operators.

Whitehall boatmen ran the watertaxi service of the waterfront. They transported men and supplies, rescued the drowning and retrieved corpses, assisted in smuggling and shanghaiing—in short, many of them did what it took to make a buck. Their boats were marvels of adaptation for the busy harbor, and sometimes took these daredevils 40 miles or more outside the Golden Gate in pursuit of profit.

"Nobody ever dropped a man through a barroom floor into the water. In other words, some said the saloon was over the water. Well, there wasn't any saloon on state property; they were all across the street. Nobody ever did that," Crowley flatly stated. [5]

In most cases, shanghaiers transported their prey overland, with horse-drawn wagons they hired or owned to convey them to waiting Whitehalls at the water's edge. The trapdoor myth romanticizes the brutality of shanghaiing—it was also not a very practical method of transporting a drunken or drugged sailor to a Whitehall boat.

Whitehall boatmen were the crucial link between ships in the stream and the waterfront. They served as water taxis, cargo-haulers and frequently were the first contact that an incoming ship had with the port. The runners whom they ferried represented all types of businesses serving ships: markets, chandleries and other providers of supplies and services as well as boarding-houses. The boatmen had to be brave, competitive and willing to run risks. Sometimes that meant breaking the law.

The craft was not without its dangers, as a colorful account in the *San Francisco Examiner* related in 1892, providing readers with a glimpse of the hazards, competitiveness and camaraderie of boatmen.

> Dummy Mike took his annual swim last night, when the waves were running high at the Golden Gate and the breeze had a tinge of the north in it. Mike's constant claim is that, "a swim wanst in a while doesn't hurt anyone," and he clings tenaciously to this idea despite the jeers . . . of his Whitehall navigating confreres. Mike's other name is Egan, and he and Buster Hart are partners in soliciting for a waterfront market . . . He and Buster were off Point Bonita late in the afternoon when they hooked onto the bark *Alex McNeil*, which was in tow of the tug *Sea King*, and skipping along at eight or ten knots. A rival butcher's runner, Dave Crowley, Sr., hooked-on astern, and Crowley and Buster Hart shinned up the *McNeil's*

side to battle for trade. Dummy Mike and Maurice Behan remained in the boats, exchanging uncomplimentary epithets.

Off Point Diablo Mike's tow line parted, and before he could move astern he was in collision with Crowley's boat. Crowley's Whitehall rolled Mike's boat and when she floated bottom up, Mike was underneath. Behan forgot the harsh words of a moment before and cut his own boat loose to go to Mike's rescue. It was hard work righting the capsized Whitehall in a rough sea, but Behan accomplished it, and hauled Mike into his boat . . . Mike kept warm by rowing home, where he arrived late at night, so little the worse for his submersion and imprisonment under the boat that he was able to meet Buster and repay scorn with scorn.

"You old tad," said Buster, "did you smash that boat?"

"Blame you," said Mike. "I suspect you'll drown me some day with yer rotten work. It's a pity Behan bothered with the likes o' you, you gray-haired old rat."

"Cuss you," rejoined Mike, impressively, "I was a fine young man when I first met you, and now all you think about is the dirty old boat. It ain't hurt a bit, an' I'm dyin' for lack of a soul-warmer."

There was a pause. "Damn you," said Mike. Buster assured himself the boat was not injured before he replied. Then he fished a quarter out of his pocket, took his gray-haired pal by the arm, and led him to a place where they sell "soul-warmers" out of black bottles at a dime a warm. And this is the way Whitehallers treat a miraculous escape from death. [6]

Among their varied tasks boatmen were called upon to fish out corpses, rescue people attempting suicide and those who accidentally fell into the Bay. The city paid $10 per corpse retrieved from the Bay, and in 1884 disbursed $480 for the 48 bodies pulled from the Bay. Boatmen received $5 for rescuing a drowning person. In 1878, $2,500 was deposited at the Merchants Exchange to reward boatmen like William Ferguson and Edward Callahan for their rescues. Boardinghouse runners William

"Hook-on" Dave Crowley, Sr. and his mate Maurice Behan . . . "None of the local Whitehallers pretend to keep up with Crowley . . . . The Whitehaller takes life as the weather gives it to him, and tows when he can, sails when he can not tow and rows when he can do neither.

"It is doubtful if any class of small-boat sailors the world over possess more skill than San Francisco's boatmen. The critical moment comes when they near a ship and make ready to 'Hook her' . . . . Hooking is an operation that requires skill, nerve and dexterity of a high order. A miss of an inch or two, the slightest error in calculation of safety distance . . . means he has lost his chance for the ship, and ten to one shot, the Whitehall is overturned.

"So he edges in close as safety permits and hangs on, ready and waiting for the runner's command, 'Now, give it to her!' A might tug at the oars, and the Whitehall shoots alongside, taking the tail of the boat at an acute angle, and the runner shoots for his mark. If he doesn't get it . . . he makes another try. Up he goes on his hook: then comes a time when his mate needs two or three pairs of hands." *San Francisco Examiner, October 8, 1893*

Wilson and John McLean recovered the body of a man floating off Meiggs Wharf in 1872. William Douglass and two other boardinghouse runners, were hooked onto the ship *Annie Fish* as she came into port. A sailor fell from the boom and the runners almost overturned their Whitehall boat when they sought to save him. They succeeded in their rescue, and the captain thanked them profusely. The runners in both cases probably were more interested in obtaining the $10 for retrieving a corpse and $5 for rescuing a drowning person.

In June of 1869 runners were up to their old tricks again. A German named Charles Braverman, about twenty years old, had been in California six months, working at the Central Pacific Railroad as a rough carpenter. His job with the Central Pacific ended and he decided to go to the Labor Exchange in search of a job. Braverman was stopped by a runner and asked if he would like to go to sea. The carpenter said he would if another German were found to go to sea with him. The runner thought that could be arranged and walked with Braverman a short distance where he introduced him to a fellow German. They went to a shipping office and Braverman was asked to sign a document, which he did. These were his shipping articles for the *Alice St. Minor*, bound for Callao, Peru. The runner, the two Germans, and a couple of other men, got into a Whitehall boat and headed for the ship. Not far from the shore everyone but the first runner and Braverman jumped from the boat. Braverman figured he had been sold out, pulled off his coat, jumped in the Bay and swam for freedom. The runner/boatman did not give up so easily—he went after his sailor and with the help of one of his decoys, pulled Braverman back into the boat. The Harbormaster, a chap named Houseman, noticed Braverman clinging to a piling near a wharf, hanging on for dear life. Houseman took Braverman by force and called Officer Guion to take charge of the reluctant sailor. Braverman was set free.

Whitehall boatman Jack Desmond committed the professional *faux pas* of allowing five seamen to escape from him as he rowed them to their new home on the *George Stetson*, bound for Queenstown. One of the escapees drowned. William Moran, Whitehall boatman, had the tip of his nose bitten off by "an infuriated whaler." The whaler was so infuriated that he swallowed the bit of nose in question. [7]

A number of boatmen who were crimps found corpses such tempting sources of bodies that they occasionally tried to pass one off as viable crew. As many as 100 people a week were estimated to die in San Francisco during the 1870s and 1880s, according to weekly contemporary newspaper tallies, and a crimp might augment his crew of breathing sailors with one who had breathed his last. When a captain asked about "that one not moving over there," the crimp would assure him that sailor "would be fine when he woke up in the morning."

Drowning in the frigid Bay or ocean was a liability of the trade when boats capsized and Whitehall boatmen passed the time when not working by practicing life-saving techniques (the boats carried no life-saving gear). Two boatmen fully dressed with their boots on intentionally capsized their boat, then righted it and bailed it out. On one such occasion off Meiggs Wharf at North Beach, local fishermen became concerned when two boatmen, one large and the other small, began arguing in the craft with the result that the smaller man wound up in the water. His antagonist promptly jumped in and rescued his watersoaked friend, demonstrating before anxious observers the techniques being practiced. The *Daily Alta* thought this good practice for the time when one of the boatmen needed to save someone actually drowning.

Tommy Crowley, Sr., a tough old bird, succeeded in tough times, as did his step-father, Dave Crowley. Aside from intense competition, the conditions on San Francisco Bay and outside the Headlands can be extremely dangerous; even if the sky is blue

San Francisco Maritime Museum N.H.P.

Abe Warner's Cobweb Palace—Located on Meiggs Wharf, Warner's saloon sported a menagerie of animals, cobwebs built up over decades (Warner never cleaned the place) and had the reputation as one of the few waterfront bars in San Francisco it was safe for a sailor to go without threat of being shanghaied. The tumble down building, complete with broken windows, served sailors and slumming socialites between 1856-1897.

and fog-free, with a calm wind in the morning, wind and fog can conspire suddenly in an afternoon to create a situation where the utmost skill is needed to survive the wild waters of the Bay. To save oneself and rescue others struggling for life is even more of a feat. Mike Fitzgerald and John Burns barely kept their Whitehall boat upright in rough seas off the Marin Headlands one stormy day. The steamer *Empire* plowed through wind-whipped whitecaps with such force that her wake swamped and capsized Fitzgerald and Burns' Whitehall. Dave Crowley, Sr., Tommy's step-father, came to their rescue, but it took two hours of constant maneuvering to pluck the men from the bottom of their boat into his without overturning his Whitehall. [8]

At other times boatmen found less law-abiding ways to supplement their income. In 1882, Customs Inspector W. A. Whaley noticed unusual goings-on around the *Arabic*, which was moored at a wharf. Climbing aboard, he watched some men lower several packages into a Whitehall boat that had silently slipped up next to the ship. Raising his pistol, Whaley threatened to shoot anyone who moved. The men on the *Arabic* dropped the contraband in the water and fled, while Whaley and a nearby Customs House boat concentrated on the Whitehall. He commanded it to halt and fired a warning shot. The boatmen continued to pull away and Whaley fired again. "I'm shot!" one of the boatmen yelled, dropping his oars, but the pair still managed to escape. The packages contained 225 pounds of refined opium, 125 pounds of crude opium, 500 high-quality flowered red silk handkerchiefs and two packages of silk cord. The street-value of the refined opium was $12 per-pound in 1882, the crude opium worth $4 a pound and the silk handkerchiefs 60 cents apiece. [9]

A major source of amusement, however, was racing. Whitehall races became a popular pastime for boatmen and spectators alike.

San Francisco Maritime Museum N.H.P.

The Annual Fourth of July Whitehall Sailing Race Pitted the Toughest Crimps on San Francisco Bay Against Each Other . . . Begun as a charity event in 1878 to relieve the suffering of a yellow fever epidemic in the southeast, the Whitehall sailing race was a mainstay of San Francisco's Fourth of July celebration for over twenty years. The shanghaiers got their boats spotless, fitted them out with new sails, and set out from Vallejo Street Wharf for the long trip to Blossom Rock, to Meiggs Wharf, on to Fort Point and back to Vallejo Street Wharf. Total distance was nine-ten miles and the winner took home $500-$100 of taxpayers' money.

The crimps christened their boats with names like *Pride of the Bay, Norwegian King* (owned by Norwegian Henry "Shanghai" Brown) or *California*. Sometimes a popular politician lent his name to that of a Whitehall boat—*Denis Kearney, Stewart Menzies,* even *Senator James G. Fair* had shanghaiers' boats carry their fame. There must have been some reason why.

San Francisco Maritime Museum N.H.P.

A Whitehall boat makes its way along San Francisco's waterfront in a race for professional prestige . . . Whitehall sailing races were a part of the scene on San Francisco Bay at least as early as 1852. The course in this race is near Mission Bay, with ships loading and unloading at Mission Rock, center left. The East Bay Hills are in the background. The date of this photograph is unknown, so the occupants of the boat can not be identified.

In the summer and early fall of 1878 a yellow fever epidemic struck the southeastern United States. New Orleans and Memphis were particularly hard hit. The *New York Tribune* reported a death toll of 8,756 by early October, 1878. All around the United States people responded to the horrors of the epidemic with an outpouring of charity. The *Daily Alta* praised "Our fellow-citizens along the City Front have started up an effort to raise a fund for the benefit of the yellow-fever sufferers . . . . generous hearts will . . . take part in this movement." The crimps decided to give a regatta to help out. Featuring sailing schooners and Whitehall boats, some of the city's most famous crimps worked "tooth-and-toe-nail" to prepare their boats for the competition. Harry "Shanghai" Wilson brought his boat *Denis Kearney* out for the event, while the following Whitehall boats came to the line for their very famous owners: Henry "Shanghai" Brown in the *Commodore Allen*; Patsy Cosgrove's *Connaught Ranger*; John Ryan's *California*; Thomas Murray with the *Pride of the Bay*; and last but not least James Laflin piloting the *Blue Duck* (also spelled the *Blue Dick* in one account). James Laflin, Joseph "Frenchy" Franklin and Andrew Peterson served on the committee of arrangements. The steamer *Contra Costa* was procured as an observation boat, with a charge of fifty cents per person.

A fleet of thirty boats, two-thirds Whitehalls and one-third keel boats, set sail from Vallejo Street Wharf on September 22, 1878 at 1:20 p.m. The course was Vallejo Street Wharf to Sausalito, Fort Point and back to Vallejo Street Wharf. The conditions were beautiful, too beautiful in fact, for there was almost no breeze and it took a long time to complete the race without full sails. Patsy Cosgrove bested the field in his *Connaught Ranger*, winning a silver pitcher donated by Commodore Allen. $300-$400 was raised by the "generous hearts" of the City Front's shanghaiing community. The event was enjoyed so thoroughly by the crimps that they formed a Whitehall Boat Club to sponsor regattas and for social purposes. The Whitehall portion of this race set the stage for future Whitehall boat races sponsored by the city of San Francisco. The crimps' regatta was sailed the Fourth of July for many years.

1882 saw the resumption of the "shanghaiers" Whitehall boat race (due to an assassination attempt on President James A. Garfield on July 4th, 1881, the Whitehall boat race was canceled in that year, along with all other activities planned for the Fourth). "Shanghai" Brown's *Norwegian King* (appropriately enough, as he hailed from the land of the fjords), Thomas Murray's *Pride of the Bay*, *Tom Crowley* sailed by Dave Crowley, Sr., and *Chief Crowley*, named for the Police Chief, with the old oarsman Henry C. Hoyt at the helm, lined up for battle against several other Whitehalls. Henry C. Hoyt pleased the policemen, most of whom had bet on their chief's namesake, when he finished a strong first. In 1883 William Fitzgerald won in the *James Sinnott*, while Dave Crowley came across the line in third place in the *Stewart Menzies*.

Whitehall sailing races continued through the 1880s and 1890s. Due to the popularity of the competition among both the participants and the public, Whitehall sailing races took place at times other than July Fourth. In late July 1884 such a race was won by David Crowley in the *Stewart Menzies*. An October, 1886, Whitehall sailing race saw John Gately in the *Belfast Maid* beat his rivals by a long way. [10]

In the late 1890s, the Whitehall *Senator James G. Fair* was piloted by Billy Clark. *Chief Lees*, piloted by Tommy Lyons, named for the police chief and the *Robert J. Tobin*, handled by Dave Crowley, Sr.'s former boatboy, Maurice Behan, entered the Fourth of July race in 1898. [11]

The builders of Whitehalls also became well known. John Twigg was one of the major ones along with Dan O'Connell, whose works were at Mason and Bay streets, J. C. Beetle from New Bedford, Massachusetts, Martin Vice, George W. Kneass, Samuel Thornton and John D. Griffin, a city supervisor and capable oarsman. [12]

Twigg was born in Ireland about 1840, moved with his wife Julia to New York before 1867 and had four children (three sons and a daughter). By 1877 the family moved to San Francisco where the Twiggs increased by three more sons. Twigg first was employed by boatbuilder Timothy Collins and subsequently worked for Martin Vice whose reputation was somewhat dubious for his penchant to fight and get into trouble. (While tending bar at a saloon at the corner of Second and Folsom streets, he shot a man in the leg). Twigg soon left Vice's employ and opened his own shop in 1881 at the corner of Ritch and King streets. Kneass' and Thornton's works were located on the same block. [13]

He built work boats as well as racing craft, counting the Crowleys among his Whitehall customers. An apprentice of Twigg's in 1898, DuVal Williams, later described Whitehalls of the period as 18 feet long with a four-and-a-half-foot beam and two-foot depth. The boats operated from wharves at the foot of Vallejo, Washington and Folsom streets, and Meiggs Wharf. [14]

Gasoline-, or naphtha-operated, launches began to be built in San Francisco in 1890 but early engines were slow and unreliable. They improved with the advent of the automobile and became practical for use in boats. Twigg built the first three gasoline launches owned by boatman Thomas Crowley, Sr., beginning with the *Jenny C.* in 1897, 36 feet long with a 35-horsepower Hercules Engine. She could carry 25 passengers and cost $1,700 to $1,800, which Crowley claimed he had gotten from selling Arctic clothing that he had bought from crews on returning whalers. The 50-foot *Crowley* followed in 1898. It transported the *Examiner* to Oakland each morning. Twigg built *The Spy* in 1900, powered by a nine-horsepower Union Engine. By 1905 Twigg had moved his shop to Illinois and 18th Street

San Francisco Maritime Museum N.H.P.

The Interior of John Twigg's Boatshop in 1899 . . . This spectacular photo shows us the inside of a working small boat workshop at the turn of the century. Tim Twigg, John Twigg's youngest son stands next to a framed out boat at the left, patterns behind him on the wall, along with a "No Smoking" sign. Obscured by the boy in left of center is father John Twigg. Two more of John's sons are at the right—oldest son Charles faces the camera in white shirt and suspenders, and Jim wears a dark shirt and vest as he rests his arm on the gunwale of a completed boat. DuVal Williams, is between the two Twigg men, in white shirt, suspenders and dark hat.

Nothing was wasted in the Twigg shop. The efficiency of Twigg's shop, along with John F. Twigg's connections forged in the California state legislature, no doubt appealed to Tom Crowley, Sr. Crowley had the Twigg shop build his first gasoline launches—a technology that launched Crowley on the path of a billionaire.

near the Union Iron Works below Potrero Hill where Kneass' Boat Shop also was located. Twigg retired and his son John took over as president of the company. [15]

DuVal Williams, Twigg's apprentice, recalled the lively activity in boatbuilding and Whitehalling along the waterfront in an oral history recorded when he was 80 years old. Born in San Francisco about 1880, he went to work at the Union Iron Works shipyard when he was 18, and then to Twigg's shop.

> I knew they were building small boats over on the beach so I walked over there . . . they were building surf boats to go to Honolulu, wooden boats. George Kneass had his shop there and at this next shop they were building about 10 of these surf boats to unload cargoes at Honolulu . . . When they got through with those 10 boats for Honolulu why they moved kit and caboodle right over to North Beach, right over there by Fisherman's Wharf . . . At that time he had about 10 men working for him and he had lots of work going on over there . . . All they had over there [at the Potrero site] was a steam box. Everything was done by hand, hand-sawed and everything. But when we moved over to the North Beach shop, that was about two blocks off of the water, [there were] no [ships'] ways over there at all. That shop was well-equipped. They had a little boiler and . . . a little steam engine and . . . a circular saw and . . . a planer . . . one big crosscut saw. The shop was built high off the street . . .

> Pretty near all of the boats that the Twiggs built had an oak keel, stem and sternpost in them and their ribs were oak, all steamed and bent . . . well-built, sturdy and strong boats. That was the kind of boat they knew how to build . . .

> I can remember Tommy Crowley coming in there . . . We built some of the first gasoline launches that Tommy Crowley ever had. I worked on Crowley's boats . . . Tommy had come up under his dad as a Whitehall man; that's the way he learned it. And I guess the old man was the top Whitehall man on the Bay. When those fellows were on the beach and they got a signal, they all made a race for that ship. The first

Whitehaller that hit the ship got the captain. Well, that was worth about $75 to bring the captain ashore. Young Tommy was a crackerjack too . . . and if there was any wind they'd go to sail. If there was no wind they'd take to the oars . . .

Another thing, to show how conservative they were, they never wasted any material. If anybody, young fellows especially, had any spare time, any . . . galvanized nails that were bent were picked up and straightened and all used again. So . . . they weren't wasteful . . . Those boat nails were kind of square with a round head and of course they countersunk every hole that they drove them into, and then they punched them in and then before they painted the boat that was all oiled . . . Some of the boats that were made very fancy and particular . . . were copper-riveted. They bored the hole, drove the rivet through, put a burr on the top and it was oiled and . . . clinched so . . . there was no rust.

Another thing about their boats: When planked . . . in between the seams, we caulked them with cotton padding all the way through; you tucked it up with big caulking mallets. Then [they] . . . were smoothed up, sandpapered nice . . . oiled with boiled oil and then . . . painted. They were sturdy boats, you could stand them on end; they were wonderfully built. They were good mechanics; they wouldn't turn out a sloppy job. [16]

John Twigg was the last of the Whitehall boatbuilders, a legend when he died in 1924 at the age of 84. [17]

Shipowners, like boatmen, were partners in the shanghaiing business although some, notably British owners, complained of the crimping system in the United States and particularly in San Francisco, with little success. While some shipowners were sincere in opposing crimping, most realized that they saved money by the system, even when it meant recruiting new crew and paying crimps "blood-money."

Shipping masters, the middle men between boardinghouse keepers and captains, were part of the system. Shipping masters allocated the number of sailors picked for crew from each boardinghouse to minimize complaints and conflict and were paid the two-months' advance for each man plus a bonus. They then distributed the money to boardinghouse keepers and boatmen, who were not known for their wise use of their new-found gains. "When they got $500 or $600 from the master, they would hit the booze," Tom Crowley, Sr., remembered of boardinghouse master Patsy Cosgrove. [18]

The *San Francisco Chronicle* in 1899 noted that three shipping masters controlled most of the placement of deepwater sailors: Tommy Chandler did the bulk of the business, with James Douglass and Fred J. Hunt picking up the rest. British sailors, although they forfeited all wages if they did not complete their voyage back to a British port, were happy to leave their ships for the higher pay of American flag ships (British sailors were paid $15 a month compared to American deepwater sailors' $20 and $40 for coastal cruises), leaving British captains in need of crew. They turned to crimps for help. The *Coast Seamen's Journal* in 1888 reprinted accusations in the British *Chambers' Journal* that British captains demanded and received kickbacks from San Francisco crimps. The practice was deplored in 1874 by the British Consul in San Francisco, William Lane Booker: "We have known cases in which the master of a ship has been paid from $10 to $15 by the crimps for each seaman he has taken off their hands in the slack season—a nice little nest-egg for a badly-paid shipmaster, and poor Jack pays in either case." The *Coast Seamen's Journal* echoed the sentiment. "When there are plenty of men to fill the ships, instead of raising the wages, the boarding masters give half the blood-money back to the British captains. It is they who demand the return—the American captains seldom get anything." The head of the shipping masters association was thought to be worth $100,000. [19]

Sailors on foreign flag ships had to sign on crews before their nation's consul. British sailors generally were recruited from a block across from the Custom House on Battery Street known as "Lime-Juice Corner," named for the lime juice fed British sailors to prevent scurvy, which gave them the irreverent moniker.

Many of the boatmen made names for themselves, the most famous of whom was Thomas "Tommy" Crowley, Sr. His step-father Dave Crowley, Sr., introduced Tommy to the boatman trade at an early age and found Tommy a fast learner. The elder Crowley began in the business in 1873. He lived at the foot of Telegraph Hill at 82 Francisco Street and worked from nearby Meiggs Wharf. He acquired the nickname "Hook-On" Crowley for his adeptness at hooking onto outbound steamers, giving Crowley's small boat a tow against flood tides beyond the Golden Gate where he would have early access to inbound ships.

Dave Crowley, Sr.'s, feats sometimes were exaggerated as in the report of a British captain who claimed to have seen two men in a Whitehall boat 40 miles west of the Farallone Islands, which would place them sixty-four miles outside the Golden Gate. The captain assumed they were blown off course in the gale-force winds and set about rescuing the boatmen. To the captain's surprise, Crowley clamored aboard and made a pitch to the captain to trade with the Golden Shore Meat Market for which Crowley was a runner. When he had finished his task, he slid down his hook into his Whitehall and set off to extol the virtues of the Golden Shore Market to yet another captain. [20]

Although unlikely that Crowley was 64 miles out to sea to solicit business, it was common practice for Whitehall boatmen to row and sail the 24 miles to the Farallones. Besides boarding-house and market runners, they often carried stevedores who offered to load a vessel with supplies once it was in port, as well as ships' chandlers seeking the vessel's business. When business was slow, a Whitehall boatman might stay outside the Gate for two or three days waiting for ships. In 1893, two Whitehall men, Lou "Buster" Hart and John "Jack the Ripper" Barr, were near the

San Francisco Maritime Museum N.H.P

The Desmonds pulled oars for Ah Sing's laundry business, but they carried runners for various shops . . . Butchers, ship chandlers and sailors' boardinghouses sent runners out in Whitehalls to solicit trade. The boatmen charged 50 cents to $1 for the runners and picked up a few dollars more for the half drunk sailors the runners enticed to desert by going ashore with them. Any wages due the sailors were forfeited, but most sailors were ready for some fun after a voyage of four or five months. Fun was not always what they got, though. Usually they stayed at a boardinghouse for two weeks or more, but if demand was brisk, they might be on dry land for only a few hours.

One of the brothers used the thole pin, where the oars rested when rowing, to control the sail when the breeze was up. Afternoons on San Francisco Bay find the wind blowing freely, a hundred years ago and today.

C.C. Stutz ran a butcher shop among the sailors' boardinghouses and was "Jack The Ripper's" boss . . . A member of the Olympic Club, Stutz may have introduced Tom Crowley, Sr., to the Olympic Club. Stutz' runner was Whitehall boatman John "Jack The Ripper" Barr.

The Olympic Club

146

A Whitehall boat "hooked-on"--On a calm day off the bar, a Whitehall boat is "hooked-on" to the bow of the British ship *Marlborough Hill*. A stout line secures a thwart near the stern of the boat to the ship. The boatman used his 10'-12' hook to climb up the side of a ship, while the boatboy tended the Whitehall as master and boatman transact trade. The job of the boatboy was to keep the boat upright and prevent it from being smashed to pieces by swells, storms or the parting of the line. The boatman's trade called for courage and salesmanship.

Farallones one night, snoozing as they waited for a ship to appear while a whale hovered nearby. At daybreak, so the story goes, the whale suddenly took umbrage at the boat's proximity, dove under the Whitehall and capsized it. Hart and "Jack The Ripper" had a cold bath but managed to survive. [21]

Boarding a ship was a feat, dangerous, and required considerable physical strength and timing. The 10-foot-long hook at the end of 30 fathoms of rope was thrown onto the ship; steps on the hook helped a boatman climb aboard. A young boatboy who acted as crew also was assigned the task of holding the Whitehall next to the side of the ship while the boatman transacted business aboard. In rolling seas a boatboy might find himself looking down at the deck of the ship one moment and up at its hull rising like a two-story building the next.

Dave Crowley, Sr., was also a fine sailor and his Whitehall frequently won first prize at Fourth of July regattas. He used his winnings to build a new boat every few years, most of which were named *Stewart Menzies* for the local ex-supervisor, a valued friend of Crowley's and of shipping master Tommy Chandler.

Tommy Crowley started working as a boatboy for his stepfather in 1890 at the age of 15 and within a short time was competing against him (Tommy's father was an Irishman, John Bannon). He bought his own boat for $80 and went into business for himself. For three or four months he stayed on the Farallones, gathering murre eggs and living with the lighthouse crew on the isolated, wind-swept rocks where sealing also was a profitable business. His first job as an independent boatman was for the Franklin Hotel at Pacific near Battery. He began to solicit business as a runner, and at an early age, knew all the crimps who worked the waterfront, recalling their names and activities in an oral history recorded many years later. [22]

"There [were] two Hawkins, Timmie and John. John was more of a sailor boardinghouse runner and Timmie was a boatman . . . The runners all had whiskey, they always carried a

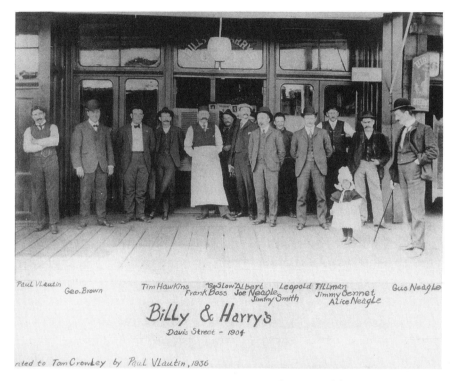

Paul Vlautin Geo. Brown Tim Hawkins "Go-Slow" Albert Leopold Tillman Gus Neagle
Frank Boss Joe Neagle Jimmy Bennet
Jimmy Smith Alice Neagle

Billy & Harry's
Davis Street - 1904

nted to Tom Crowley by Paul Vlautin, 1936

Courtesy of the Bancroft Library

Billy & Harry's, Davis Street Saloon, 1904 . . . Paul Vlautin presented Tom Crowley Sr., with this rare photograph of a group of crimps. Billy & Harry's saloon stood at 631 Davis Street. Paul Vlautin, with arms folded at the extreme left, had his restaurant at 629 Davis. His father ran Paul's Restaurant at 715 Davis as early as 1860—when crews boarded upstairs.

Second from the left is George Brown, son of Henry "Shanghai" Brown. Billy & Harry's place may have been run by George's brother, Henry "Shanghai" Brown Jr. and Billy Jordan, long-time boardinghouse keeper, bare-knuckle boxer and fight referee. Fourth from the left is Tim Hawkins, a "well-known crimp," who left San Francisco as the shanghaiing trade slowed.

To the right, little is known of "Go-slow" Albert, but Joe Neagle was a well-known Whitehall boatman. Whitehall boatman Jimmy Sinnot, fourth from the right, operated one of Tom Crowley's gasoline launches for years.

couple of flasks with them . . . They [would] talk to the sailors in the focsle, give them a couple of drinks and some of them would pack up and go ashore right away." The first thing a runner did on boarding an incoming ship was to cry out, "Are any of Murray's boarders here?" Any sailors who answered were offered the whiskey flask, which went around to the crew with little resistance from captains. By the time Crowley became a Whitehall boatman, crimping had become an accepted institution of more than 40 years.

Runners boarded ships in violation of the prohibition against doing so before a ship docked, a rule aimed at cutting down the large amount of smuggling that went on through the port of San Francisco, as well as attempting to control runners. That was one reason why the boatmen went outside the boundaries of the Golden Gate to meet ships. Popular commodities for smuggling were whiskey, brandy and cordials that British captains, who were less well paid than their American counterparts, smuggled in for extra money. In 1872 Captain Bolt of the British bark *Albert the Good* was arrested for smuggling liquor into the country without paying the required duties. The captain was suspected when federal agents noticed an unusual amount of constant traffic by sailors visiting Maiden Lane—the site of several whorehouses—for more than its female attractions. Upstairs in one establishment the agents found Bolt dispensing brandy from a two-gallon container. A search of his ship turned up several barrels of liquor worth $1,000 to $2,000. [23]

Ships from Asia carried opium, the preferred illegal drug of the 19th century. Whitehall boatman, "were out there [boarding ships] and their business . . . finished long before the customs ever" appeared. Occasionally the boatmen were caught, however. Crowley was once detained on Angel Island for violating a quarantine order imposed by federal agents during a bubonic plague outbreak in San Francisco in 1904. He had gone aboard a ship before it had been released from quarantine. (In previous years, the city had been responsible for managing quarantines on inbound vessels, which had not been handled very effectively). [24]

Crowley thought of sailors as like compliant goats who would do anything they were told to do. Others on the waterfront constantly made fun of them. As one old seaman told Crowley, after being paid off with one dollar after a two-year whaling voyage, "Well, I did not make much but I had a good long ride." [24]

Tommy Crowley said that if a Whitehall boatman ever allowed the escape of a shanghaied sailor from his boat—that would be the end of the boatman's business. Sailors being rowed out to a ship usually knew what was going on; sometimes they would resist. "Then I'd use the footstretcher on 'em. That would quiet 'em down." An oak block three feet wide, the footstretchers were very effective weapons.

Crowley said of boardinghouse masters "They always wanted to be a big fellow, he wanted to be a big fellow, and they'd go up there to the 'Bank Exchange Saloon' [where Joseph Hayes had met his fate], which was located at the corner of Montgomery and Washington. There, they would drink a lot of booze . . . Some of them got into bad repute because they didn't have money to pay their bills. Running a boardinghouse you got to pay for grub, and one thing and another. They hit upon a pretty good plan. Years ago, there was quite a few butcher shops like the 'Golden Gate Market' on Davis Street. The liver . . . of the animals was thrown away, dumped overboard. They discovered that liver was a pretty good thing, so they went down and they packed the liver home, and the sailors living there, ate liver for breakfast . . . lunch and . . . dinner. After two or three days of that they'd go mad. 'For Christ sakes, get me a ship; I'll take anything as long as I get away from liver!'" [25]

Once a ship's business was obtained, Whitehalls carried supplies brought to the wharves in wagons from four to 10 o'clock in the morning. After Crowley began operating gasoline

A whale hunt (top) . . . "Anything might happen in the next few moments. The whale might run—he might turn back and attack the boat with open jaws or 'sound' (dive)."

Rendering whale oil (bottom) . . . "Dense black smoke by day, and illuminated sails and rigging at night, disclosed the proximity of a whaler. Day and night the try works were kept going until all the blubber had been rendered. The furnace consisted of two large iron kettles, beneath each was a separate fire grate, and under all a shallow pan of water as a safeguard." *Gordon Grant quotations and drawings from Greasy Luck, 1932*

A "Nantucket sleigh ride." The boat followed the whale at a speed of fifteen or more knots per hour. As the whale tired, the line grew shorter, and the boat drew closer to the whale's flank. The mate stood ready to exercise his privilege of delivering the final thrust. A Nantucket sleigh ride often took the boat miles beyond the horizon.

launches, he got the job of taking the morning newspapers across the Bay. In the past they had been rowed to Oakland each morning in a Whitehall boat by Billy Pinckney who operated a stand next to the Young America Saloon, at the corner of Howard and Steuart streets.

Crowley's stepbrothers, Dave and John, began working for him soon after he went on his own along with a German named "Dutch" Albert. Tommy solicited business and the stepbrothers worked at the waterfront supplying ships or ferrying passengers. They frequently slept at the boathouse where, in Albert's case, he lived at the Vallejo Street Wharf; Crowley also had a boathouse at Meiggs Wharf.

A ship signaled a request for boatmen by running up a red flag which set off a mad rush of boatmen with runners swarming toward the ship. They learned about incoming vessels at the Marine Exchange where word was flashed that a ship was entering the harbor. Early arrivals to the Whitehalls sometimes tossed their competitors' oars in the water to slow them down. Boatmen did not carry water or food with them, getting it from a pilot boat, tug or incoming ship if they needed supplies. Crowley was afraid the other fellows would call him "a softie" if he took a sandwich with him when he was outbound. [26]

Crowley displayed a savvy business acumen early in his career. Former state Assemblyman Bill Gately was a rival whose trade Crowley wanted. According to one of Crowley's long-time employees, William McGillivray, Gately also enjoyed the pleasures of the Barbary Coast. "Bill Gately . . . had a launch about three docks down, and he was running opposition, and probably going out bringing captains in from the ship. One day [Crowley] said to Bill, 'Why don't you bring your boat down to my float where it's more convenient and run from there?' He was a competitor. So Bill says, 'You don't mind, Tom?' He says, 'No.' Well, the next thing you know Bill was tying his boat up with the Crowley boats and going and getting captains and pocketing the money, and sleeping in Crowley's boathouse. He had a bunk up there. He used to drink an awful lot, you know. But he was a very nice fellow. I was . . . sleeping one time upstairs in the boathouse, and Bill come down after he'd been drinking for quite awhile, and all of a sudden—I don't know—he got out of bed and run out and he disappeared. There used to be a place called 'Spaza's' steak joint about three blocks up there on Drumm Street. He ran out. So I said to him later on, 'Bill, what happened to you?' 'Well,' he said, 'Mac, I was drinking for about a week there, and you know when I went to bed, I looked at the window and there was a cow looking in the window. He had a glass head on him and he had electric lights in his eyes. And he was looking at me, you know? I got kinda scared . . . Then you know the clock that I have along side of me? That was a little girl singing. I could hear this little girl singing. That ticking was a song . . . That was all right, but I got scared and I pulled the covers over my head and a cannon went off in the room, and I jumped up, and that's when I ran out, and I went over to 'Spaza's' steak joint, and I sat there all night, just drinking coffee until daylight in the morning. I was afraid to go back to bed again.'" [27]

Billy Clark, whose boathouse was next to Crowley's at Vallejo Street Wharf, was another competitor. One day Crowley and Clark, also known as "Suck Eggs," reached an incoming ship at the same time. As Clark climbed up the rope ladder, Crowley scampered over his back and headed for one end of the ship, Clark for the other. Crowley found the captain first and won all the ship's business that day.

Henry Peterson was another neighbor whose business Crowley eventually took over. McGillivray thought it was because he was too "easy going" and hampered by the fact that he, too, "was quite a drinker." Crowley persuaded the harbor commissioners to let him put a fence between his boathouse and Peterson's to prevent people from entering Crowley's and going

Courtesy Dolphin Club

Professional Oarsman Henry Peterson was a long-time Whitehall boatman and started a fleet of gasoline launches about the time Tom Crowley, Sr., built up his fleet . . . The two competitors were located next to each other and worked very hard to get business from the other. Peterson became so exasperated after Crowley had the State Harbor Commissioners put a fence up between their two boathouses that he finally said to Crowley, "'Tom, you're nothing but a rat!' Crowley shot back, 'You're such a big rat, they can put a saddle on you.'"

through to his competitor. Peterson fought the fence but it stayed, and after a year, he took off part of the end, allowing passage between the two boathouses. "Tom, you're nothing but a rat!" Peterson finally told Crowley, who shot back, "You're such a big rat, they can put a saddle on you.'"[28]

Crowley, a short but well-proportioned man, was one of the few, if not the only, Whitehall boatmen to join two exclusive clubs, the Commercial and Olympic clubs, whose members included the city's elite businessmen and leaders. "He didn't have much schooling but he could talk to anybody, talk business to them, and he'd tell them just what he thought, used perfect language," said McGillivray.

Crowley did not join the Olympic Club to row but to box and was known not to duck a fight. On one occasion, "He had a big load of silver in his pocket, it weighed his pants down. He collected from sailors coming off the battleships on his boats. And [one] fellow was a four-round prize fighter, and he had something against [Crowley] and Tom bawled him out, and . . . started fighting with him. Tom was trying to fight with one hand and hold his suspenders up with the other. He was afraid he'd lose the money—he thought more of the money. And he'd fight with this hand and then that hand. That was down there on Vallejo Street Wharf. And the fellow licked him . . . That'll show you what kind of fighter he was. He come in and he was wiping the blood off his face, and he got all the money out of his pocket and he said, 'Mac, put it in the safe. I'll get that fellow some other time.' One time the fellow did come back around the front there . . . He lived over in North Beach. Tom saw him and he went out after him. And he beat the hell out of him—he didn't have any money in his pocket then. He took off his coat and his hat and he went after the feller. And he just plowed him and knocked him down . . . knocked him down three or four more times, and the fellow never came back anymore."[29]

Crowley was fond of telling stories, and one that was often repeated on the waterfront concerned salmon bellies that ships carried in big barrels to feed the crew. A fellow named Charlie Barlow had gotten a barrel from a ship and brought it to Meiggs Wharf one night. Many Chinese worked as packing hands or fishing on ships operated by Alaska Packers. They preferred to be buried in native soil, so if one died on board, the usual way to "store" the body until the ship returned to port was to pickle it in a barrel. Barlow's hair stood on end when, expecting to find salmon bellies in his barrel, he opened it to see a pickled Chinaman. [30]

A newspaper article from October 22, 1892, observed that the practice of shipping deceased Chinese back to their homeland from San Francisco was an old practice even then.

Crowley had memories of seeing large vessels line the harbor as far around as Mission Bay, at Sausalito, initially an Italian fishing village and Oakland. Deepwater ships tied up at the wharves near the Barbary Coast. Steuart Street was the favorite location of boardinghouses for coastal sailors because the wharves nearby catered to vessels in the coastal trade. Coal schooners from British Columbia and the Black Diamond Mines in Contra Costa County berthed at Folsom Street Wharf. Brick, hay, lumber and cord wood was unloaded off scow or lumber schooners in Mission Creek channel between Third and Fourth streets.

Crowley grew with the times and built his business from a few Whitehalls and motorized launches to a large fleet that included barges, tugs and sightseeing boats that continued to operate more than 100 years after he first took to the sea. He survived not only tough competition and difficult economic times but the dangers of working in the Bay and ocean beyond.

Peter Burns, an Irishman of "unlimited . . . beam and muscular development," began pulling a Whitehall boat the same

San Francisco Maritime Museum N.H.P.

The Desmond brothers row their Whitehall boat northwest from Vallejo Street Wharf . . . The strong flood tide as one approached Meiggs Wharf made it essential to have two men rowing a Whitehall, if they could not sail. Two strong oarsmen could take such a boat to the Golden Gate to meet an incoming ship in about an hour from Vallejo Street Wharf. Many boatmen used Meiggs Wharf as their base, about fifteen to twenty minutes closer. Alcatraz Island is just visible over the nearer man's oar to the right.

Fred Plaisted faced world's champion Ned Hanlon in Toronto, Canada, in May 1878 . . . After defeating Hanlon at Boston's Fourth of July regatta in 1877, a match race was negotiated between Plaisted (top left) and Hanlon (top right). Stephen Roberts (bottom), champion oarsman of the 1830s and New York alderman, acted as referee. Hanlon won easily.

Originally from Maine, Plaisted worked as a Whitehall boatman in San Francisco from 1867 through 1874. He helped captains procure crews for their ships, which meant he helped shanghai men. *Author's Collection*

NEW YORK, SATURDAY, MAY 18, 1878.

year as Dave Crowley, Sr. "I went out to the Heads in a 19-foot Whitehall boat to throw a hook on a clipper ship in 1873. We were in the business of meeting barks out on the bar to get orders for food supplies, for I represented butchers in those days. It was a long pull out there. Two men were in each Whitehall, and when one hooked onto a brig his partner had to be at the oars to keep the boat in line at the stern of the ship . . . English vessels were the best markets for the butchers' runners for they always came in from the long trips short of food. American barks were usually well-stocked, but fresh meats were always wanted . . . Dave Crowley, Sr., was representing Wilson's market with me, and the other big market was the Golden Gate on Davis and Clark streets." Burns and another oarsman, Charles Olsen, "a Norwegian of Herculean frame," as a newspaper described him, competed against one another in a memorable race from the foot of Market Street around Goat [Yerba Buena] Island and back in 1882. [31]

Another well-known boatmen who gained fame as a racing competitor was Frederick A. Plaisted from Maine. His father and grandfather purportedly were sea captains. Plaisted followed them to sea at the age of 14 on the schooner *Ellen M. Doughty*. He made his way to San Francisco where he took up the trade of a Whitehall boatman, carrying captains to shore when they "wished to recruit a new crew or cargo for the Orient," as he later described it. He also was a powerful rower, winning his first Whitehall race on the Bay in 1867. The prize was $500 in gold. That convinced the 18-year-old, a tall man for the time at five feet, ten-and-a-half inches and weighing 160 pounds, that rowing would be his life's work. [32]

He learned about a man in Shanghai who had issued a challenge to anyone in the world to row a race for $10,000. Plaisted worked passage to Shanghai by stoking boilers of the Pacific Mail Steamship's *Yokohama* for the 28-day journey. It is a little unclear why Fred Plaisted would work his way to Shanghai after winning what must have been a princely sum of $500 in 1867. Could he himself have been shanghaied? Possibly. It was only after winning the race in China that he discovered the purse would be paid in Chinese dollars, worth a fraction of the amount in U.S. dollars. Plaisted kept on competing, however, in the eastern United States and even as far away as Sydney, Australia. He must have lost that race because he later admitted that he remembered only victories.

More rowing races were conducted on the East Coast and for larger purses than in San Francisco. Fifty-thousand people watched the Boston Regatta on July 4, 1877, in which a black oarsman and former inmate of Sing Sing prison, "Frenchy" Johnson, was the crowd favorite in the professional sculling race. Plaisted, however, shot to the front at the start. Johnson and world champion Ned Hanlon closed on him toward the final lap but Plaisted crossed the finish line in 14:24 minutes over the two-mile course, the fastest time on record.

In 1883, Fred and Wallace Ross, a Canadian oarsman, opened a saloon in Pittsburgh, Pennsylvania. Fred liked the work and, when queried on his plans for the coming year, said he was not sure he would join the boys that year, as there was more money to be made in selling mint juleps than selling races.

John L. Sullivan, the famed pugilist, was one of Fred's visitors at his Pittsburgh saloon in 1883. The pair of professional athletes were under the sponsorship of Jim Keenan. Plaisted was pressed into service on occasion when John L. needed to keep his skills sharp. Fred boxed as Sullivan's sparring partner. "'I was crazy to spar with John L., but he couldn't find anybody else and he had to have someone,'" Fred reasoned. For the rest of his life Plaisted carried scars over his ears and on his forehead as testimony to Sullivan's fistic prowess. [33]

Fred continued rowing and repairing boats in Philadelphia until shortly before his death. Fred passed away in 1946 at the age of 96.

Accounts vary as to the number of boatmen who plied the trade. Crowley's rival, Henry Peterson, believed there were 60 during their hey day, while another boatman, Ed McCarthy, estimated between 80 and 100. Whatever the number, the boatman's profession died about 1904-1905, a casualty of the gasoline-powered launch. As McCarthy put it, "Joe Kane built a gasoline launch called the *Brisk*, and Tom Crowley built one that he named the *Jenny C.*, after his sister. Then Crowley built a whole fleet of them, and Henry Peterson built a fleet, and the boatmen were through." [34]

Footnotes

1 Asbury, pp. 213, 217

2 Dillon, pp.191 and 210 and Camp, p. 212

3 Edward Connors, ms., J. Porter Shaw Library

4 *South of Market Journal*, "Memories," John Roberts, March 1927, p.15

5 Thomas Crowley, ms., J. Porter Shaw Library

6 *San Francisco Examiner*, August 31, 1892, p.4, col.4

7 *San Francisco Chronicle*, September 26, 1878, p.3, col. 8; *Daily Alta*, February 7, 1872, p.1, col.2; April 9, 1872, p.1, col.2 and June 24, 1869, p.1, col.1

8 *Daily Alta*, August 21, 1882, p.1, col.4 and *San Francisco Examiner*, October 8, 1893, p.20, col.3

9 *Recollections of the San Francisco Waterfront*, interview of Thomas Crowley, Sr. by Willa Baum and Karl Kortum, 1967, p. 4

10 *Daily Alta*, October 4, 1878, p.1, col.7; September 17, 1878, p.2, col.1; September 20, 1878, p.1, col.4; September 18, 1878, p.1, col.4; September 20, 1878, p.1, col.4; September 22, 1878, p.1, col.5; September 23, 1878, p.2, col.2; September 25, 1878, p.2, col.3; July 1, 1882, p.1, col.2; July 5, 1882, p.1, col.2 and July 5, 1883, p.1, col.2

11 Thomas Crowley, Sr. Scrapbook and *San Francisco Call*, July 4, 1898

12 Census data for San Francisco, 1880. John D. Griffin started building boats in San Francisco by 1865. He also built up a political following by participating in rowing races and sponsoring informal noontime boxing matches at his boatbuilding establishment at 218 Steuart Street. Those with a grudge were encouraged to enter Griffin's ring and settle their differences there. One day the caulkers and longshoremen in the crowd witnessed a rare treat—a boxing match between two one-armed sluggers. John D. Griffin offered to back the winner against any one-armed boxer in the world.

13 *San Francisco Chronicle*, February 21, 1882, p.3, col. 4

14 *Recollections of The San Francisco Waterfront*, Willa Klug Baum and Karl Kortum, 1967, pp.252-3; "San Francisco's Oldest Rowing Clubs," John Bielinski, *Wooden Boat*, May/June 1981, p.47

15 *Recollections of the San Francisco Waterfront*, Willa Klug Baum and Karl Kortum, 1967

16 Transcript of an oral history with DuVal Williams, pp. 14-25

17 *San Francisco Chronicle*, September 23, 1924, p.6, col.8

18 *Recollections of the San Francisco Waterfront*

19 *San Francisco Chronicle*, June 18, 1899, p.2, col.1 and *Coast Seamen's Journal*, Vol.1, no. 50, p.1, October 10, 1888. When a glut of sailors existed in late 1883, boardinghouse keepers were forced to pay a $10 fee to captains for each man the captain took off the boardinghouse masters' hands. The Sailor's Home at this time reduced wages for deepwater sailors to $20 per month, and pushed the monthly rate for coastal sailors from $40 to $30.

20 *San Francisco Examiner*, October 8, 1893, p.20, col.3

21 Ibid

22 *Recollections of the San Francisco Waterfront*, interview of Thomas Crowley, Sr., by Willa Baum and Karl Kortum, 1967, p.1; p.4; p.14. Also see Thomas Crowley ms., J. Porter Shaw Library, p.2. Tom Crowley, Sr., was very proud of his rise from boatman to billionaire. As early as 1933, Asbury acknowledged Crowley's contribution for material incorporated in *The Barbary Coast*. Thirty-four years later, Baum and Kortum put together an oral history of Crowley that runs, including photographs, over three-hundred pages.

23 *Daily Alta*, February 21, 1872, p.1, col.8

24 *Recollections of the San Francisco Waterfront*, p.61

25 Thomas Crowley ms., J. Porter Shaw Library, p.7

26 *Recollections of the San Francisco Waterfront*, p.29

27 *Tugboats and Boatmen of California: 1906-70*, interview of William J. McGillivray by Ruth Teiser, 1971, p.74-5

28 Ibid, p.80, 49

29 Ibid, p.95, 96

30 Ibid, p.97

31 *San Francisco Newsletter*, February 25, 1882, p.7; *San Francisco Subway*, 1924

32 Maine census, Cumberland County, 1850; *Portland (Me.) Press Herald*, May 2, 1946; *Philadelphia Evening Bulletin*, November 3, 1938

33 *Portland (Me.) Press Herald*, May 2, 1946; *Philadelphia Evening Bulletin*, December 27, 1927; *New York Times*, July 5, 1877, p.3, col.5; *New York Clipper*, October 27, 1883, p.523; *Philadelphia Record*, November 2, 1940 and *Philadelphia Evening Bulletin*, November 3, 1941

34 "Riptides," *San Francisco Chronicle*, Robert O'Brien, November 15, 1950, p.16, col.4

A GROUP OF WHALE HUNTERS ON HOWARD-STREET WHARF.
[Sketch d by an "Examiner" artist.]

Sutro Library

Whale Hunters on Howard Street Wharf in 1893 . . . An artist for the *San Francisco Examiner* drew his impression of whalers back from the hunt. Saloons and a whaling bark figure as a backdrop for these colorful men who had braved the bitter cold of the Arctic and the danger of enraged whales. One of the crew of the whaler *Cape Horn Pigeon* bore a fresh scar (so he said) where the fluke of a bowhead whale grazed his cheek.

The oil and bone were the only part taken from a whale. "The hide is peeled away from him as readily as the skin from an orange." The price of whalebone was $5-$6 per pound in 1893; the average whale yielded 1,800 pounds of bone and 80-100 barrels of oil. The poorer quality bone found its way into women's corsets and dress stays. The finest whalebone became fiber as delicate as silk. In the 1890s, many silk dresses consisted mainly of whalebone fiber, as the bone gave strength and elasticity lacking in pure silk.

The 1893 article quoted Captain Wells, a whaler for many years, as saying, "It won't be long before the whale, like the buffalo, will be a thing of the past. In fact, we have killed about all the largest ones now." But it would be many years before international agreements halted commercial whaling.

Courtesy Bancroft Library

Funeral of Police Captain C. W. Dakin and T. J. Hennessy Leaves The Hall of Records, Feb. 4, 1906 . . . San Francisco's Hall of Records rotunda saw the gathering of mourners for the long march down Market Street.

It took twenty years to build City Hall: after April 18th, in just days fires destroyed most of the city records. As the ruins were cleared away, what had appeared to be stone columns, were cement stuffed with rolls of newsprint. Politically awarded contracts were a big part of the city's political system.

Corruption existed before and after "Blind Boss" Chris Buckley ran San Francisco in the 1880s. Martin Kelly, the Republican counterpart to Buckley in the 1890s, gave his opinion that Buckley "developed a knack for colonizing the boardinghouses and turning tricks in the rough work of the primaries." This power base among the sailors' boardinghouses of San Francisco's First Ward gave the shanghaiing community influence over the affairs of the city. The crimps did not just have power with the city's politicians—in many cases, they were the city's politicians.

Politics Among The Shanghaiers

We can do business without [Isaac] Friedlander, or
anybody else.

Thomas Chandler, quoted at a Democratic convention.

A seemingly minor case of municipal corruption in San
Francisco in 1874 sheds light on how politicians could benefit
from the resources of the shanghaiing system. Three employees
of the County Clerk's Office, Joe Casey and two others, were
accused of forging poll-tax receipts and embezzling the proceeds.
Joe Casey's brother, Henry Casey, was implicated in the scheme
a few days later. Henry Casey had some prominence in state
politics, holding the office of secretary of the state Democratic
Party.

Henry Casey and his friends heard of the warrant issued for
his arrest while Casey was in Sacramento, and his friends hatched
an escape plan. Joseph "Frenchy" Franklin, Republican County
Committeeman for San Francisco and well-known crimp, approached the crewmen of the sloop *Mary E. Donovan* (so their
story went) with a request to go on a fishing trip to Half Moon
Bay. The sloop hired, it proceeded up to Benicia to pick up another party who turned out to be Henry Casey. They fished off
the Marin Headlands for one-and-a-half hours, then Franklin

wanted to try the fishing at Half Moon Bay. Once at Half Moon Bay, Franklin and Casey fished for a short time then went on shore even as one of Casey's friends made his way from San Francisco to Half Moon Bay with a horse and buggy. The buggy arrived, and Henry Casey made his escape. [1]

Eleven other vessels departed San Francisco the same day the *Mary E. Donovan* left with its fugitive cargo. Those most in the know believed Henry Casey made his escape to another country on one of the foreign ships in the fleet after leaving the Bay in the *Mary E. Donovan*. The story told by the crew was fabricated to protect themselves from prosecution for aiding a fugitive. The fact the *Daily Alta* did not report was that the sloop *Mary E. Donovan* was owned by crimp James Laflin.

The marriage of James Laflin's twenty year old daughter Ann to John G. Paton was the social event of the crimping community in late May, 1886. The marriage took place at St. Dominic's Church, with a reception at Laflin's home at 2924 Washington Street. "Dancing was indulged in to a late hour. The presents were numerous. The house was profusely decorated with rare flowers." Former Board of Supervisors' member John T. Sullivan attended the reception with his wife. Tommy Chandler's residence at 1115 Montgomery was next door to the residence of John T. Sullivan, member of the Board of Supervisors, shoe factory and shoe-store owner, oarsman with the Pioneer Rowing Club and, according to the *San Francisco Newsletter*, a friend of the boatmen and boardinghouse masters who made their living shanghaiing sailors. (Hibernia Bank founder and Police Commissioner Robert J. Tobin also was a Pioneer Rowing Club member. Tobin owned North Beach property allegedly used as houses of prostitution). A politician living next to a long-time crimp does not prove corruption. Attending the wedding and reception of the daughter of a man who had actively shanghaied crews for over thirty years is quite another thing. John T. Sullivan was under the influence of the crimping community without a doubt. A Mrs.

Cannavan also attended. The Cannavans were important political figures in San Francisco. [3]

In the early 1870s, the officers and members of the Seamen's Boarding House Masters' Association were a powerful group politically: president Tommy Chandler was a Democratic County Committeeman from the First Ward; "Frenchy" Franklin and Edwin C. Lewis held both Republican County Committeeman positions from the First Ward (and both were future state assemblymen); Dick Chute was secretary of the state Republican Party, while Edward Warren Casey was former secretary of the state Democratic Party. Edwin C. Lewis, an Englishman 38-years-old in 1873, was vice president and secretary of the association. Tommy Chandler served as president for more than 10 years (1872 to 1883), while Richard Chute, a boss in the Republican Party, was general manager in the 1870s. [4]

Tommy Chandler was a crimp who protected his professional interests from inside the political ring. Chandler was actively involved in Democratic Party politics by 1870. He nominated Hugh J. O'Reilly, for First Ward supervisor in that year. Ironically, he lost to Stewart Menzies whom Chandler would appoint as a delegate to the state convention the following year. Menzies ran a longshoremen's business specializing in British shipping, and enjoyed a clean reputation as a member of the Board of Supervisors but his close association with the known crimp Chandler suggests that Menzies was subject to influence by boardinghouse keepers in his ward, the First. The First Ward included the Barbary Coast, Meiggs and Vallejo Street wharves on the waterfront where Chandler and his colleagues did their business. Chandler's office was at 518 Battery Street, next to the offices of Stewart Menzies. According to Tommy Crowley, Sr., if a captain needed a sailor, his man could always find Tommy Chandler at Stewart Menzies.'

Chandler served as sergeant-at-arms at the Democratic Convention in Sacramento in 1871, where he was responsible for maintaining order among delegates and collecting money to pay convention expenses. Locally, the Democrats were sharply divided that year and Chandler stayed in the old-line Jack Mannix-Owen Brady camp. [5]

He was a power in the party, facing down challenges to the Democratic County Committee from people such as grain and shipping tycoon Isaac Friedlander when they did not agree with Chandler's and his cohorts' positions. "We can do business without Friedlander, or anybody else," Chandler was quoted as saying. He also had been elected foreman of Fire Hose Company Number 1 by the Board of Fire Commissioners in 1870. Chandler was paid $45 per month for the honor, a good monthly wage for a working man in 1870, but just a little gravy for Tommy. The Fire Department had become a hotbed of political activity in the 1870s under Sam Rainey. Rainey was one of the Democratic political bosses to run the city in the 1870s, along with Captain Al Fritz, who came by his title from the Gatling Gun Battery he commanded, and Matt Fallon, a San Francisco politician in the local Democratic Party since the 1850s. Fritz, Rainey and Chandler were hard-fisted men of action who got things done in San Francisco as the city underwent wrenching changes in the 1870s. Fritz and Fallon also trained as their apprentice the aspiring politician Chris Buckley. It was a free-wheeling time for party politics in San Francisco. The *Daily Alta* called the 1872 Democratic primary a "farce . . . any and everybody could vote, whether entitled or not . . . Whiskey and money were freely dispensed by the friends of the various candidates," and 17 arrests for violence were made. [6]

After his accident with a derringer, Chandler briefly receded from the public eye. In June, 1873, he ran unsuccessfully for the Democratic County Committee, but bounced back to his old position on the Democratic County Committee in 1875, aligning

Chris Buckley in Fire Department uniform . . . Buckley rose from humble beginnings to run San Francisco Democratic politics for a decade. While working for Tom Maguire selling Pisco Punch at The Snug Saloon (the predecessor of the Bank Exchange Saloon), Buckley apprenticed under Republican boss Bill Higgins. Under the patronage of Al Fritz, Buckley climbed the Democratic ranks in the 1870s. With Al Fritz' death under mysterious circumstances, Buckley stepped into the void to run the San Francisco Democratic Party. *Photo Courtesy Wm. Bullough*

Looking natty for the camera, Alex Greggains was a popular figure in San Francisco for decades . . . Greggains was a professional boxer whom the "Blind Boss" hired as his bodyguard. Buckley's biographer, William Bullough, credits Greggains with keeping the Boss to a strict regime which maintained Buckley in good physical condition. When Chris Buckley died in 1922, Greggains was at his bedside.

Alex ran a boxing club in San Francisco for many years. He was popular enough South of Market that the *South of Market Journal* mentioned Greggains among its reminiscences several times. *Photo San Francisco Public Library* himself closely with Chris Buckley. In 1877 and 1879 he served on the Democratic County Committee, this time in the A.J. Fritz/Chris Buckley camp. In 1893 Chandler's long service to the party was paid off with an appointment as deputy collector for the Internal Revenue Service, considered a political plum doled out by the County Committee. He was chosen over 2,200 other applicants and held the position until September 1899. Chandler's son Thomas W., carried on his father's waterfront tradition as a shipping master. Thirty-three years old in 1896, the younger Chandler ran for the state senate in that year as a Republican. He was described as, "Large of physique and generous of heart, he is popular along the waterfront, where he is known and respected. Having been engaged as a shipping master for a number of years he stands well with the commercial community." [7]

After his stint as Chris Buckley's dogcatcher, Joseph "Frenchy" Franklin rose to higher office: He was elected Assemblyman as a Republican from the 26th district in 1884. Franklin served on that party's county committee in the 1870s and '80s and in 1876 was a delegate to the state convention along with fellow Republican boardinghouse owners Edwin Lewis and "Shanghai" Brown. Franklin and Edwin Lewis had the most power of any of the Republican crimps within the First Ward: three months after the series of conventions and primaries began in July, 1882, Franklin was named the only member of the Republican County Committee from the First Ward; Edwin C. Lewis was a delegate to the state Republican convention. The crimps by the mid-1880s had built strong bases in both political parties and held positions of influence in the city's hierarchy as well as the state legislature, thus were able to protect their business interests.

Democratic political bosses, Chris Buckley and Al Fritz, their rivals, Owen Brady and Jack Mannix, and Republican William T. Higgins courted and patronized crimps for one reason—the boardinghouses were ready sources of help at election time. It was there that politicians recruited men to vote regularly and often—for the same candidate. They were known as "repeaters" and were crucial to winning elections. [8]

Franklin served only one term in the Assembly as a Republican but ran again in 1890, this time as a Democrat. He was beaten in a Republican sweep that year by a fellow boardinghouse keeper, George Lewis.

The old boardinghouse keepers/politician alliance showed serious signs of deterioration by 1890, though. The rise of the economic power of South of Market sailors' boardinghouses and the challenge of the Coast Seamen's Union impacted the old deep-water sailors' boardinghouses at the North End, as they were called. Political alignments changed as well in the early 1890s. The death of William T. Higgins in 1889 and the rise of Martin Kelly and Phil Crimmins saw old lions of the crimping trade like "Frenchy" Franklin and Edwin Lewis abandon the Republican Party for the more congenial Democratic Party. Kelly and Crimmins drew their boardinghouse "repeater" support from the Third Street corridor. They did not need the North End boardinghouse association. [9]

On the Democratic side, Chris Buckley had fled the country and Sam Rainey kept a low profile as reform threatened to take hold after a series of grand jury investigations into graft. Dick Chute became caught up in the net of the graft prosecutors; but Chute had left San Francisco to collect fees as a lobbyist in Sacramento. In the absence of Buckley, Max Popper ran one faction of the San Francisco Democratic machine in the early 1890s. The sailors' boardinghouse keepers fell into his faction.

Popper took the reins of the State Democratic Party as its chairman in 1892. The appointment of "Frenchy" Franklin and John T. Sullivan to the State Democratic Committee helped the crimps hold on to some power. Popper was not about to turn the reins of power back to Buckley, Rainey or anyone else without a fight. [10]

Author's Collection

**Martin Kelly inherited the Republican mantel after the death of
William T. Higgins . . .** Higgins' power base was rooted, in part, among
the sailors' boardinghouses along Davis, Vallejo and Battery streets. With
the death of Higgins and political decline of Buckley on the Democratic
side, Martin Kelly's "repeaters" from the Third Street boardinghouses
brought a shift in political power to the South of Market area. Kelly teamed
up with Phil Crimmins to run San Francisco for the Republican Party in the
early 1890s—just as corruptly as Buckley had before them.

Sam Rainey poses for a studio camera . . . Rainey became active in the San Francisco Fire Department and turned his department into his political power base for over twenty years. Volunteer fire departments were usually very active politically in 19th century American cities. Rainey worked under Chris Buckley when Buckley took over leadership of the Democratic Party after Captain Al Fritz' death. The rising tide of reform caused the "Blind Boss" flee the country, while Rainey, despite his girth, made himself scarce. Sam Rainey was always a sub-boss, never the boss. *Photo San Francisco Public Library*

Thomas W. Chandler followed his famous father's footsteps into crimping and politics . . . Young Thomas was a shipping master and participated in the Republican Party. He made an unsuccessful bid for a state senatorial seat in 1896—he did not achieve the fame of his popular father. *Photo San Francisco Public Library*

Other crimps who rose to political power were William H. Gately and Al P. Mordaunt, both active in Buckley's Democratic machine, which was built on a system of clubs in each electoral district. In 1888 Gately was secretary of the 44th Assembly District Club and Mordaunt active in the 31st district. Gately, a Whitehall boatman and John Gately's brother, won a Democratic primary race over fellow crimps Chandler and Franklin in 1892, and went on to win an assembly seat. The North End sailors' boardinghouses lie in the 45th Assembly District, an area bounded by Kearny Street on the west, Market Street to the south and San Francisco Bay to the east and north. To run for this assembly seat, Popper supported William H. Gately, a Whitehall boatman and opponent of Sam Rainey's control of San Francisco's fire department. John Gately, Bill's brother, did not hesitate in criticizing Rainey in the newspapers. Bill Gately won the assembly seat by a two-to-one margin, but his victory had a price. [11]

Shortly after the victory over his Republican opponent, Gately was attacked, which dramatized the peril of antagonizing the fire department in 19th century San Francisco. Gately walked down Pacific near Kearny Street at 5:30 a.m. on November 11, 1892, when four or five toughs from the fire department accosted him. Bill and John Gately had refused to support the Rainey-Kelly-Crimmins alliance when demanded to by their fire department superior (the San Francisco fire department still had elements of a volunteer organization in 1892), and threw their badges at the feet of District Engineer O'Shaughnessey, their departmental boss. The fire department toughs did not want a completely paid department (it would curtail their opportunities for graft) and wanted to know why Bill Gately would vote for a paid department. Gately replied that he thought the idea of paid firemen a good one and, secondly, the fire department politicians had worked against him. "The department worked against me, and I'll take a scalp in return, if I can," Gately had told his attackers, provoking them to beat him with brass knuckles, a blackjack and butt of a pistol. He managed to survive the brutal attack. [12]

Footnotes

1 *Daily Alta*, October 4, 1874, p.1, col.3; October 9, 1874, p.1, col.4 and p.2, col.3 and October 10, 1874, p.1, col.3

2 *San Francisco City Directory, 1876*, B.C. Vandall, p.23

3 *Daily Alta*, September 18, 1886, p.8, col.1. Laflin's friend John T. Sullivan, the politician and shoe store owner, invested in whaling. In 1884 Sullivan held the principal block of stock controlling the Arctic Whaling and Trading Company. The connection with Laflin would have helped Sullivan in the whaling industry, but the shoe business suffered three years later and Sullivan had to declare bankruptcy. He assigned his assets to his fellow oarsman, John D. Griffin. See *Daily Alta*, October 25, 1884, p.1, col.1 and July 8, 1887, p.8, col.3

4 Camp, pp. 206-7

5 Ibid, July 14, 1871, p.1, col.2; July 29, 1871, p.1, col.2; August 18, 1871, p.1, col.1; August 19, 1871, p.1, col.1 and September 1, 1871, p.1, col.2

6 *Daily Alta*, August 16, 1870, p.1, col.1; June 27, 1871, p.1, col.2; April 9, 1872, p.1, col.4; May 3, 1871, p.1, col.2; July 14, 1871, p.1, col.2; July 29, 1871, p.1, col.2; August 18, 1871, p.1, col.1; August 19, 1871, p.1, col.1; September 1, 1871, p.1, col.2; July 16, 1872, p.1, col.3; May 27, 1871, p.1, col. 4. William A. Bullough, *The Blind Boss and His City: Christopher Augustine Buckley & Nineteenth Century San Francisco* (Berkeley and Los Angeles, Ca. : University of California Press, 1979), p.65. The night that Democratic boss Captain Al Fritz committed "suicide," Sam Shear, Fritz' business partner in Recreation Grounds and other ventures, tried to make off with the receipts of an athletic competition Harry Maynard and Shear were sponsoring. Fritz' death left the way clear for "Blind Boss" Chris Buckley to take over leadership of the city's Democratic Party. Shear was later appointed by the "Blind Boss" as head of the House of Corrections in 1883. See *San Francisco Chronicle*, May 28, 1881, p.3, col.5

7 *Daily Alta*, July 10, 1875, p.1, col.1; July 15, 1875, p.1, col.4; July 22, 1875, p.1, col.5; July 28, 1875, p.1, col.4; August 2, 1875, p.1, col.2; August 3, 1875, p.1, col.5;October 9, 1877, p.1, col.1; August 12, 1879, p.1, col.4; and August 14, 1879, p.1, col.3; *Daily Alta*, December 2, 1871, p.1, col.2; June 8, 1872, p.1, col.2; June 3, 1873, p.1, col.1; July 10, 1875, p.1, col.1; July 15, 1875, p.1, col.4; July 22, 1875, p.1, col.5; July 28, 1875, p.1, col.4; August 2, 1875, p.1, col.2; August 3, 1875, p.1, col.5; October 9, 1877, p.1, col.1; August 12, 1879,

p.1, col.4; and August 14, 1879, p.1, col.3; *San Francisco Call*, September 30, 1896, p.9, col.5; *The New York Clipper*, May 30, 1885, p.174, col.4

8 *Daily Alta*, June 3, 1873, p.1, col.1

9 *San Francisco Bulletin*, September 4, 1917, p.9, col.2

10 *San Francisco Examiner*, July 17, 1892, p.5, col.2 and July 28, 1892, p.5, col.4

11 Ibid, August 20, 1892, p.3, col.1 and August 27, 1892, p.4, col.6

12 Ibid July 24, 1888, p.1, col.5 and October 5, 1888, p.1 col.2; *San Francisco Examiner*, July 17, 1892, p.5, col.2 and July 28, 1892, p.5, col.4; August 20, 1892, p.3, col.1 and August 27, 1892, p.4, col.6, and November 12, 1892, p.4, col.5

Billy Clark, an early rival of Tom Crowley, Sr., in his Whitehall boatman days, sits with his arms folded . . . The scene is Harry Hanson's sailors' boardinghouse at 12 Union Street. Hanson is the man holding the dog. The date is 1893. To the right is 10 Union Street, where proprietors George and Harry Lewis also served sailors. George Lewis was a state assemblyman from San Francisco in 1890.

Economics Overcome the Law

Seamen...are deficient in that full and intelligent responsibility for their acts that is accredited to ordinary adults, and [need] the protection of the law in the same sense in which minors and wards are entitled to the protection of their parents and guardians. *Arago* decision, U. S. Supreme Court ruling, 1897. (quoted from *A Historical Dictionary of the U.S. Merchant Marine and Shipping Industry Since the Introduction of Steam*, de la Pedraja, p.56-7)

Shanghaiing continued to flourish in San Francisco until about 1910, with isolated incidents in the 1920s. In 1853, 1864 and 1870, state laws were enacted to regulate runners but enforcement was proportionate to the influence that crimps had on police and politicians—rendering the laws ineffectual. Police responded to pressure from ship captains and owners by arresting runners who boarded ships illegally but fines were light and prison sentences virtually non-existent. As crimps became more involved in local politics in the 1870s, they gained the upperhand over anti-shanghaiing efforts. The anti-shanghaiing forces continued with little success through the 1880s and '90s.

Even when laws were passed at the federal level, the ever resourceful crimps found a way for economics to transcend the law. If money could be made selling a sailor, then the crimps were determined to make that money.

The first action by the California legislature against shanghaiing echoed the 1847 San Francisco town council ordinance against desertion of sailors. In 1853, the legislature made enticing a sailor to desert from a ship a misdemeanor. In 1864, the state legislature set misdemeanor penalties for people who boarded vessels in San Francisco's harbor before it was docked at a wharf without oral permission from the master or written permission from ship owners. The same measure (Supplement 18 to the Consolidation Act of 1856 for the City and County of San Francisco) also made it illegal to entice or persuade crew to desert a ship. It was aimed at controlling the worst abuses of boardinghouse runners. But the penalties were light—a $100 fine or 50 days in jail. Harbor Police were not terribly effective in enforcing it, and runners and crimps carried on pretty much as if the law did not exist. [1]

In 1870, the California legislature established a Marine Board in San Francisco to license boardinghouse keepers and shipping masters—an effort to regulate both boardinghouses and runners. In 1871, the board issued four licenses to shipping offices and 26 to sailors' boardinghouses. Fourteen boardinghouses closed that year. One of the board's members was Police Chief Patrick Crowley. [2]

A boardinghouse owner, William Moore, challenged the board's constitutionality and refused to pay the license fee. The annual license fee was $50 for a sailors' boardinghouse and $100 for a shipping office. Moore's defense argued against the legislature's right to interfere with congressional authority to regulate interstate commerce. The prosecution defended the law on grounds that it did not interfere with commerce but merely protected sailors against the excesses of runners' soliciting them on ships. The Twelfth District Court ruled against the licensing but upheld the law's constitutionality. [3]

The *Daily Alta* newspaper in an 1871 article entitled, "Abuse of Seamen" recounted horror stories about shanghaiing which continued despite the Marine Board's existence. One example was the boarding of the bark *Chotham* by runners who clubbed and beat sailors, removed them by force, including the captain's son, who was taken from his bed to a boardinghouse. Twelve of the sailors were shipped within 24 hours to another ship, the *Cultivator*, for which shanghaiers received $60 per man. The article laid responsibility for such abuses to the Marine Board's siding with the crimps. It actually "interfered [with] and compelled the sailor to submit to be plundered" in cases where they refused to ship out after signing articles of agreement because boardinghouse masters took their advance money. The board, ostensibly created to protect sailors, prevent cruelties against them, promote commerce and safeguard the port's reputation was, in fact, protecting what it was supposed to regulate. [4]

A disgruntled ship captain, in a letter to the *Daily Alta*, claimed that the board's rules actually interfered with seamen's rights to choose employment by prohibiting them from taking jobs outside of boardinghouse channels (unless they lived in their own homes, which virtually none did). Could such a rule be legally enforced, he wondered? Boardinghouse keepers decided to make sure that it was, preventing seaman from non-Seamen's Boarding House Masters' Association houses from getting jobs. To make their point, crimps refused to provide crew to one ship left at anchor until a week or so after it was due to sail. [5]

Joseph "Frenchy" Franklin and Edwin Lewis entered San Francisco Republican County Committee politics, with Tommy Chandler on the Democratic side, as part of the boardinghouse masters' plan to exert as much political power as possible in the city and state to further their interests. In its first attempt to eliminate shanghaiing, the Federal Government enacted the United States Shipping Act of 1872. The initial success of the Act

THOMAS CHANDLER

San Francisco Public Library
Thomas Chandler, Sr., circa 1900 . . . Tommy Chandler procured crews for British ships and advertised himself as a shipping master in *The Men of California, 1900-02.* A crimp and member of the powerful San Francisco Democratic County Committee for over thirty-five years, and president of the Seamen's Boarding House Masters' Association for many years, Chandler was a bare-knuckle boxer who moved easily among the rich and powerful men of California.

frightened San Francisco's crimps so much that they stepped up their active political involvement.

The Shipping Commissioners' Act of 1872 required that sailors sign shipping articles in front of a commissioner appointed by a federal circuit court, before a voyage. Section 11 of the 1872 Act provided for a $100 fine for anyone demanding or receiving any remuneration for obtaining employment for a seamen or a non-seaman seeking work as a seaman. This was a blow at the shipping masters who charged a fee for placing men on a ship. The most important provisions were contained in Sections 17, 18 and 19, which provided that advances could be paid *only* to the sailor, his wife or mother. This was a direct threat to the sailors' boardinghouse masters. Vessels in the coastal trade were exempt from the Act. Crews were to be paid off only in the Shipping Commissioner's office. Section 25 authorized the Shipping Commissioner to settle any disagreements between a captain and his crew. The fine for illegally boarding a ship was set at $200. Shipping agents could continue to serve as intermediaries but could be paid only by a merchant, not by fees deducted from a sailor's wages. If advances could be stopped, shanghaiing would stop. Shipping commissioners were to be appointed by U. S. circuit courts and compensated by fees charged for placing sailors on ships, an aspect that critics feared encouraged collusion between shipowners and commissioners. But the *Daily Alta*, a champion for sailors, heralded the legislation as protecting the rights of both merchants and seamen. [6]

What Congress failed to realize was that sailors' boardinghouses kept sailors going when they were not needed aboard a ship and that few sailors had cash to pay their boardinghouse bills. The boardinghouse masters extended credit to seamen. Congress also underestimated the resourcefulness of the crimping community.

The first U. S. Shipping Commissioner appointed in San Francisco was Colonel Jonathan D. Stevenson, who gained fame as head of Stevenson's Regiment, a group of New York volunteers who arrived in San Francisco in 1846. He set up his office in July, 1872, in three large rooms rented at the northeast corner of Jackson and Front streets and announced his intention to enforce the law with gusto. [7]

Commissioner Stevenson declared that no advances would be paid thereafter to shipping or boardinghouse masters. The law, however, initially exempted coastal vessels, a loophole that was remedied by a Philadelphia judge the following November. That effectively put an end to crimps' sources of income and the next month they declared war on the shipping commissioner. They would see to it that he got no business. Stevenson responded by posting a notice along the waterfront that 100 sailors were needed and could apply at his office. He next swore out warrants for the arrest of two of the city's longest-standing shipping masters, Lewis C. Hunter and Abel F. Scott, for placing crews without going through his office. He was finding all the sailors he needed, he said, to which the boardinghouse masters' association responded that several ships were sitting in the stream waiting for crews.

The *Daily Alta* publicized Stevenson's announcements, listing vessels that sought crew who could be hired through the commissioner's office. "As long as the quarrel continues," the newspaper opined, sailors would "remain on shore drinking free rum." Crimps resorted to hanging around the commissioner's office when crews were paid off, waiting to entice them to a good drunk, then set them up in their boardinghouses. [8]

Stevenson was determined, however, that no "blood-money" or bonuses would be paid to intermediaries and that any money that changed hands would be legal tender paid to sailors themselves. The effect was that British captains stopped paying "blood-money" to crimps, although the need for crews was great to transport cargoes from a large California wheat harvest. American captains and ship owners, realizing that $143,000 reportedly had been paid in "blood-money" to shipping masters over a five-month period, followed suit, publishing a memo declaring their refusal to pay members of the Seamen's Boarding House Masters' Association and agreeing to support Stevenson in enforcing the law. A few members of the association urged compromise with Stevenson, but the majority felt they could win the battle by defying the determined commissioner. The association announced publicly that its members would refuse to supply sailors for a year, if necessary, if their regular fees were not paid. Stevenson held firm and the captain of the British bark *Lapwing* stated that he would stay in port for six months if he had to rather than pay "blood-money" to any more crimps. [9]

Boardinghouse masters began to intimidate sailors with threats of violence if they sought employment at the commissioner's office. American ship captains, A. R. West of the *Arracan* and the captain of the *Robert L. Lane*, formed bodyguards for sailors so they could go to the commissioner's office in safety. Crimps retaliated by sending their strongest runners to threaten sailors as they entered or left Stevenson's second-floor office, pulling them off the stairs. Harbor police had to be summoned to restore order on at least one occasion. [10]

Sailors continued to find work through the commissioner's office and as the year ended, only seven months after the law's enactment, it appeared less and less likely that the boardinghouse system could survive its impact. Crimps were prepared to intimidate sailors but not confront police. So they organized a march with banners flying and a band blaring out tunes, in a pathetic attempt to rally public support for their side. The *Daily Alta* sneered at the effort, and British shipowners telegraphed support of their captains' refusal to continue paying crimps. Boardinghouse masters threatened next, in desperation, to withhold sea chests of sailors who sought jobs without their permission.

A rumor circulated in December, 1872, that boardinghouse keepers would no longer do business through shipping masters

Courtesy Bancroft Library

General B. Griffin Barney, Deputy Shipping Commissioner . . .
Barney was Shipping Commissioner Jonathan D. Stevenson's Deputy
when this Taber photograph was taken in 1880. The United States
Shipping Act of 1872 required all sailors to sign articles of agreement
before the Shipping Commissioner. Republican boss Dick Chute ef-
fected a compromise with Republican Stevenson which allowed the
boardinghouse system to continue.

California Historical Society, San Francisco. Photographer: Redington, St. Louis Art Studio, San Francisco. FN-27723

504 Battery Street, circa 1879-80 . . . Over a dozen commission merchant and ship and custom house brokers located their offices opposite the Custom House on Battery Street. The offices of shipping masters Edward N. Laffey and George Naunton were on this block in 1880. After he became a shipping master in 1886, Tommy Chandler set up his office at 518 Battery, next to his old friend Stewart Menzies.

but would furnish sailors to any ship that needed them. Other rumors warned that crews would be supplied by men sent by rail from New York. It would be cheaper to pay their transcontinental fare than "blood-money," as railroads had agreed to lower fares in cooperation with ship owners. Crimps countered by offering to supply sailors to British captains at a monthly rate of $40 per sailor, dropped to $35 when the captains resisted and $30 for American ships (the British ships were pressed to sail with their grain cargoes). In effect, the crimps were beaten. Sailors were again the losers—their wages were lowered to $25 per month. [11]

With the New Year of 1873 came a new pair of officers for the Seamen's Boarding House Masters' Association. The powerful new team of Richard Chute as secretary (and secretary of the state Republican Party) and Edward Warren Casey, treasurer (former secretary of the state Democratic Party), were recruited. Stevenson himself was a Republican and could work with the association's new officers. They set up an office in the same building where the commissioner was housed and began a publicly-announced cooperative relationship. Stevenson agreed to tell the association when crews were needed and Chute agreed to supply men from a daily list of eligible applicants. When a sailor was hired, his boardinghouse was notified and any claims by the boardinghouse master against the sailor for outstanding bills presented to Chute. Chute and Casey deducted five percent from the advances paid as a commission for cashing any due bills, or notes payable, after the sailor departed port. Chute and Casey now played the role formerly filled by shipping masters.

Richard Chute's power to forge this compromise stemmed from his ability to deliver votes to his preferred candidate in Republican Party primaries. Dick Chute and Chris Buckley, before Buckley became a Democrat, apprenticed under William T. Higgins, the Republican Party boss from the 1860s until his death in 1889. Higgins operated from his saloon on Davis Street in the midst of the sailors' boardinghouses, as politics in San Francisco loosened up after the defeat of the People's Party.

Chute had ties to the boardinghouses through the political system, having used their boarders to deliver votes for the Republican Party candidates he backed—men who voted repeatedly for candidates at various polling places. Boardinghouse keepers, by supplying "repeaters" on election days, garnered favors from both political parties. If officials at a particular polling place objected, boardinghouse runners and their friends used strong-arm tactics to overcome any objections. The payoff for the repeaters would be a drink or two, maybe a dollar. Sailors' boardinghouses were a natural site for Chute and Buckley to recruit repeaters. One of "Blind" Chris Buckley's Republican opponents in the 1890s, Martin Kelly, declared that Buckley had "developed a knack for colonizing the boardinghouses and turning tricks in the rough work of the primaries." [12]

In 1879, San Francisco's County Registrar of Voters Kaplan found in four precincts alone fifty-five men from boardinghouses who never resided at the addresses listed in their registration materials, or had moved from the reported address months before. Kaplan believed hundreds fell into the category of "repeaters." The First Ward was more highly organized than wards South of Market or other outlying areas of the city. Sailors' boardinghouse keepers satisfied not only the demand for sailors but also were in a position to satisfy the political needs of the city's bosses by supplying "repeaters."

Stevenson now found himself in a position to help the boardinghouses. When there was a glut of sailors on the market, British captains demanded reverse "blood-money" —$10 to $30 for each man taken off their keepers' hands. The association complained about this reverse "blood-money" and Stevenson took action against the captains. [13]

The future for shipping masters, however, was not promising, and in 1873 Abel F. Scott retired from the business, burning his books in a large bonfire and locking the doors to his once-thriving office. As a parting shot, he sued the commissioner for favoring the boardinghouse association by refusing to place sailors whom Scott had presented to him for the ship *Prussia.* "Shanghai" Brown was one of the witnesses for the commissioner and the new system, glad not to have to pay ship captains to rid himself of excess boarders. The result of Scott's suit was that new rules were drafted and the suit was dropped. [14]

The changes wrought by the Shipping Commissioners' Act were to be short-lived, however. British captains resorted again to paying "blood-money" when there was a shortage of seamen and the old system was resumed later in 1873. Boardinghouse keepers were happy to have their cash-flow back. To further blunt Stevenson's recent victories, Harbor police informed him that they no longer would accept the $3 reward for every deserter returned to a ship. [15]

In early 1874, the *Daily Alta* called for the abolition of the state Marine Board, saying it had been a failure, filled no function after the establishment of the federal commissioner and was merely an opportunity for gubernatorial appointments. In June, two years after it had passed the law, Congress effectively nullified the Commissioners' Act for deepwater ships other than whalers and in December, 1875, the California legislature repealed the Marine Board Act. The U.S. Shipping Commissioner maintained a register which included names of all sailors who had shipped before him. (This became the forerunner of attempts by shipowners to use a grading system for seamen maintained by an employment book. The shipowners system was despised by sailors). Crimps resorted to old tactics by falsifying names on the commissioner's register while loading shanghaied victims aboard outbound ships. [16]

The crimps had won that round.

San Francisco Maritime Museum N.H.P.

The ship *Amazon* in full sail . . . One of boardinghouse keeper John Daly's sailors tried to ship on the *Amazon* through a rival master to avoid paying his boarding bill. Daly brought the sailor, Charles O'Brien, before Judge Hale Rix. The judge dismissed charges.

They also benefited from enactment of a state law in 1889 that made it a criminal offense not to pay a boardinghouse or hotel bill. It allowed innkeepers to put a lien on baggage or other property of guests who owed them money and to sell such property to recover the costs of unpaid bills. That was especially helpful when boardinghouse keepers stole sailors from one another, leaving lodging masters with unpaid bills. By 1890 more and more cases came to light of boardinghouse keepers stealing sailors from each other. Let the other guy pay the bills and I'll pocket the money was the philosophy. Boardinghouse keeper John Daly prosecuted one of his sailors, Charles O'Brien, for defrauding an innkeeper, when O'Brien tried to ship through a rival boardinghouse keeper on the ship *Amazon*. Judge Hale Rix dismissed charges.

"Shanghai" Nelson accused the Sailor's Home superintendent of pulling a similar stunt when Nelson lost two of his boarders one night and was stuck with their bills. The two men admitted signing false names on their shipping articles in order to run out on Nelson and their bills. [17]

The boardinghouse association began to lose its power, however, as conditions changed dramatically in the 1890s. Three major reasons caused the changes. The city was developing south of Market Street with new boardinghouses as competition. Secondly, the Sailor's Home, subsidized by the city with low rent and having a large reserve of men, aggressively found jobs for sailors at less cost to ships. Finally, a union was formed in 1885 to represent coastal sailors—the Coast Seamen's Union.

Competition rapidly grew that challenged traditional boardinghouses and their long-time control over the sailors' job market. The Sailor's Home's rent of $1 a year enabled it to operate with much lower overhead costs than private boardinghouses. [18]

Andrew Furuseth, "Emancipator of the Sailor" . . . Furuseth led the Coast Seamen's Union as its secretary for decades. Although Furuseth fought shanghaiing for years, it was the death of sail that killed the practice. His efforts through tough times kept the union together and ultimately Furuseth accomplished his goal of civil rights and respect for seamen.

The Coast Seamen's Union, founded in 1885, called a strike in 1886 that slowed the placement of crews on coastal vessels by harassing non-union men from sailing on coastal vessels. In an anonymously-published statement, a shipowner decried that sailors in the past had been "content" with their employers and "satisfied" with their boardinghouses. "A condition generally satisfactory alike to the shipowner and sailor has been radically changed by the acts of political demagogues and mercenary agitators, who as leaders of the Coast Seamen's Union, now seek to pose in the philanthropic role of the 'Sailors' Savior.'" Shipowners accused the union of depriving them of freedom to employ whomever they wished and the union argued for living wages and a closed-shop system in which only its members would be hired. Union sympathizers frequently boarded coastal ships in an effort to talk "scab" workers off crews, and sometimes resorted to force, trying to tear the lumber schooner *Irma*'s cook away from its wheel as he hung on for dear life and spiriting three men off another boat, the *Dora*, delaying its departure until replacements could be found. [19]

The economic climate was not conducive to the union's cause at the end of 1886. Some 1,200 sailors were idle in San Francisco in 1886, and if union sailors refused to work for the wages offered, others were readily available to take the jobs. Many members left the union in order to work, resorting to the Shipowners' Association office for placement. The next year the Knights of Labor, needing to consolidate its resources on other fronts, withdrew support of the Coast Seamen's Union, leaving it to fight its battles alone. It was further hampered in its militant efforts by police specially detailed to protect non-union sailors from attack.

One success the Coast Seamen's Union achieved was the decision by United States Labor Commissioner Tobin to hold hearings in San Francisco to solicit testimony concerning conditions relating to shipping sailors from this port. A key provision prohibited the payment of advances to anyone but a sailor's family members. Men such as R.L. David, George Fogle, James Cohen and Louis Levy who supplied clothing to seamen admitted they helped men find jobs as sailors. They swore they never charged a commission from the men. Sailors' boardinghouse masters John Kane and Adolph Classen denied charging an advance; fellow boardinghouse masters John Munroe and Peter McMahon said they did discount a sailor's $40 advance note from $2.50 to $5 if they did not know the person cashing the note. George Roeben, who had been in the sailors' boardinghouse business over 35 years by 1887, denied he ever discounted advance notes.

The Laflin Record gives the lie to statements that a commission, or an advance, was never paid to clothiers or charged by them. George Fogle had signed for several advances and Louis Levy's signature is one of the most frequent in Laflin's book.

Although nothing came from the Labor Commissioner's hearings of material benefit to the Coast Seamen's Union, they did serve as a forum for the grievances of coastal sailors against a system aligned against them. Andrew Furuseth had the astuteness to recognize that public opinion on the side of the sailor was a very powerful thing. The union's newspaper, the *Coast Seamen's Journal*, and Furuseth's frequent trips to Washington, D.C., to lobby Congress were the two most powerful weapons sailors had in their favor in the fight for recognition of their civil rights. [20]

Congress responded with other laws aimed at curbing shanghaiing. In 1884 it passed the Dingley Act, named for its sponsor, Maine Senator Nelson Dingley, Jr. At the same time, Congress established the Bureau of Navigation in the U. S. Department of Treasury (part of the executive branch of government) and a U. S. Commissioner of Navigation to which shipping commissioners reported. In 1886 Congress abolished the practice of compensating commissioners with fees paid by shipowners. The Dingley

San Francisco Maritime Museum N.H.P.

   The wreckers move in on the last old wooden waterfront structure to escape the 1906 earthquake and fire . . . Fred Offernan's Saloon is captured by John W. Proctor's lens as one of the last landmarks of the shanghaiing era is about to fall.

Act specifically prohibited payment of advances on sailors' wages, providing that all payments be made only to a seamen, his wife, mother or other relative. Although the Shipping Commissioners' Act of 1872 attempted to legislate advances to wife, mother or other relative only, that act was amended into ineffectiveness in 1874. [21]

The new law struck at the heart of crimps' livelihoods by outlawing their practice of receiving advance money to settle boardinghouse bills. The law also reinforced the prohibition against runners' boarding vessels before they were docked and passengers and cargo unloaded. W. Lane Booker, the British Consul, moralized that the new law would force sailors to be more careful with their money in order to pay bills and result in fewer drunken sprees. But 24 deepwater boardinghouses and another 29 South-of-Market establishments catering to coastal sailors announced that they would not place sailors unless the customary advances were paid. At the time, crews for grain ships were in demand for the passage around Cape Horn to England, and it was in captains' and boardinghouse keepers' interests to evade the new law, which they did openly. It was common knowledge on San Francisco's waterfront that no ship left the city in 1884 without advance monies first being paid to boarding masters, who refused to ship out sailors otherwise. [22]

Another reform law was enacted in 1895 with the help of a San Francisco congressman, former judge James Maguire, who won his seat in 1892 and again in 1894 with the backing of the Coast Seamen's Union. Maguire successfully pushed the act named for him that exempted *coastal* sailors from arrest for desertion and prohibited the hated payment of advance money. That law, too, though laudable in intent, was largely ignored. Seamen suffered another set-back when the U. S. Supreme Court in 1897 issued the *Arago* decision (Robertson v. Baldwin), which reaffirmed that sailors had few rights as citizens because they were vulnerable and needed to be cared for or treated like helpless children. "Seamen are . . . deficient in that full and intelligent responsibility for their acts that is accredited to ordinary adults, and [need] the protection of the law in the same sense in which minors and wards are entitled to the protection of their parents and guardians," the Court stated. Sailors, it concluded, had to be protected from themselves and therefore were not subject to the Constitution's Thirteenth Amendment that prohibited involuntary servitude. [23]

By 1899, there was a shortage of seamen because of the Spanish-American War and Klondike Gold Rush. Henry "Shanghai" Brown, Jr. and Johnny Savory were charged with violating the allotment law in connection with sailors named Svenson and J. McDonald in that year. Their accuser was Andy Furuseth of the Coast Seamen's Union. United States Court Commissioner Heacock dismissed the charges and the sailors were shipped out. Brown said after the case was dismissed that "the sailors were stool pigeons for certain persons who had an enmity against the shipping masters." He was speaking of Furuseth.

Tommy Crowley, Sr., no friend of unions, later intimated that Furuseth and the union were behind the bombing of One-Eyed Curtin's boardinghouse in 1893 and openly accused the union of blowing up a boat, the *Ethyl and Marion*, that ferried non-union crews to ships. The union passed a resolution to hurt John Curtin, John Kane, Al Mordaunt, Adolph Classen and John Munroe in any way possible. A number of blasts occurred during the period which were attributed to union activists. The bad publicity that they gave the union tested Furuseth's ability to recover public sentiment and hold the union together. [24]

One of the union's crusades was to expose, through its publication, the *Coast Seamen's Journal*, the fact that the Sailor's Home was "the largest crimp joint in the world." In 1875 a known crimp, Andrew Peterson, had become one of the Home's superintendents, forced to resign a few years later along with superintendent John Duff for allegedly shanghaiing boarders. The Home continued to be suspect, however, under its new superintendent Daniel Swannack, who took over in 1880. He was accused of mismanagement and of smuggling in liquor, strictly against the Home's rules for sobriety. The union asked the Board of Supervisors to investigate the Home as one of the worst such establishments for sailors in the city. Despite a clean bill of health from the supervisors, criticism of the Home continued. [25]

It was no safe haven for poor sailors. They were ill-treated if they refused to ship out when offered the chance or if they tried to find other lodgings. The low rent from the city permitted the Sailor's Home operators to make a big profit. Swannack admitted to the board's police committee in 1888 that the Home had taken in $32,500 from sailors the previous year and that he had made a profit of $19,000 after paying bills and the five percent of gross receipts due the Home's sponsor, the Ladies' Seamen's Friend Society. The board nevertheless extended the Home's lease for another three years. Swannack resigned but was retained until a replacement could be found. On New Year's Eve he was arrested with two other men, a stableman and longshoreman, for beating and taking the clothes of a lodger who tried to leave the Sailor's Home. Swannack defended his action by claiming the sailor owed $40 and repeatedly refused to ship out. Swannack also sent a letter to the *Daily Alta* extolling the Home's virtues and his management of it. As a Salvation Army captain put it, Swannack "went there a poor man and in a few years he became rich." The Ladies' Society was unhappy with the bad publicity the Home was receiving and barred reporters from its February, 1889 monthly meeting, when they considered a replacement for Swannack. A *San Francisco Chronicle* reporter learned that the sole applicant was the former city jailer, "Hangman" John Rogers, a cohort of boss Buckley's and a known crimp. [26]

The principal objection that the union had to the Sailor's Home was its willingness to place sailors at below-union wages—as much as $5 or $10 below the going rate of $30 per month. Boardinghouse keepers also were threatened by the Home. "Frenchy" Franklin told the supervisors in 1889 that the ladies of the Sailor's Home were being "hoodwinked" by Swannack and that the Home was an unfair competitor to boardinghouses like his. Board members decided to visit the Home themselves and talk to sailors living there. Just before Christmas, members of the committee paid a visit to the Sailor's Home to elicit opinions of the sailors living there as to their treatment. Several sailors said the Home's runners promised the sailors a kickback, or blood-money, if the sailors would stay at the Home. The promised money was never received. Complaints were frequent about the Home not being heated. The residents had to continue moving around to stay warm. Bedclothing was also inadequate.

The union sponsored a march in the mid-1880s when the Home placed sailors on a ship for $20 per month, and fiery speeches denounced Swannack. Activists threatened to prevent the ship, *Forest Queen*, from sailing but instead a delegation was named to meet with Swannack. He refused to see them, further angering the union. In 1888, police spokesmen said the Sailor's Home caused more trouble than any other boardinghouse in the city. [27]

The Sailor's Home was founded in 1856 by the Ladies' Aid and Protection Society for the Benefit of Seamen. The organization later changed its name to the Ladies' Seamen's Friend Society. Their building on Davis Street was in such bad condition that they moved to a building at the southwest corner of Battery and Vallejo streets in 1863. The Sailor's Home in the old U.S. Marine Hospital was the creation of an unusual degree of cooperation between local, state and federal officials. In 1875, a concerted effort was made by men such as A.M. Winn and A.K.

Stevens to have the Sailor's Home moved from its old quarters to the roomy site on Rincon Hill. Dedicated to preventing drink among sailors, it also seemed to be dedicated to gauging sailors whenever possible and at least as dedicated to working against the other boardinghouse keepers of San Francisco.

The Federal government gave the U.S. Marine Hospital to the City and County of San Francisco for use as a Sailor's Home. The California state legislature agreed to pay expenses of improving the building so it would not tumble down Rincon Hill (the building was closed as the Marine Hospital after the earthquake of 1868). The city leased the building to the Ladies' Seamen's Friends Society for one dollar per year. [28]

The Sailor's Home on Rincon Hill had capacity for 150 sailors, four or five times the number that could stay at the average sailors' boardinghouse in San Francisco. What this meant was that the Sailor's Home could always be counted on to put downward pressure on sailors' wages because of its low operating cost and large number of men who could be released at rates lower than other boardinghouses could afford to charge—and the Home still made money for its crimp/operators.

In 1891, the city's Chamber of Commerce set up a committee to investigate the "blood-money" problem, naming former Supervisor Stewart Menzies as chairman. The union decried the fact that sailors' views would not be considered and called the investigation a waste of time. The committee's report, however, estimated that some 3,000 sailors had been shipped from San Francisco in 1889 with $40 per-head going into crimps' hands, a total of $120,000 in illegal payments. It blamed British shipowners for allowing crewmen to desert in order to hire cheaper crew, and proposed that two "competent and reliable persons" representing each flag be hired to manage the placement of seamen on both British and U. S. vessels. Tommy Chandler, a friend of Menzies,' was hired as British shipping master. [29]

Stewart Menzies began life in Gold Rush San Francisco as a stevedore and rose to prominence as part of the city's elite . . . Menzies served on the Board of Supervisors in the 1870s. Tommy Chandler appointed Menzies to the state Democratic convention in 1871. Years later, the favor was repaid when Menzies recommended his friend Tommy Chandler to the newly created position of British shipping master. As Tom Crowley, Sr., put it years later, "'If a captain needed a crew, he could always find Tommy Chandler at Stewart Menzies.'" *Photo San Francisco Public Library*

John T. Sullivan, member of Chris Buckley's Board of Supervisors and shoe store owner . . . Sullivan parlayed his popularity as an oarsman with the Pioneer Rowing Club among the boatmen and boardinghouse masters of his First Ward into election to the Board of Supervisors.

Sullivan's connections to the world of shanghaiing are shadowy—he attended the wedding of James Laflin's daughter, a long time crimp, and had a home next to Tommy Chandler in the 1100 block of Montgomery Street. *Photo The Olympic Club*

Courtesy Dr. Albert Shumate

The Sailor's Home—This building went from ominous to sinister after it was taken over by the Ladies' Seamen's Friends Society. Built in 1852 as the U.S. Marine Hospital, it became transformed into the Sailor's Home in 1875. One of the few sailors' boardinghouses without a barroom, its reputation was so bad that only foreign sailors frequented the place. Known as the "largest crimp joint in the world," a succession of superintendents ran the institution for their private gain rather than for the benefit of sailors new to a strange port (this was the connotation of the term "Sailor's Home" in the rest of the world). Ironically, a saloon graces the foreground of this photo.

By late 1891, the competitive pressure caused by the Sailor's Home compelled ten boardinghouses to leave their association and ally themselves with the Sailor's Home, giving it temporary domination over the hiring system. In January, 1893, the Ladies' Seamen's Friend Society applied to the Board of Supervisors for a ten year lease renewal. The annual rental would continue at one dollar per year. Supervisor James Ryan, of the Seventh Ward, where the Home was located, strenuously objected to renewal of the lease on the grounds that the superintendent, Captain Melvin Staples, was paid $25,000 annually. This was in 1893 dollars. Approval of the lease was recommended anyway.

A newspaper account reveals the Sailor's Home contained small rooms, often without windows in the sleeping quarters, poorly prepared food, little heat and no medical care for those who became sick. As the Salvation Army captain had put it, the previous superintendent had entered the Sailor's Home a poor man and left it rich. The Sailor's Home also had a skillful runner known as "Young Johnny." This was Johnny Ferem.

A few days later the former chaplain of the Sailor's Home, James B. Campbell, told his version of how the Home was run to the Health and Police Committee of the Board of Supervisors: the Sailor's Home was run for all the money which could be pumped from it. Some of the directors were respectable but they did not spend enough time to learn anything beyond the surface. The only patrons were foreign sailors, who did not realize the reputation of the place. Campbell accused Mrs. Sykes, one of the "ladies," of being in on the mismanagement and financial abuses surrounding the Home. Supervisor Ryan mentioned accusations that certain of the "lady managers" were known to borrow $100 to $200 from the superintendent, with no repayment plan offered or required. Campbell had heard similar rumors. When Campbell tried to correct the abuses he was fired. [30]

Other action against the crimping system was taken when the British Consul General, J. Courtney Bennett, brought charges in 1902 against two men for enticing seamen to desert the British ship *Stronsa*. The following year the consul charged the Sailor's Home with operating as a crimp establishment under the guise of a charitable institution, and instigated an investigation of the matter by the U. S. Commissioner of Navigation. The consul presented as evidence a letter from Ferem, then superintendent, to the captain of a British ship, setting out terms for placing sailors on his vessel. The Home continued to operate, however. [31]

In early 1899, Congress lowered the allowable advance from two months' wages to one month's wage in an effort to decrease the abuse of sailors. The land shark combine simply demanded—and received—a "blood-money" bonus sufficient to make up the difference in their cash-flow.

The only amusing item concerning the Sailor's Home was noted by the *San Francisco Examiner* in 1893. The Sailor's Home was ostensibly dedicated to the sobriety of sailors and undertook to have its residents take the pledge. No saloon existed on the premises. The charge was made that the chapel was filled on Sundays only by bribing sailors to attend. The most common form of bribe was a drink or its monetary equivalent. [32]

Even the devastating earthquake and fire that nearly destroyed the city in April, 1906, did not end shanghaiing. A crimp who tried to board a ship that September met with a skipper who promised to fill him full of holes if he touched the vessel. He backed off. Congress made another effort to outlaw shanghaiing in 1906, and President Theodore Roosevelt signed the act on June 28, 1906. This attempt at eliminating shanghaiing, entitled "An Act to Prohibit Shanghaiing in the United States," imposed heavier penalties than previous acts (a $1,000 fine and one year in prison), but focused solely on those who enticed a man to go onto a vessel through threats, misrepresentations or getting the quarry drunk or under the influence of drugs. It did not even attempt to prevent payment of advances. But by 1909 the crimping business was so poor that one particularly infamous one, Timothy Hawkins, was forced to ship out. [33]

Shipping masters nevertheless existed as middlemen between boardinghouses and sailors until Congress passed the La Follette Act in 1915, to regulate conditions governing maritime employment, authored by Progressive Wisconsin Senator Robert M. La Follette during the presidential administration of President Woodrow Wilson. The La Follette Act eliminated imprisonment for desertion; prohibited advance payments; established requirements for able-bodied seamen; improved conditions aboard ship for sailors; and, in a gesture to make the bill more acceptable to members of Congress reluctant to help sailors only three short years after the sinking of the *Titanic*, set lengthy requirements for life rafts and boats and preservers, and other safety procedures. [34]

It was not until the death of the age of sail during World War I (1914-19) that shanghaiing truly ended as the demand for sailing crew died. Stories still circulated, however, of shanghaiing cases for Alaska Packers ships during the 1920s.

San Francisco's waterfront settled into a more lawful state with the end of shanghaiing, a system which enslaved men for over sixty years in the city by the Bay. The system was perpetuated by the political power of crimps, motivated by the money they once made, and shipowners who cooperated with them.

Footnotes

1 *Municipal Reports, 1875-6*, pp.819-21. The Consolidation Act of 1856 for the City and County of San Francisco was passed by the California Legislature in 1856 and remained the basic framework of municipal government in San Francisco until 1898. The Consolidation Act of 1856 <u>decreased</u> the size of San Francisco and made every effort to achieve low cost government by eliminating duplication. By the late 1860s, the Act was woefully inadequate for a large city. See Bullough, pp.54-7.

2 *Daily Alta*, June 8, 1872, p.1, col.2

3 Ibid, May 8, 1871, p.1, col.2

4 Ibid, April 9, 1874, p.1, col.1

5 Ibid, February 27, 1871, p.1, col.6

6 *A Historical Dictionary of the U.S. Merchant Marine and Shipping Industry Since the Introduction of Steam*, Rene de la Pedreja, 1994, p.568; *Daily Alta*, August 21, 1884 and de la Pedreja, p.102

7 *Daily Alta*, August 7, 1872, p.1, col.1

8 Ibid, December 3, 1872, p.1, col.2; December 4, 1872, col.1, col.2; December 5, 1872, p.1, col.3 and December 10, 1873, p.1, col.4

9 Ibid, December 7, 1872, p.1, col.1; December 8, 1872, p.1, col.2; December 10, 1872, p.1, col.3 and December 11, 1872, p.1, col.1

10 Ibid, December 12, 1872, p.1, col.1

11 Ibid, December 17, 1872, p.1, col.2; December 19, 1872, p.1, col.2 and December 20, 1872, p.1, col.2; Ibid, December 27, 1872, p.1, col.2

12 *The Blind Boss and His City*, Bullough, p.17; *The Daily Alta*, August 21, 1879, p.1, col.1

13 Ibid, January 4, 1873, p.1, col.1; January 6, 1873, p.1, col.1 and January 8, 1873, p.1, col.3

14 Ibid, February 28, 1873, p.1, col.3; March 21, 1873, p.1, col.1 and March 22, 1873, p.1, col.3

15 Ibid, March 8, 1873, p.1, col.1; March 19, 1873, p.1, col.1 and March 20, 1873, p.1, col.2

16 Ibid, April 9, 1874, p.1, col.1

17 *Daily Alta*, September 24, 1889, p.1, col.3; September 25, 1889, p.8, col.3 and September 26, 1889, p.1, col.4; *Amendments to the Civil Code, Twenty-First Session, 1875-76*, State of California, pp.78-9

18 Ibid, October 20, 1891, p.4, col.2, November 2, 1891, p.3, col.3 and November 12, 1891, p.4, col.4

19 *The Daily Alta,* August 23, 1886, p.2, col.2; August 27, 1886, p.1, col.5 and August 31, 1886, p.1, col.5

20 Ibid, September 28, 1886, p.1, col.6 and November 4, 1886, p.2, col.3; December 17, 1887, p.8, col.1; *San Francisco Examiner,* August 19, 1892, p. 4, col.3; *Daily Alta*, July 1, 1887, p.1, col.4; July 6, 1887, p.1, col.6; July 7, 1887, p.1, col.6 and July 22, 1887, p.1, col.6

21 *Daily Alta*, August 21, 1884 and de la Pedreja, p.102

22 Ibid, August 7, 1884, p.1, col.2; July 17, 1884, p.1, col.3 and August 6, 1884, p.1, col.3; October 25, 1884, p.8, col.1 and December 2, 1884, p.1, col.2

23 See de la Pedraja, pp. 336, 56-7. Four sailors signed shipping articles in San Francisco to ship to Chile by way of Oregon. When their ship, the *Arago*, arrived in Oregon, they deserted. They claimed they had never left the coastal trade and were therefore not subject to arrest. According to de la Pedraja, the outraged captain decided to make an example of the men by dragging them in chains through the streets. Appeals by the Andrew Furuseth's International Seamen's Union brought the case to the United States Supreme Court. On January 25, 1897, the justices rendered their decision (see William Standard, *Merchant Seamen: A Short History of Their Struggle)*, a decision which organized labor saw as the "'Second Dred Scott Decision.'" The California Legislature passed Assembly Joint Resolution No. 27, expressing its indignation at the Court's decision, a decision the Resolution considered "a menace to the personal rights of every other class of workers." Although shipowners shied away from use of arrest for desertion, at least when men were plentiful, it was not until passage of the La Follette Act in 1915 that imprisonment for desertion in the merchant marine was eliminated.

24 *Recollections of the San Francisco Waterfront*, p. 170

25 Dillon, pp.197-9

26 *Daily Alta*, November 24, 1888, p.1, col.4; December 29, 1889, p.8, col.3; January 1, 1889, p.2, col.4 and January 2, 1889, p.7, col.6; *San Francisco Examiner*, January 23, 1893, p.3, col.5; *San Francisco Chronicle*, February 7, 1889, p.5, col.5

27 *Daily Alta*, August 14, 1885, p.4, col.3; November 9, 1889, p.1, col.2 and December 25, 1889, p.4, col.3; September 5, 1885, p.1, col.2; August 26, 1888, p.8, col.3

28 Ibid, February 26, 1878, p.2, col.3. Menzies' report underestimated the number of sailors shipped out in 1890 by a factor of two or three times. According to the Laflin record, James Laflin alone shipped out 1900 men and officers or the whaling and sealing fleets, paying $70,000 in advances. With five other shipping masters sending seamen out on deepwater and coastal vessels, probably 6,000-8,000 sailors were shipped out. Advances may have been $200,000-$250,000 annually.

29 *The Coast Seamen's Journal*, volume IV, no. 33, p.4; volume IV, no. 36, p.5 and volume IV, no. 42, p.5

30 *San Francisco Examiner*, October 29, 1891, p.3, col.7 and November 10, 1891, p.8, col.4; *San Francisco Examiner*, January 23, 1893, p.3, col.5; January 28, 1893; September 8, 1893, p.3, col.3

31 *San Francisco Call*, April 14, 1899, p.12, col. 7 and April 19, 1899, p.12, col.2; *San Francisco Examiner*, July 31, 1894, p.7, col.4; May 27, 1902, p.7, col.6; *Morning Call*, January 1903

32 *San Francisco Examiner*, September 8, 1893, p.3, col.3

33 Interview of Captain James Allen, p.8; *Morning Call*, July 24, 1906, p.12, col.4

34 Manuscript of crews of whaling vessels from the J. Porter Shaw Library; de la Pedraja, pp. 295-6. Woodrow Wilson waited until one hour before Congress adjourned to sign the La Follette Act. Furuseth was allowed to see Wilson to persuade him to sign, and the "Emancipator of the Seamen" reportedly fell on his knees and begged the President to sign. Wilson did; this time the combination of strong legislation and the death of sail sounded the death knell of crimping.

Drawing and quotations from Gordon Grant's Greasy Luck!, 1932

Choosing whale boat crews . . . According to marine artist Gordon Grant who made this sketch on board a whaler: "Soon after the ship was on her course, the crew was mustered and divided into two watches—starboard and larboard— . . ." Grant wrote that, "The mate steered the boat until the harpooner struck the whale. They thereupon changed places and the latter became 'boatsteerer.' The boatsteerer ranked next to the officers, were quartered aft and had a separate mess."

James Laflin and the Shipping of Whaling Men

Davis Street must have been quite a fascinating area in 1867: in that year clothier Louis Levy's establishment was at 607 Davis, while George Fogle operated from 506 Davis, between "Shanghai" Brown's sailors' boardinghouse at 504 and Thomas Murray's Golden Gate House at 510 Davis. For those who thought they might find refuge across the street, William Harris, another clothier involved with shanghaiing, awaited them at 507 Davis. [1]

These shanghaiers and many more signed the pages of the Record Book kept by James Laflin. The Laflin Record gives us a rare glimpse into the operation of shipping sailors on whaling and sealing vessels from 1886-1890. Many surprises are hidden in the pages of this document of payments to crimps over a four-year period. One of the biggest discoveries is that retail clothiers on the waterfront received a larger proportion of payments of sailors' advance wages than did saloon keepers. Boardinghouse keepers, of course, were paid the largest amount. Not only did almost one-third of all advances in 1886-7 go to retail clothiers, those payments went primarily into the hands of two men—Louis Levy and Gussie Stein. The Laflin Record indicates George Fogle, Gussie Stein and Louis Levy were three clothiers who supplemented their income by bringing in new whaling men.

Louis Levy used newspaper "Help Wanted" ads to recruit young men for whalers. In 1890 Walter Noble Burns responded to such an ad for "the adventure of the thing"— he was not shanghaied. Burns wrote a book, *One Year On A Whaler*, documenting his experiences. At the end of the voyage, under Captain William T. Shorey, Burns ran from the whaling bark *Alexander*, and never set foot on a whaler again. [2]

As for Levy, he was still using the want ad method for recruiting whaling crews in 1902. One such ad read:

> "WANTED—Young men to go on a cruise in the South Seas. No experience required. Apply to L. Levy, Battery and Jackson streets."

The crew of the *John and Winthrop* complained to the press in Honolulu that of twenty-four seamen on board the bark, nineteen had been shanghaied by Levy with the simple want ad above. Levy took the $40 advance money which was supposed to go to each man and kept it. When the men opened the bags their friend Louis Levy had given them for their advance, they found one pair of heavy shoes, two pairs of stockings, one suit of heavy underwear, one light woolen cap and one bottle of whiskey. This was supposed to get them through a winter in the Arctic. One crewman vowed not to touch his bag, but would return the contents on his arrival in San Francisco back to his friend Levy. None of the men aboard the *John and Winthrop* were able to escape, however. [3]

The details revealed by the Laflin record demonstrate the complexities of shanghaiing in San Francisco in the late 1890s. A man who signed as Captain Jack shipped only Japanese men. He

San Francisco Maritime Museum N.H.P.

A rare photograph of the businesses of two long-time crimps side-by-side . . . In 1907, after the earthquake and fire had destroyed all of the north of Market sailors' boardinghouses, John Kremke and Joe Harris set up shop at 407 and 409 Drumm Street. Kremke, who had received a payment from long-time shanghaier James Laflin as early as 1887, used the popular name Young America Saloon—two other saloons with the same name existed at this time. Joe Harris supplied clothing to sailors, usually at inflated prices.

John Ryan and John Anderson, both very bad apples in the shanghaiing community, operated separate sailors' boardinghouses at these addresses in the early 1870s. Even the hellish inferno which wiped most of San Francisco from the face of the earth could not eliminate the crimps, who rose like mutant phoenixes from the ashes of the city by the Bay.

signed in English as Captain Jack, and in Chinese with the characters meaning Japan. A number of women received advances for sailors delivered—Mrs. Gomes,' Mrs. Edgar's and Mrs. Stein's names are found frequently in the pages of the Laflin Record. Mrs. Gomes made her mark, a small x, when she was paid. Elizabeth Murray almost always picked up the advances in her husband Tom's name—either he sent her down to get the money or she, afraid he would drink up all the money, got the payments before Tom could.

Representatives of the Sailor's Home grace the pages of the Record. Daniel Swannack and Leroy D. Fletcher, successive superintendents of the Home, received payments, but usually their runner John Ferem, signed for the due bills. Ferem wrote his name as Fjerem in the 1880s; he became one of the most notorious of the Sailor's Home's many notorious superintendents in the latter years of its existence.

Harry "Horseshoe" Brown, Nils "Shanghai" Nelson, Dick Ahlers of the Old Ship Saloon, Ed Mordaunt, John T. Callender, Thomas Murray, Billy Jordan, John Curtin, Harry Lewis, George Lewis, Martin Brunsen and John Cardoza are famous shanghaiers who autographed Laflin's book for payments received when they brought in sailors. Curtin's signature is so irregular, sometimes not even complete, that it is safe to conclude John was either illiterate, had a neurological problem or was very drunk when he came to Laflin's shipping office. It is impossible to say what percentage of the men shipped by Laflin were shanghaied. Henry Ewald, who was sent out as a greenhand and surgeon by Louis Levy, could not have gone willingly unless he were a very strange character. Ewald, who left San Francisco on December 21, 1889, on the bark *Eliza*, brought $50 for Levy.

Five separate tables follow the footnotes of this appendix. Table 1 includes payments made to the top twenty shanghaiers in 1886 and 1890. Harry "Horseshoe" Brown leads the list in 1890, receiving 182 of the 1,169 advances, for 16 percent of all advances and $9,310, 13 percent of the total of $71,066.55 paid out by Laflin in 1890. Louis Levy received 101 sailors' advances in 1890, while Nils "Shanghai" Nelson was third with 62 advances. Mrs. Edgar struck a blow for early women's equality, being paid for 46 advances, placing her in fourth place.

Table 2 lists female shanghaiers receiving advances from James Laflin in 1887 and 1890.

Table 3 sorts payment of advances in our two study years by four occupational groups for those individuals who could be identified in San Francisco City Directories. Not surprisingly, sailors' boardinghouse keepers and shipping masters were paid more advances than anyone else, 438 out of 1,169 in 1890, 37 percent of the total. Unexpectedly, clothing outfitters received more than twice as many advances as saloonkeepers in both periods. Louis Levy was paid more money—$5,940—in 1887 than any other shanghaier.

Table 4 presents the average advance paid by occupational position.

Table 5 includes raw data from the Laflin Record for 1887 and 1890 of all advances paid by Laflin. It is sorted by crimp name, and includes occupation, number of and dollar amount of advances received in both years, and compares 1890 to 1887.

James Laflin received the salutation of captain in later life, a term of respect for long-time inhabitants of San Francisco's waterfront. Captain James Laflin died June 14, 1905, at the age of 73.[4]

Footnotes

1 1867 Langley, San Francisco City Directory

2 Walter Noble Burns, *One Year On A Whaler* and United States Criminal Case #2822, Criminal Register #5, San Francisco, California. Shorey was charged with cruelty to seaman John Rentford after this voyage, Shorey's second offense for cruelty. Rentford charged Shorey with assaulting him with the barrel of the captain's revolver, then inflicting cruel and unusual punishment on Rentford by forcing the sailor to work constantly on deck for twenty-four consecutive days, with no more than four hours of sleep a night. Peter Laflin, James son, acted as surety for Shorey. Even though Rentford produced an eyewitness to the beating, the court found Shorey, a black man, not guilty. Burns provides a description of the assault and subsequent punishment in his book.

3 Charles Page Scrapbook, Vol. 1, p.22, J. Porter Shaw Library

4 San Francisco City Directories 1859, 1860, 1861, 1862, 1890-95, Great Register of Voters, 1873, *San Francisco Chronicle*, June 15, 1905, p.13, col.3 and *Morning Call*, June 15, 1905, p.5, col.3

Table 1
Top 20 Shanghaiers Receiving Advances from James Laflin, 1887 and 1890

Crimp Name	Occupation	1887 # of Adv. Received	Amount Received	1890 # of Received	Amount Received	1890 Over	Over/Under 1887
arry "Horseshoe" rown	Sailors' boardinghouse keeper	42	$2,070	182	$9,310	140	$7,240
ouis Levy	Clothier	68	$5,940	101	$7,285	33	$1,345
il "Shanghai" elson	Sailors' boardinghouse keeper	29	$1,420	62	$3,250	33	$1,830
rs. Edgar				46	$2,735	46	$2,735
Woodworth	Sailors' boardinghouse keeper	30	$1,645	43	$2,500	13	$855
m Wynn				42	$1,830	42	$1,830
homas Murray	Sailors' boardinghouse keeper	10	$800	41	$2,615	31	$1,815
ussie Stein	Clothier	38	$2,535	39	$2,717	1	$182
artin Brunsen	Saloon	4	$160	31	$1,555	27	$1,395
hn W. Wilson				28	$1,485	28	$1,485
ter Gaffney	Sailors' boardinghouse keeper	19	$1,150	23	$1,195	4	$45
ick Ahlers	Old Ship Saloon	7	$750	22	$1,390	15	$640
te McMahon				20	$1,445	20	$1,445
is Nunez	Clothier	2	$270	19	$1,509	17	$1,239
hn W. Williams	Sailors' boardinghouse keeper	6	$565	19	$1,345	13	$780
Frank & Son	Clothier	11	$1,265	18	$2,532	7	$1,267
anuel Brooks	Porter	7	$620	18	$1,066	11	$446
orge Brown				18	$910	18	$910
Freitas		2	$170	16	$1,450	14	$1,280
Mordaunt	Sailors' boardinghouse keeper	27	$1,560	15	$860	(12)	($700)
Total		302	$20,920	803	$48,984	501	$28,064

Table 2
Female Shanghaiers Receiving Advances from James Laflin, 1887 and 1890

Crimp Name	Occupation	1887 # of Adv. Received	Amount Received	1890 # of Adv. Received	Amount Received	1890 Over/	Over/Under 1887
Magdalena Lutz		1	$100.00			(1)	$(100.00
Maria Santa Williams				1	$100.00	1	100.00
Mary Mathewson				1	13.00	1	13.00
Miss Nettie Choen				1	150.00	1	150.00
Mrs. A. Murphy				1	100.00	1	100.00
Mrs. Cathcart		1	60.00			(1)	(60.00
Mrs. Cohen		6	680.00	1	50.00	(5)	(630.00
Mrs. Cushing		1	70.00			(1)	(70.00
Mrs. Edgar				46	2,735.00	46	2,735.00
Mrs. F. Kane				1	30.00	1	30.00
Mrs. Gavin		2	100.00			(2)	(100.00
Mrs. Gillespie				1	60.00	1	60.00
Mrs. Anna Gomes		3	200.00	8	480.00	5	280.00
Mrs. Greenway				1	25.00	1	25.00
Mrs. Hamilton		3	210.00			(3)	(210.00
Mrs. Harris				1	200.00	1	200.00
Mrs. Harty		1	50.00			(1)	(50.00
Mrs. Isabel Kerr				1	30.00	1	30.00
Mrs. Jackson		1		1	30.00	1	30.00
Mrs. M. Lutz		1	40.00			(1)	(40.00
Mrs. Martindale		1	100.00			(1)	(100.00
Mrs. Mary Martin				1	50.00	1	50.00
Mrs. McCarthy		2	100.00			(2)	(100.00
Mrs. Powell				1	140.00	1	140.0
Mrs. Roby		1	50.00			(1)	(50.00
Mrs. Roeben				2	80.00	2	80.00
Mrs. Roehi		1				(1)	
Mrs. Sheehan				2	100.00	2	100.0
Mrs. Stein				7	360.00	7	360.0
Mrs. Sweeney		3	185.00			(3)	(185.00
Mrs. Whalen		1	100.00			(1)	(100.00
Mrs. Williams				1	30.00	1	30.0
Mrs. Wright		11	640.00			(11)	(640.00
Pauline Lang				1	185.00	1	185.0
Total		39	$2,685.00	80	$4,948.00	41	$2,263.0

Table 3
Shanghaiers Receiving Advances from James Laflin, 1887 and 1890

Crimp Name	Occupation	1887 # of Rec'd	Amount Rec'd	1890 # of Rec'd	Amount Rec'd	1890 Over/Under 1887	
Dick Ahlers	Saloon	7	$750.00	22	$1,390.00	15	$640.00
D. Heins	Saloon	3	610.00			(3)	(610.00)
Fred Nobman	Saloon	2	100.00			(2)	(100.00)
Martin Brunsen	Saloon	4	160.00	31	1,555.00	27	1,395.00
Ed Melander	Saloon	10	725.00	3	150.00	(7)	(575.00)
G. Theopolis	Saloon	10	1,015.00			(10)	(1,015.00)
Jim Barton	Saloon	6	340.00			(6)	(340.00)
J. Drake	Saloon	4	280.00			(4)	(280.00)
Otto W. Lilkenley	Saloon	3	90.00			(3)	(90.00)
	Subtotal	49	$4,070.00	56	$3,095.00	7	($975.00)
J. Purdy	Runner	3	$195.00			(3)	($195.00)
F. Walton	Shipping master	4	230.00			(4)	(230.00)
J. Cushing	Shipping agent	2	100.00			(2)	(100.00)
Henry Brown	Sailors' b.h.	42	2,070.00	182	9,310.00	140	7,240.00
Nils Nelson	Sailors' b.h.	29	1,420.00	62	3,250.00	33	1,830.00
J. Woodworth	Sailors' b.h.	30	1,645.00	43	2,500.00	13	855.00
Thomas Murray	Sailors' b.h.	10	800.00	41	2,615.00	31	1,815.00
Peter Gaffney	Sailors' b.h.	19	1,150.00	23	1,195.00	4	45.00
John W. Williams	Sailors' b.h.	6	565.00	19	1,345.00	13	780.00
W. Lane	Sailors' b.h.	33	1,740.00	15	775.00	(18)	(965.00)
Ed Mordaunt	Sailors' b.h.	27	1,560.00	15	860.00	(12)	(700.00)
Billy Jordan	Sailors' b.h.	7	325.00	8	400.00	1	75.00
William Thompson	Sailors' b.h.	13	655.00	7	360.00	(6)	(295.00)
M. Martin	Sailors' b.h.	3	180.00	7	535.00	4	355.00
John Curtin	Sailors' b.h.	6	370.00	5	261.50	(1)	(108.50)
George Lewis	Sailors' b.h.	2	100.00	5	330.00	3	230.00
Harry Lewis	Sailors' b.h.	6	320.00	2	110.00	(4)	(210.00)
Joseph Franklin	Sailors' b.h.	1	100.00	2	100.00	1	-
John T. Callender	Sailors' b.h.	13	1,045.00	1	100.00	(12)	(945.00)

Table 3
Shanghaiers Receiving Advances from James Laflin, 1887 and 1890

Name	Type						
P. Mackey	Sailors' b.h.	7	310.00	1	50.00	(6)	(260.00)
David Swannack	Sailors' b.h.	15	900.00			(15)	(900.00)
John Williams	Sailors' b.h.	14	1,345.00			(14)	(1,345.00)
W. Williams	Sailors' b.h.	10	460.00			(10)	(460.00)
Charles Olson	Sailors' b.h.	8	545.00			(8)	(545.00)
John Munroe	Sailors' b.h.	6	400.00			(6)	(400.00)
F. Cunha	Sailors' b.h.	5	580.00			(5)	(580.00)
Charles Reed	Sailors' b.h.	4	215.00			(4)	(215.00)
Henry Brown #1	Sailors' b.h.	4	185.00			(4)	(185.00)
John Cardoza	Sailors' b.h.	3	250.00			(3)	(250.00)
Joe Enos	Sailors' b.h.	2	350.00			(2)	(350.00)
George Roeben	Sailors' b.h.	1	50.00			(1)	(50.00)
	Subtotal	335	$20,160.00	438	$24,096.50	103	$3,936.50
Louis Levy	Clothier	68	$5,940.00	101	$7,285.00	33	$1,345.00
Gussie Stein	Clothier	38	2,535.00	39	2,717.00	1	182.00
Luis Nunez	Clothier	2	270.00	19	1,509.00	17	1,239.00
Ed Frank & Son	Clothier	11	1265	18	2532	7	1,267.00
Samuel Lanzet	Clothier	8	945	8	600	0	(345.00)
George Fogel	Clothier	5	285	1	30	(4)	(255.00)
John Kremke	Clothier	1	100			(1)	(100.00)
	Subtotal	133	$11,340.00	186	$14,673.00	53	$3,333.00
Manuel Brooks	Porter	7	$620.00	18	$1,066.00	11	$446.00
Ben Reyes	Laborer	8	400				(400.00)
	Subtotal	15	1020	18	1066	11	46
	Total	532	$36,590.00	698	$42,930.50	174	$6,340.50

Table 4
Average Advance Paid per Position by James Laflin, 1887

Position in Crew	# of Advances Paid	Amount
Steward	26	$103.10
Steerage Boy	19	46.58
Seaman (ordinary)	17	44.12
Seaman (able bodied)	464	50.16
Previous boatsteerer	7	72.86
Hunter	3	33.33
Greenhand (1 was asst carpenter)	55	56.18
Fireman	13	108.50
Engineer	9	106.70
Cooper (4 not paid an advance)	21	100.20
Cook/Steward (5 not paid an advance)	26	93.46
Chief Engineer	6	241.70
Carpenter (1 no advance)	8	105.00
Cabin Boy	22	48.16
Blacksmith	13	79.62
Asst Engineer	8	135.00
Asst Cooper, blacksmith	2	57.50
5th mate (2 no advance)	10	197.50
4th mate (11 no advance)	10	212.00
3rd mate (17 no advance)	10	246.00
2nd mate (16 no advance)	12	297.10
1st mate (24 no advance)	6	229.00
Total	767	$72.06

Table 5
Shanghaiers Receiving Advances from James Laflin, 1887 and 1890

| Crimp Name | 1887 | | 1890 | | 1890 o/(u) 1887 |
	# of Rec'd	Amount Rec'd	# of Rec'd	Amount Rec'd	
29 Pacific St.	1	60.00			(1) (60.00)
A. Baker	1	75.00			(1) (75.00)
A. Bander			1	60.00	1 60.00
A. Franklin			2	95.00	2 95.00
A. Greenberg			1	30.00	1 30.00
A. Jackson	1	60.00	1	50.00	- (10.00)
A. Johnson			5	250.00	5 250.00
A. Lopes			2	110.00	2 110.00
A.M. Reis	1	60.00			(1) (60.00)
A.P. McDonald			1	50.00	1 50.00
A.W. Smith	1	60.00			(1) (60.00)
Abbott	2	120.00			(2) (120.00)
Abelman			1	50.00	1 50.00
Advance but not to crimp	3	100.00			(3) (100.00)
Ah Poo	1	100.00			(1) (100.00)
Al White			2	70.00	2 70.00
Anna Gomes	2	100.00			(2) (100.00)
Antonio Prato			1	50.00	1 50.00
Antonio Vierra			2	170.00	2 170.00
August Prato			1	50.00	1 50.00
B. Baroni	2	110.00			(2) (110.00)
B. Dauman			1	20.00	1 20.00
B. Hickey	1	150.00			(1) (150.00)
Ben Prages	1	65.00			(1) (65.00)
Ben Reyes	8	400.00			(8) (400.00)
Ben Sales			10	560.00	10 560.00
Billy Jordan	7	325.00	8	400.00	1 75.00
C. Anderson			1	50.00	1 50.00
C. Brown			1	50.00	1 50.00
C. Byrne	1	60.00			(1) (60.00)
C. Dickey			2	25.00	2 25.00
C. Peterson	1	30.00			(1) (30.00)
C. Schroeder			1	50.00	1 50.00
C. Sorenson			1	50.00	1 50.00
C. Tanaka			1	50.00	1 50.00
C.A. Richter	1	100.00			(1) (100.00)
C.F. Dean	10	680.00			(10) (680.00)
C.J. Christenson			4	200.00	4 200.00

Table 5
Shanghaiers Receiving Advances from James Laflin, 1887 and 1890

Name						
Capt. Crew			1	20.00	1	20.00
Capt. Hallett			1	50.00	1	50.00
Capt. Jack	16	815.00			(16)	(815.00)
Capt. L. Williams	1	50.00			(1)	(50.00)
Capt. Lewis			8	713.05	8	713.05
Capt. McKenna	1	50.00			(1)	(50.00)
Capt. Thaxter			1	100.00	1	100.00
Capt. William			1	20.00	1	20.00
Carroll			1	25.00	1	25.00
Cash	1	45.00			(1)	(45.00)
Charles Olson	8	545.00			(8)	(545.00)
Charles Reed	4	215.00			(4)	(215.00)
Charles Bolling	1	60.00			(1)	(60.00)
Charles Chepplers			1	40.00	1	40.00
Charles Porter	1	60.00			(1)	(60.00)
Coleman	1	60.00			(1)	(60.00)
Collier	1	40.00			(1)	(40.00)
D. Burk	1	100.00			(1)	(100.00)
D. Heins	3	610.00			(3)	(610.00)
D. O'Connell	1	100.00			(1)	(100.00)
D. Terullo			1	100.00	1	100.00
David Swannack	15	900.00			(15)	(900.00)
Delfino Lopes			1	50.00	1	50.00
Dick Ahlers	7	750.00	22	1,390.00	15	640.00
Dr. Smith	1				(1)	-
E. Johnson	2	120.00			(2)	(120.00)
E. Morton	1	60.00			(1)	(60.00)
E. Peterson			1	50.00	1	50.00
E.B. Dean			1	20.00	1	20.00
E.H. Hanson			1	100.00	1	100.00
E.O. Wester			1	30.00	1	30.00
Ed Frank & Son	11	1,265.00	18	2,532.00	7	1,267.00
Ed Jones			1	50.00	1	50.00
Ed Melander	10	725.00	3	150.00	(7)	(575.00)
Ed Mordaunt	27	1,560.00	15	860.00	(12)	(700.00)
F. Brightman			1	175.00	1	175.00
F. Conception	1				(1)	-
F. Cunha	5	580.00			(5)	(580.00)
F. Fogel	4	325.00			(4)	(325.00)
F. Martin	1	60.00			(1)	(60.00)
F. Walton	4	230.00			(4)	(230.00)
Fogel	1	50.00			(1)	(50.00)

Table 5
Shanghaiers Receiving Advances from James Laflin, 1887 and 1890

Frank Marshall			1	50.00	1	50.00
Fred Nobman	2	100.00			(2)	(100.00)
Freeman	1	50.00			(1)	(50.00)
G. Digham	1	50.00			(1)	(50.00)
G. Franklin	1	120.00			(1)	(120.00)
G. O'Brien			2	100.00	2	100.00
G. Samstrither	1	120.00			(1)	(120.00)
G. Strand			7	210.00	7	210.00
G. Theopolis	10	1,015.00			(10)	(1,015.00)
G.M. Wilson			1	50.00	1	50.00
Gardner	1	10.00	1	25.00	-	15.00
Geo. McLaughlin	1	50.00			(1)	(50.00)
George Brown			18	910.00	18	910.00
George Cashell			3	150.00	3	150.00
George Fogel	5	285.00	1	30.00	(4)	(255.00)
George Lewis	2	100.00	5	330.00	3	230.00
George Roeben	1	50.00			(1)	(50.00)
George T. LeFleche			2		2	-
Ginger Malag			1	70.00	1	70.00
Gorman			2	50.00	2	50.00
Gray & Mack	1	50.00			(1)	(50.00)
Gus A. Roemer			1	150.00	1	150.00
Gus Johnson			2	70.00	2	70.00
Gus Sound			3	350.00	3	350.00
Gussie Stein	38	2,535.00	38	2,717.00	-	182.00
Guthrie	1	60.00			(1)	(60.00)
H. Bulton	1	60.00			(1)	(60.00)
H. Kneeman	1	50.00			(1)	(50.00)
H. Koizimi			9	560.00	9	560.00
H. Kolkstein	1	100.00			(1)	(100.00)
H. Krumman	2	100.00			(2)	(100.00)
H. Lettici	1	60.00			(1)	(60.00)
H. Lichow	1	300.00			(1)	(300.00)
H. Lithier	2	250.00			(2)	(250.00)
H. Lorentzen			1	20.00	1	20.00
H. Reuther (572 Folsom)	2	100.00			(2)	(100.00)
H. Roeben	1	150.00			(1)	(150.00)
H. Wilson			8	300.00	8	300.00
Hamilton	1	150.00			(1)	(150.00)
Harry Lewis	6	320.00	2	110.00	(4)	(210.00)
Henry "Shanghai " Brown	42	2,070.00	182	9,310.00	140	7,240.00

Table 5
Shanghaiers Receiving Advances from James Laflin, 1887 and 1890

Name						
Henry Bradhoff	4	200.00			(4)	(200.00)
Henry Brown No. 1	4	185.00			(4)	(185.00)
Henry Stumer	1	50.00			(1)	(50.00)
Hukey	1	150.00			(1)	(150.00)
J. Baker			1	50.00	1	50.00
J. Boyes			1	30.00	1	30.00
J. Cohen	1	60.00			(1)	(60.00)
J. Colbert	1	50.00			(1)	(50.00)
J. Cushing	2	100.00			(2)	(100.00)
J. Despasath	3	150.00	1	125.00	(2)	(25.00)
J. Drake	4	280.00			(4)	(280.00)
J. Duffy			12	555.00	12	555.00
J. Ferguson	1	100.00			(1)	(100.00)
J. Gillison	1	150.00			(1)	(150.00)
J. Hines			4	210.00	4	210.00
J. Keenan			2	150.00	2	150.00
J. Knowland			1	250.00	1	250.00
J. Meyer	1	300.00			(1)	(300.00)
J. Munroe			1	100.00	1	100.00
J. Munson	2	180.00			(2)	(180.00)
J. Oppenheimer			2	230.00	2	230.00
J. Purdy	3	195.00			(3)	(195.00)
J. Sheehan			1	50.00	1	50.00
J. Woodworth	30	1,645.00	43	2,500.00	13	855.00
J.C. Herold			1	75.00	1	75.00
J.H. Seebe			1	50.00	1	50.00
J.M. Johnson			1	30.00	1	30.00
Jacob Graber	1	100.00	13	1,110.00	12	1,010.00
Jacob Horne	1	100.00			(1)	(100.00)
James Laflin			3	81.20	3	81.20
James Murray			1	30.00	1	30.00
James Osranurr			1	30.00	1	30.00
James Bryne	1	60.00			(1)	(60.00)
James Douglas	1	50.00			(1)	(50.00)
James Wakeman	1	100.00			(1)	(100.00)
Jerry Sheen	1	50.00			(1)	(50.00)
Jim Barton	6	340.00			(6)	(340.00)
Jor Antone			13	925.00	13	925.00
Joe Enos	2	350.00			(2)	(350.00)
Joe Ferro	10	735.00	1	180.00	(9)	(555.00)
Joe Peters			2	310.00	2	310.00
John Admith	2	200.00			(2)	(200.00)

Table 5
Shanghaiers Receiving Advances from James Laflin, 1887 and 1890

Name						
John Cardoza	3	250.00			(3)	(250.00)
John Curtin	6	370.00	5	261.50	(1)	(108.50)
John D. Griffin			1	80.00	1	80.00
John Finn			1	30.00	1	30.00
John Kane			1	50.00	1	50.00
John Kremke	1	100.00			(1)	(100.00)
John Langford			4	230.00	4	230.00
John Miller			1	150.00	1	150.00
John Munroe	6	400.00			(6)	(400.00)
John O'Brien	2	110.00	1	70.00	(1)	(40.00)
John T. Callender	13	1,045.00	1	100.00	(12)	(945.00)
John T. Williams			3	225.00	3	225.00
John W. Williams	6	565.00	19	1,345.00	13	780.00
John W. Wilson			28	1,485.00	28	1,485.00
John Walker	1	30.00			(1)	(30.00)
John Williams	14	1,345.00			(14)	(1,345.00)
Joseph "Franchy" Franklin	1	100.00	2	100.00	1	-
L. Newman	1	100.00			(1)	(100.00)
L. Shillegar			2	60.00	2	60.00
Lamones	1	60.00			(1)	(60.00)
Lisbon House-John Cardoza	1	125.00			(1)	(125.00)
Louis Barner			2	55.00	2	55.00
Louis Levy	68	5,940.00	101	7,285.00	33	1,345.00
Louis Perralto			2	115.00	2	115.00
Luis Niman	1	50.00			(1)	(50.00)
Luis Nunez	2	270.00	19	1,509.00	17	1,239.00
M. Amarat	1	65.00			(1)	(65.00)
M. Dotles & Co.	1	50.00	2	60.00	1	10.00
M. Freitas	2	170.00	16	1,450.00	14	1,280.00
M. Hartman	1	50.00	1	75.00	-	25.00
M. Kilden	1	500.00			(1)	(500.00)
M. Lopes			2	100.00	2	100.00
M. Martin	3	180.00	7	535.00	4	355.00
M. McCarthy	1	90.00			(1)	(90.00)
M. Silva			1	50.00	1	50.00
M. Smith	1	60.00			(1)	(60.00)
M.B. Almada			1	20.00	1	20.00
M.J. Flavin			1	50.00	1	50.00
Magdalena Lutz	1	100.00			(1)	(100.00)
Manuel Brooks	7	620.00	18	1,066.00	11	446.00
Manuel Silva	1	70.00			(1)	(70.00)
Maria Santa Williams			1	100.00	1	100.00

Table 5
Shanghaiers Receiving Advances from James Laflin, 1887 and 1890

Martin Brunsen	4	160.00	31	1,555.00	27	1,395.00
Martin Joseph			1	60.00	1	60.00
Mary Mathewson			1	13.00	1	13.00
Maurice Roach			1	48.80	1	48.80
McCarthy	3	320.00			(3)	(320.00)
Mellocraft			1	80.00	1	80.00
Miss Nettie Choen			1	150.00	1	150.00
Morgan			1	125.00	1	125.00
Mr. Butler	1	120.00			(1)	(120.00)
Mrs. A. Murphy			1	100.00	1	100.00
Mrs. Cathcart	1	60.00			(1)	(60.00)
Mrs. Cohen	6	680.00	1	50.00	(5)	(630.00)
Mrs. Cushing	1	70.00			(1)	(70.00)
Mrs. Edgar			46	2,735.00	46	2,735.00
Mrs. F. Kane			1	30.00	1	30.00
Mrs. Gavin	2	100.00			(2)	(100.00)
Mrs. Gillespie			1	60.00	1	60.00
Mrs. Gomes (Anna?)	1	100.00	8	480.00	7	380.00
Mrs. Greenway			1	25.00	1	25.00
Mrs. Hamilton	3	210.00			(3)	(210.00)
Mrs. Harris			1	200.00	1	200.00
Mrs. Harty	1	50.00			(1)	(50.00)
Mrs. Isabel Kerr			1	30.00	1	30.00
Mrs. Jackson			1	30.00	1	30.00
Mrs. M. Lutz	1	40.00			(1)	(40.00)
Mrs. Martindale	1	100.00			(1)	(100.00)
Mrs. Mary Martin			1	50.00	1	50.00
Mrs. McCarthy	2	100.00			(2)	(100.00)
Mrs. Powell			1	140.00	1	140.00
Mrs. Roby	1	50.00			(1)	(50.00)
Mrs. Roeben			2	80.00	2	80.00
Mrs. Roehi	1				(1)	-
Mrs. Sheehan			2	100.00	2	100.00
Mrs. Stein			7	360.00	7	360.00
Mrs. Sweeney	3	185.00			(3)	(185.00)
Mrs. Whalen	1	100.00			(1)	(100.00)
Mrs. Williams			1	30.00	1	30.00
Mrs. Wright	11	640.00			(11)	(640.00)
N. Muller			1	180.00	1	180.00
N. Peterson	1	125.00			(1)	(125.00)
N. Snyder	1	35.00			(1)	(35.00)

Table 5
Shanghaiers Receiving Advances from James Laflin, 1887 and 1890

Name						
Nils "Shanghai" Nelson	29	1,420.00	62	3,250.00	33	1,830.00
No adavnce or monthly wage	138				(138)	-
Other-officers, boatsteerers, et al	121	16,135.00			(121)	(16,135.00)
Otto W. Lilkenly	3	90.00			(3)	(90.00)
P. Mackey	7	310.00	1	50.00	(6)	(260.00)
P.A. Damell	1	100.00			(1)	(100.00)
P.A. Johnson			5	240.00	5	240.00
Pauline Lang			1	185.00	1	185.00
Pedro Silva	9	530.00			(9)	(530.00)
Pete McMahon			20	1,445.00	20	1,445.00
Peter Gaffney	19	1,150.00	23	1,195.00	4	45.00
R. Cohen			3	150.00	3	150.00
R. Lavigne			1	250.00	1	250.00
R. Sweeney			10	500.00	10	500.00
R.V. Silveira			12	990.00	12	990.00
R.W. Smith	1	60.00			(1)	(60.00)
Rodriques & Roposa			1	60.00	1	60.00
Roeben	1	150.00			(1)	(150.00)
Rogers & O'Brien			1	50.00	1	50.00
S. Label			1	30.00	1	30.00
S. Santos	5	310.00			(5)	(310.00)
S. Simonds			1	15.00	1	15.00
S.A. Nunes			1	200.00	1	200.00
Sailor's Home			2	100.00	2	100.00
Sam Wynn			42	1,830.00	42	1,830.00
Samuel Lanzet	8	945.00	8	600.00	-	(345.00)
T. Ahlman	1	50.00	2	60.00	1	10.00
T. O'Neil			1	15.00	1	15.00
T.F. Cunha	1	100.00			(1)	(100.00)
Thomas C. Fry			1	40.00	1	40.00
Thomas Murray	10	800.00	41	2,615.00	31	1,815.00
V. Pangolini			2	100.00	2	100.00
W. Bennett	1	50.00			(1)	(50.00)
W. Boundy	1	100.00			(1)	(100.00)
W. Britton	1	50.00			(1)	(50.00)
W. Graham			1	50.00	1	50.00
W. Laflin			5	250.00	5	250.00
W. Lane	33	1,740.00	15	775.00	(18)	(965.00)
W. Shaw	1	50.00	5	250.00	4	200.00
W. Williams	10	460.00			(10)	(460.00)
W.E. Maher			1	50.00	1	50.00
W.H. Huges	1	50.00			(1)	(50.00)

Table 5
Shanghaiers Receiving Advances from James Laflin, 1887 and 1890

Walter Benson			5	195.00	5	195.00
Watson	3	130.00			(3)	(130.00)
William Thompson	13	655.00	7	360.00	(6)	(295.00)
Wilson	2	110.00			(2)	(110.00)
Wm. Bendt			1	50.00	1	50.00
Wm. Britton	1	50.00			(1)	(50.00)
Wm. Clark			1	50.00	1	50.00
Wm. McCarthy			2	100.00	2	100.00
Wm. Sharo	4	200.00			(4)	(200.00)
	1005	68,070.00	1168	71,066.55	163	2,996.55

Glossary

Advance Money Two months advance wages was given in a sailor's name by shipowners during most of the late 19th century. The advance was intended to outfit the sailor for his trip, settle any bills due to original creditors and provide for the man's family while he was at sea. In practice, especially in San Francisco, the two months advance was issued directly to the sailors' boardinghouse master or other shanghaier. The sailor never saw the money.

Articles of Agreement The document containing all particulars relating to the terms of agreement between the master of the vessel and the crew. Sometimes called ship's articles or shipping articles. It contained the nature, description and capacity of all members of the crew, the amount of wages to be received and provisions to be served. Articles of Agreement were considered to form a legally binding contract in the 19th century—frequently a shanghaied man's signature was forged to Articles and the courts forced a man to go to sea, if he were to seek a legal remedy. *International Maritime Dictionary*

Blood-Money Fee given by a shipmaster to a crimp or boardinghouse keeper for the procurement of a seaman. *International Maritime Dictionary*. Blood-money came to have more specialized meanings along the San Francisco waterfront: to some it meant a bonus paid to shanghaiers when demand for sailors was strong, over and above the two months advance money; when demand for seamen was slow, reverse blood-money was frequently paid by boardinghouse keepers to captains, especially of British ships, to get rid of the hungry sailors with no way of paying off their bills.

Crimp Someone, who by force or trickery, persuades men to serve in the army, navy or merchant marine. The *Oxford Companion to Ships and the Sea* notes that the first usage of the word crimp, in this sense, occurs in 1638. By the late 19th and early 20th centuries, San Francisco had become the most notorious port in the world for crimping.

Forecastle Usually abbreviated to fo'c'sle, or focscle, in maritime literature. The forecastle raised deck, at the fore end of the vessel, formed the living quarters for crew members, and was cramped, dank, dirty, and frequently, foul smelling.

Gunwale The upper edge of the vessel's or boat's side. *International Maritime Dictionary*

"Illegal boarding" The practice by Whitehall boatmen, the runners they carried and boardinghouse masters of coming aboard an incoming vessel before the vessel was securely tied up at its dock. Early California law sought to control shanghaiing—enticing crewmen to desert their ship with promises of a good job, women or a good drunk—by making boarding a vessel without permission of the captain a criminal misdemeanor.

Impressment Forced service in the British military forces. The Parliamentary legality was first set down in 1556. Impressing resistant Americans into the Royal Navy became a significant cause for the War of 1812.

Runner A runner operated between a business on shore and ships arriving in San Francisco. The business the runner represented could be a meat market, ship chandlery or a sailors' boardinghouse. Sailors' boardinghouse runners did the dirty work of the shanghaiing trade—they gave bad whiskey to incoming sailors, making it easier to entice men to desert their ship and leave behind wages due. These same runners doubled as the muscle which enforced the bidding of the boardinghouse master.

Sailors' boardinghouse keeper One who operates a boardinghouse catering to sailors. The bulk of shanghaiing was done by sailors' boardinghouse keepers or their runners. Few working-class men or women could buy a home in the 19th century and apartments or flats were too expensive for the lower working-class. Sailors fell into this category. Hundreds of boardinghouses served the needs of lower working-class, and low class, individuals. Along the waterfront, both north of Market and south of Market, more than fifty boardinghouses existed which provided food and lodgings to sailors. The master made sure he had the first opportunity to ship a boarder out as a sailor, and claim one or two months of the sailors' pay.

Shanghaiing The term coined in San Francisco for the older usage, crimping—namely, someone taken by force or trickery to serve on a board a vessel. The Pacific voyage to Shanghai was indirect, often requiring a trip around the world to return to San Francisco; surviving such a voyage was not assured.

Shipping master The shipping master acted as go-between, or market maker, for ships' captains and shipowners on the demand side, and sailors' boardinghouse masters and other approved providers of sailors during the days of shanghaiing. It was all but impossible for a sailor to get a job by approaching a captain directly in cities like San Francisco, where crimps had tremendous economic and political clout.

 Shipping masters like Tommy Chandler or James Laflin signed contracts with agents of shipowners to supply their vessels with sailors in port. The shipping master position was much more prestigious than the average sailors' boardinghouse keeper—the shipping master decided how much business each shanghaier got when crew was needed. Old business associates of Laflin's like Harry "Horseshoe" Brown and Nils "Shanghai" Nelson got the lion's share.

Slopchest A chest containing a complement of clothing, boots, oilskins, tobacco, blankets, etc. for the use of seamen. Any of the contents may be sold during the voyage to members of the crew. *International Maritime Dictionary*. Typically, 19th century ships deducted any slopchest purchases from the wages due a sailor. The combination of slopchest deductions for a poorly outfitted sailor, sometimes priced at three or more times their value, and the sailor's advance, which the boardinghouse keeper received, meant the sailor was paid off with next to nothing at voyage's end.

Whitehall boats Most authorities agree that the Whitehall boat was perfected near Whitehall Landing in New York harbor, near the time of the War of 1812. Tom Mendenhall, in his book *A Short History of American Rowing,* refers to passengers in Whitehall boats exhorting their boatmen to race one another in the 1790s. Built with a plumb stem and wineglass transom, these relatively light craft made perfect harbor boats. The Whitehall became extremely popular in New York, Boston, Philadelphia and San Francisco, until made obsolete by the gasoline-powered launch. The overall length of commercial boats varied from 18.5 feet to as long as 22 feet. Whitehalls were much preferred by the shanghaiing community: they could be rowed or sailed by one or two men; they were fast, could bear a load and were quite rugged.

Bibliography

Newspapers and Periodicals

California Police Gazette

Coast Seamen's Journal

Sea Breezes

South of Market Journal

San Francisco Morning Call

Portland (Me.) Press Herald

New York Clipper

Philadelphia Evening Bulletin

San Francisco Chronicle

New York Times

San Francisco Newsletter

Philadelphia Record

San Francisco Examiner

San Mateo Gazette

San Francisco Magazine

San Francisco Daily Sun

San Francisco Daily Alta California

San Francisco The Elevator

San Francisco Daily Evening Bulletin

San Francisco Pacific Appeal

San Francisco The California Star

Government Records and Reports

Acts Amendatory to the Codes of California, Twenty-First Session, 1875-6 (Sacramento, Ca.: State Printing Office, 1876)

Federal Government. Records of the Work Projects Administration, Record Group 69. *Ship Registry and Enrollments, 1848-1910, for the Port of San Francisco* (Washington, D.C.: 1941)

Index To The Laws Of California, 1850-93 (Sacramento, Ca.: State Printing Office, 1894)

Legislative Sourcebook: The California Legislature and Reapportionment, 1849-1965 (Sacramento, Ca.: Assembly of the State of California, 1965)

San Francisco, *Great Register of the City and County of San Francisco, 1873* (San Francisco: A.L. Bancroft, 1873)

San Francisco, *Great Register of the City and County of San Francisco, 1867* (San Francisco: Towne and Bacon, 1867)

San Francisco Municipal Reports, 1875-76, 1884-85

San Francisco Subway (Sacramento, Ca.: California State Printing Office, 1925)

Ship's Articles and Crew Lists, 1856, Record Group 36, Box 16, *Haidee* and *Kate Hooper*

U.S. Bureau of the Census. Census data for San Francisco, 1852, Volume 6

U.S. Bureau of the Census. *Eighth Census of the United States, 1860. Volume 7. Population.* (Washington, D.C.: Government Printing Office)

U.S. Bureau of the Census. *Ninth Census of the United States, 1870. City of San Francisco, Ward 1* (Washington, D.C.: Government Printing Office)

U.S. Bureau of the Census. *Tenth Census of the United States, 1880. San Francisco City*, (Washington, D.C.: Government Printing Office, 1883)

U.S. Bureau of the Census. *Twelth Census of the United States, 1900. San Francisco City*, (Washington, D.C.: Government Printing Office)

U.S. Bureau of the Census. *Seventh Census of the United States. 1850. Cumberland County, Maine, Roll 251* (Washington, D.C.: Government Printing Office)

United States Statutes At Large, Vol. 18, part 3, (Washington, D.C.: Government Printing Office, 1875)

Directories and Reference Books

Bancroft, Hubert Howe, *History of California*, vol. VI (San Francisco: History Co., 1888)

Compiled by D.M. Bishop & Co., *San Francisco City Directory, 1876*, (San Francisco: B.C. Vandall, 1876)

Davis, Winfield J., *The History of Political Conventions in California, 1849-1892* (Sacramento, Ca.: California State Library, 1893) de T. Abajian, James, compiler, *Blacks In Selected Newspapers, Censuses, And Other Sources: An Index To Names And Subjects, Vol. 1* (Boston, Massachusetts: G.K. Hall & Co., 1977)

de Kerchove, Rene, *International Maritime Dictionary* (New York: Van Nostrand Reinhold Company, 1983)

de la Pedreja, Rene, *A Historical Dictionary of the U.S. Merchant Marine and Shipping Industry Since the Introduction of Steam*, (Westport, Connecticut: Greenwood Press, 1994)

Handy Block-Book, (San Francisco: Hicks-Judd, 1894)

Insurance Maps of San Francisco, California (New York: Sanborn Map and Publishing Co., 1887)

Kemp, Peter (ed.), *The Oxford Companion To Ships And The Sea*, (London: Oxford University Press, 1976)

Laflin, James, *List of Officers Composing the Whaling Fleet of San Francisco, Cal.* (San Francisco, Ca.: James Laflin; issued annually, 1886-1906; Laflin, Peter J., 1907-08)

Press Reference Library. Notables of the West, vol. I (New York: International News Service, 1913)

San Francisco City Directories for the mentioned years

Simpson, J.A. and Weiner, E.S.C. (eds.), *The Oxford English Dictionary* (Oxford: Clarendon Press, 1989)

Wolfe, Wellington C., ed., *Men of California, 1900-02* (San Francisco: The Pacific Art Company, 1901)

Books

Asbury, Herbert, *The Barbary Coast : An Informal History of the San Francisco Underworld* (New York: Knopf, 1933)

Bailey, Hiram P., *Shanghaied Out of 'Frisco in the '90s* (London: Heath Crenton, 1938)

Barry, Theodore Augustus and Patten, Benjamin Adam, *Men and Memories of San Francisco, California in the "Spring of '50"* (San Francisco: A.L. Bancroft, 1873)

Beasley, Delilah Leontine, *The Negro Trailblazers of California* (New York: Negro Universities Press, 1919)

Brown, Richard Maxwell, *Strain of Violence* (New York: Oxford University Press, 1975)

Bullough, William A., *The Blind Boss and His City: Christopher Augustine Buckley & Nineteenth Century San Francisco* (Berkeley and Los Angeles, Ca.: University of California Press, 1979)

Burns, Walter Noble, *A Year With A Whaler* (New York: The MacMillan Company, 1919)

Coffman, William Milo, *American in the Rough* (New York: Simon and Schuster, 1955)

Cross, Ira B., (ed.), *Frank B. Roney: Irish Rebel and California Labor Leader* (Berkeley, Ca.: University of California Press, 1931)

Dillon, Richard H., *Shanghaiing Days* (New York, New York: Coward-McCann, 1961)

Hendry, F.C. (Shalimar), *From All The Seas* (Edinburgh and London: William Blackwood & Sons Ltd., 1933)

The History of the Olympic Club, (San Francisco, Ca.: The Art Publishing Company, 1893)

Inkersley, Arthur, *Souvenir, San Francisco Yacht Club, 1900* (Sausalito, Ca.: San Francisco Yacht Club, 1900)

Martin, William Camp, *San Francisco: Port of Gold* (Garden City, New York: Doubleday & Company, Inc., 1947)

Mullen, Kevin J., *Let Justice Be Done*, (Reno and Las Vegas: University of Nevada Press, 1989)

Olmsted, Roger R. and Nancy L., *San Francisco Waterfront* (San Francisco, 1977)

Recollections of the San Francisco Waterfront, Thomas Crowley, Sr., interviewed by Karl Kortum and Willa Klug Baum, (Berkeley, Ca.: University of California Press, 1967)

Rhodes, Frederic Cecil, *Pageant Of The Pacific Being The Maritime History Of Australasia , 2 volumes* (Sydney, N.S.W.: F.J. Thwaites, 1937)

Schimmel, Jerry F., *An Old Ship From the Gold Rush* (San Francisco: Prepared for the Token and Medal Society Journal, 1992)

Shaw, Frank Hubert, *White Sails and Spindrift* (New York: Odyssey Press, 1947)

Taylor, William, *Seven Years' Street Preaching In San Francisco, California; embracing incidents, triumphant death scenes, etc. . . .* (New York, Carlton & Porter, 1856)

Tugboats and Boatmen of California: 1906-70, interview of William J. McGillivray by Ruth Teiser (Berkeley, Ca.: University of California Press, 1971)

Walsh, James P., *The San Francisco Irish, 1850-1976* (San Francisco: The Society, 1978)

Articles

Berg, Annemarie, "Johnny Devine: Alias, the Shanghai Chicken," *The California Highway Patrolman,* v.38, no.2, April 1974, pp.14-5, 34-5, 38-40

Bielinski, John, "San Francisco's Oldest Rowing Clubs", *Wooden Boat*, May/June 1981,

Morphy, Edward, "San Francisco Thoroughfares," San Francisco *Chronicle*

O'Brien, Robert, "Riptides," *San Francisco Chronicle*

"San Bruno prize fight, 119 rounds," *La Peninsula,* v.5, no.2, May 1949, p.8

Transcripts of Oral History Interviews

Captain Alexander McKenzie ms. by Jack McNairn, J. Porter Shaw Library

Captain James Allen ms., J. Porter Shaw Library

Captain Alfred C. Hansen ms., J. Porter Shaw Library

Captain Edward Connors ms., J. Porter Shaw Library

Captain John E. Johnson ms., J. Porter Shaw Library

Captain F. N. Lyons ms., J. Porter Shaw Library

Hans Hansen ms., J. Porter Shaw Library

Johann Carlson ms., J. Porter Shaw Library

Max DeVeer ms., J. Porter Shaw Library

George W. Kimble ms., J. Porter Shaw Library

Thomas Crowley ms., J. Porter Shaw Library

DuVal Williams ms., J. Porter Shaw Library

Manuscript of crews of whaling vessels, 1906-08, 1909-12, 1913-28, J. Porter Shaw Library (San Francisco: Peter J. Laflin)

Miscellaneous

Crowley, Sr., Thomas, Scrapbooks
The Laflin Record. A Record of Men and Ofiicers Shipped by the
  Whaling and Sealing Fleets from San Francisco, Ca., and Recipients
  of Sailors' Advances, 1886-1890
"San Francisco City Licenses 1850-1856," microfilm Roll No. 2-86
United States Criminal Court Case No. 1210, California District
"Whitehall Boatman" pamphlet file, J. Porter Shaw Library

Index

Y

Also by Bill Pickelhaupt

Club Rowing on San Francisco Bay, 1869-1939

The story of the old rowing clubs of the Bay— their early competitions and later role in bringing to reality Daniel Burnham's vision of an Aquatic Park for the people of San Francisco.

"Pickelhaupt is masterful in chronicling the various races these clubs would launch against each other . . . A particularly beautiful photograph . . . eerily echoes Thomas Eakins' painterly masterpiece . . . ."
Kevin Starr
author *Americans and the California Dream* series

"A helluva great book on old-time San Francisco,"
Tom Cahill
former San Francisco Police Chief

Paperback. 100 pages. 32 photographs. ISBN 0-9647312-0-7
$12.95 plus $2.25 shipping. California residents add $1.10 sales tax

Send check or money order to:

Flyblister Press
1706 Irving Street
San Francisco, California 94122

Cover design: Bill Pickelhaupt, Malcolm E. Barker, Larry Van Dyke
Text design: Bill Pickelhaupt and Malcolm E. Barker
Copy editor: Lucille Matthews
Typefaces: Garamond and Titanic
Printed and bound by Edwards Brothers, Michigan
on 60 lb. Finch Opaque